高等院校立体化创新经管教材系列

实用会计英语

于 丹 任 梦 主 编

李 玥 任 彬 段佳萌 副主编

清华大学出版社
北京

内 容 简 介

本书充分体现了高等职业教育的特色,理论内容简明、概括,注重培养学生的职业素养,突出了实用性这一重要特点。本书包括 11 章内容,每章均包含学习目标、听力练习、至理名言、微型案例、正文、课后练习以及阅读材料 7 个部分,每节开始都有一段听力练习和一小段英文对话,以便提高读者与会计英语相关的听力和口语能力;末尾都有词汇和注释,方便读者记忆和阅读,并对一些重要内容,例如会计科目、财务报表等表格以中英文对照的方式进行了列示。

本书所选内容涵盖会计导论、会计循环、财务报表以及流动资产、非流动资产、负债、所有者权益等会计要素的确认、计量和报告等问题,并引入了财务报表分析、管理会计、审计、国际会计协调等相关会计知识领域的内容。

本书是为教学需要编写的,既可以作为普通高等院校会计专业英语课程的教学用书,也可以作为工程硕士和其他相关专业学生的学习用书,还可供会计专业人士参考。本书旨在帮助读者掌握大量会计专业术语的英文表达,同时使读者获得一定的会计知识,提高其英语水平。

图书在版编目(CIP)数据

实用会计英语/于丹,任梦主编. —北京:清华大学出版社,2022.8(2024.2重印)
高等院校立体化创新经管教材系列
ISBN 978-7-302-61306-0

Ⅰ. ①实… Ⅱ. ①于… ②任… Ⅲ. ①会计—英语—高等学校—教材 Ⅳ. ①F23

中国版本图书馆 CIP 数据核字(2022)第 121257 号

责任编辑:陈冬梅
封面设计:刘孝琼
责任校对:周剑云
责任印制:宋 林
出版发行:清华大学出版社
   网 址:https://www.tup.com.cn, https://www.wqxuetang.com
   地 址:北京清华大学学研大厦 A 座 邮 编:100084
   社 总 机:010-83470000 邮 购:010-62786544
   投稿与读者服务:010-62776969, c-service@tup.tsinghua.edu.cn
   质量反馈:010-62772015, zhiliang@tup.tsinghua.edu.cn
   课件下载:https://www.tup.com.cn, 010-62791865
印 装 者:三河市人民印务有限公司
经 销:全国新华书店
开 本:185mm×260mm 印 张:17.75 字 数:428 千字
版 次:2022 年 9 月第 1 版 印 次:2024 年 2 月第 2 次印刷
定 价:49.80 元

产品编号:093235-01

前　　言

习近平总书记在中国共产党第二十次全国代表大会上的报告中明确指出，要办好人民满意的教育，全面贯彻党的教育方针，落实立德树人根本任务，培养德智体美劳全面发展的社会主义建设者和接班人，加快建设高质量教育体系，发展素质教育，促进教育公平。本书在编写过程中力求深刻领会党对高校教育工作的指导意见，认真执行党对高校人才培养的具体要求。

随着经济全球化和会计准则的国际协调，我国急需培养国际化的会计专业人才。相关课程内容的合理设置和实用教材的引导是人才培养的重要基础。目前，国外引进的原版教材篇幅较长且与我国正在执行的会计准则存在较大差异，在内容体系方面并不完全适合国内学生学习需要。基于此，我们结合多年的会计专业英语及双语教学实践，考虑国内学生的学习特点和教学需要，编写了本教材。

本书以中国会计准则为基础，以美国会计准则和国际会计准则为主要参考对象，用英语对会计基本原理、会计循环及会计要素的确认、计量和报告等问题进行了阐述，并引入了财务报表分析、管理会计、审计、国际会计等相关会计知识领域内容。本书在充分考虑高等院校教学培养目标的基础上，在编写过程中注重突出以下特点：

第一，本书在参考了大量国外原版会计英语教材资料及以往会计英语教材的基础上，结合我国目前的会计知识体系，进行了系统的整合和构建，使内容更容易被中国读者接受。

第二，为了方便记忆和阅读，本书每小结末尾都附有词汇表，对课文内重要或不易理解的语句都用下划线标出，并在课文后进行翻译。

第三，本书每篇课文后附有大量习题和一篇阅读材料，旨在巩固和拓展读者所学的内容，并提高读者的英文综合能力。

第四，本书在对应章节中列示了会计科目中英文对照表、财务报表中英文对照表、国内外著名会计机构网址等，便于读者阅读和查询。

本书是为教学需要编写的，旨在帮助读者掌握大量会计专业术语的英文表达，同时使读者获得一定的会计知识，并提高读者英语水平，因此本书既可以作为普通高等院校的会计专业英语课程教学用书，也可以作为工程硕士生和其他相关专业学生的学习用书，还可供会计专业人士阅读参考。

本书由辽宁石油化工大学的于丹、任梦、李玥、任彬、段佳萌拟定全书写作大纲并总纂定稿。感谢连云港徐圩港口投资集团有限公司运营事业部王壮总经理的支持与配合。

在写作过程中，编者参阅了国内外大量的专著、教材和网络资源，在此谨向所有参考文献的作者表示诚挚的感谢。由于编者水平有限，书中难免存在不足之处，恳请广大读者不吝指正。

编　者

目　　录

Chapter 1　An Introduction to Accounting
会计导论

Learning Objectives

- Understand accounting and accountants　了解会计学和会计人员
- Identify the main users of accounting information　识别会计信息使用者
- Discuss the underlying assumptions of financial accounting　讨论会计假设
- Discuss accounting recognition and measurement principles　讨论会计认证和会计衡量标准
- Use the accounting elements and the accounting equation　学会使用会计要素和会计等式

Listening Practice　听力练习

Chapter 1 English Listening.mp3

第 1 章听写原文翻译和答案的音频见右侧二维码。

Dictation: *Listen and complete the passage with the words or phrases according to what you've heard from the speaker.*

Accounting is a special _____1_____ of business. The purpose is to provide useful information for different users in order to make their decisions. These users may include owners, managers, _____2_____, government agencies, customers, labor unions, and competitors. There are three basic accounting elements on the balance sheet: assets, liabilities, and owner's _____3_____. The relationship between the three basic accounting elements is expressed in the accounting equation. This accounting equation shows that assets are equal to equities. Equities are divided into liabilities and owner's equity. When any two of the elements are known, the third can be _____4_____, under the business entity principle, the accounting elements are affected by each other. At all times, the accounting equation must be in _____5_____.

Wisdom　至理名言

Financial statements are like fine perfume; to be sniffed but not swallowed.
财务报表就像上等的香水；闻而不咽。

 Mini Case 微型案例

Rosa Scarlett opened a bar. She deposited $14,000 into a bank account opened specially for her business—Scarlett's Bar. She bought equipment, supplies, inventories, sustained debt and paid expenses. After the first month's operation, she summarized her transactions occurred. The total sales revenue was $15,000, and the expenses paid was $4,745. However, she was wondering about the issues as follows:

- How come that her net income reaches $10,255?
- What are the total assets of her bar at the end of the month?
- How much debt did she sustain during the month?
- How does her accountant present all the financial information?

1.1 Accounting and Accountants
会计学和会计人员

A conversation between A—an accountant and S—a freshman majoring in accounting.

S: Accounting is sometimes described as the language of business. What is meant by this description?

A: The purpose of any language is to convey information. Accounting uses its own special words and symbols to communicate financial information that is intended to be useful for economic decision making by managers, shareholders, creditors and many others.

S: What's the difference between bookkeeping and accounting?

A: Bookkeeping is only a small part of accounting, and probably the simplest part, for it is only the recording of transactions, and generally it is mechanical. Generally speaking, accounting includes not only the recording of economic data, but also interpretation of accounting information, financial management, auditing, tax planning, accounting analysis, forecasting and so on.

S: That means being an accountant is much more difficult than being a bookkeeper, right?

A: Right. One can become a skilled bookkeeper in a few months and even in a few weeks, while it takes quite a few years of efforts to become a qualified accountant.

What is Accounting

Accounting is a system that **identifies, measures, records**, and **communicates** relevant, reliable, and comparable information about an organization's **business activities**. [1] The accounting process consists of:

(1) Identification—the observation of activity and the selection of particular events that are

evidence of economic activities to an entity;

(2) Measurement—the quantification of the events in monetary terms;

(3) Recording—the keeping of a chronological diary of the measured events [2];

(4) Communication—the preparation and distribution of **financial statements** to users.

Accounting is therefore, also considered as a method of **figuratively** recording business transactions which make possible portrayal of the operating results and state of affairs of an organization.

We must guard against a narrow view of accounting. The most common contact with accounting is through credit approvals, checking accounts, tax forms, and payroll[3]. These experiences are limited and tend to focus on the bookkeeping parts of accounting. **Bookkeeping** is the recording of transactions and events, either manually or electronically. This is just one part of accounting. Accounting also identifies and communicates information on transactions and events, and it includes the crucial processes of analysis and interpretation.

Technology is a key part of modern business and plays a major role in accounting. Technology reduces the time, effort, and cost of bookkeeping while improving clerical accuracy. Some small organizations continue to perform various accounting tasks manually, but even they are impacted by technology. As technology has changed the way we store, process, and summarize masses of **data**, accounting has been freed to expand. [4] Consulting, planning, and other financial services are now closely linked to accounting. These services require sorting through data, interpreting their meanings, identifying key factors, and analyzing their implications.

Who are Accountants

An **accountant** is a practitioner of accounting, and they can be categorized based on the kinds of organizations they work in.

Private accountants are the accountants employed by a particular business firm, perhaps as a chief accountant, **controller**, or financial vice president. The scope of activities and responsibilities of private accountants varies widely. They offer services such as general accounting, **cost accounting**, **budgeting** and internal **auditing**. Private accountants are frequently referred to as **administrative or management accountants**, or, if they are employed by a manufacturing concern, as industrial accountants. [5]

Public accountants are the accountants who render accounting services on a fee basis, and staff accountants employed by them. In public accounting, an accountant may practice as an individual or as a member of a public accounting firm. Because of the complexity of today's business structure and increasing regulations by **governmental agencies**, members of public accounting firms tend to specialize in one of the three general services: auditing, taxation, and management advisory services. And public accountants who have met a state's education, experience, and examination requirements may become **certified public accountants**, which are commonly abbreviated as CPAs.

Government accountants work in the public sector, maintaining and examining the records of governmental agencies and auditing private businesses and individuals whose activities are subject to government regulations or taxation.[6] In China, all branches of government, as well as non-profit organizations, employ accountants, and all these accountants, like those in private industry, work on a salary basis rather than pay/paying a fee.

Vocabulary

accounting	*n.* 会计；会计学
identify	*vt. & vi.* 确认；识别，认出
measure	*vt. & vi. & n.* 计量；测量
record	*vt. & vi. & n.* 记录
communicate	*vt. & vi.* 传达，表达；沟通，交流
business activity	经营活动，业务活动
financial statement	财务报表
figuratively	*adv.* 形象地，比喻地
bookkeeping	*n.* 记账，簿记，管账
data(复数 datum)	*n.* 资料，材料，数据
accountant	*n.* 会计人员，会计师
controller	*n.* 管理者；财务总管
cost accounting	成本会计
budgeting	*n.* 预算
auditing	*n.* 查账；审计；审计学
administrative or management accountant	管理会计师
governmental agency	政府机构
certified public accountants (CPA)	注册会计师

Notes

[1] Accounting is a system that identifies, measures, records, and communicates relevant, reliable, and comparable information about an organization's business activities. 会计是用来确认、计量、记录和传递有关组织的经营活动信息的相关性、可靠性、可比性的系统。

[2] the keeping of a chronological diary of the measured events 被计量事项按时间顺序予以记录

[3] credit approvals, checking accounts, tax forms, and payroll 信贷(信用)审批，支票账户，纳税申报表格以及工资单

[4] As technology has changed the way we store, process, and summarize masses of data, accounting has been freed to expand. 由于技术已经改变了我们储存、处理、汇总大量数据的方法，会计得以自由发展。

[5] Private accountants are frequently referred to as administrative or management accountants, or, if they are employed by a manufacturing concern, as industrial accountants. 企业(专用)会计师通常被称为管理会计师，如果受雇于制造业企业，就被称为工业会计师。

[6] Government accountants work in the public sector, maintaining and examining the records of governmental agencies and auditing private businesses and individuals whose activities are subject to government regulations or taxation. 在公共部门工作的政府会计，负责记录和检查政府机构账务，审计其活动受政府管制或具有纳税义务的企业和个体。

1.2   Users of Accounting Information
会计信息使用者

A conversation between A—an accountant and S—a freshman majoring in accounting.

S: Who are the external users of accounting information?

A: They could be various individuals and institutions, such as lenders, shareholders, directors, customers, suppliers, governmental agencies.

S: It's not an easy job for accountants to provide useful financial information to all these groups and individuals, because their needs will vary according to their purposes.

A: It's not easy. They are usually interested in the financial position and the operating results of a business. The gathering and presentation of this information for external financial reporting is known as financial accounting.

S: What about internal users?

A: They are often referred to as "management", who need various types of accounting information for the day-to-day operations of the business, for evaluating current operations and for planning the future operations.

People receiving accounting reports are termed as the users of accounting information. The type of information that a specific user will require depends upon the kinds of decisions that the user must make. Users of financial information are generally divided into two groups: external users and internal users.

External Information Users

External users of accounting information are not directly involved in running the organization. They include **shareholders (stockholders)**, lenders, directors, customers, suppliers, regulators, lawyers, **brokers,** and the press.[1] External users have limited access to an organization's information. Yet their business decisions depend on information that is reliable, relevant and comparable.

Financial accounting is the area of accounting aimed at serving external users by providing them with **general-purpose** financial statements. The term "general-purpose" refers to the broad

range of purposes for which external users rely on these statements.

Each external user has special information needs depending on the types of decisions to be made. Lenders loan money or other resources to an organization. Lenders look for information to help them **assess** whether an organization is likely to **repay** its loans with **interest**. Shareholders are the owners of a **corporation**. They use accounting reports in deciding whether to buy, hold, or sell **stock**. Shareholders typically select a **board of directors** to oversee their interests in an organization. Since directors are responsible to shareholders, their information needs are similar. External **auditors** examine financial statements to verify that they are prepared according to accounting principles. **Employees** and **labor unions** use financial statements to judge the fairness of wages, appraise job prospects, and **bargain** for better wages. Regulators often have legal authority over certain activities of organizations. For example, **tax authorities** require organizations to file accounting reports in computing taxes. **Securities** regulators require reports for companies that sell their stock to the public.

Accounting serves the needs of many other external users. <u>Voters, legislators, and government officials use accounting information to monitor and evaluate government receipts and expenses.</u> [2] Contributors to nonprofit organizations use accounting information to evaluate the use and impact of their donations. Suppliers use accounting information to judge the soundness of a customer before making sales **on credit**, and customers use financial reports to assess the staying power of potential suppliers.

Internal Information Users

Internal users of accounting information are those directly involved in managing and **operating** an organization. They utilize the information to help improve the efficiency and effectiveness of an organization. **Management accounting** is the area of accounting that serves the decision-making needs of internal users. <u>Internal reports are not subject to the same rules as external reports and instead are designed with the special needs of internal users.</u> [3]

There are several types of internal users, and many are **managers** of key operating activities. For example, research and development managers need information about projected costs and revenues of any proposed changes in products and services; purchasing managers need to know what, when, and how much to purchase; human resource managers need information about employees' payroll, benefits, performance, and compensation; production managers depend on information to monitor costs and ensure quality; marketing managers use reports about sales and costs to target consumers, set prices, and monitor consumer needs, tastes, and price concerns.

Both internal and external users rely on internal controls to monitor and control company activities. <u>Internal controls are procedures set up to protect company property and equipment, ensure reliable accounting reports, promote efficiency, and encourage adherence to company policies.</u> [4] Examples are good records, physical controls, and independent reviews.

Vocabulary

shareholder	*n.* 股东；股票持有者
stockholder	*n.* 股东；股票持有者
broker	*n.* (股票、外币等)经纪人
general-purpose	*adj.* 多方面的，多种用途的；通用的
assess	*vt.* 评定；估价
repay	*vt. & vi.* 偿还
interest	*n.* 利益；利息
corporation	*n.* 公司；法人；社团，团体
stock	*n.* 股份，股票
board of directors	*n.* 董事会
auditor	*n.* 审计员
employee	*n.* 雇工，雇员，职工
labor union	*n.* 工会
bargain	*vi.* 讨价还价；达成协议
tax authorities	税务机关
securities	*n.* 有价证券
on credit	赊欠，赊账
operate	*vt. & vi.* 经营；管理
management accounting	管理会计
manager	*n.* 经理；管理人

Notes

[1] They include shareholders (stockholders), lenders, directors, customers, suppliers, regulators, lawyers, brokers, and the press. 他们(外部信息使用者)包括股东、出借方、董事、客户、供货商、监管者、律师、经纪人以及传媒。

[2] Voters, legislators, and government officials use accounting information to monitor and evaluate government receipts and expenses. 投票者、立法者以及政府官员使用会计信息来监督和评价政府的收入及费用。

[3] Internal reports are not subject to the same rules as external reports and instead are designed with the special needs of internal users. 内部报告不需遵守外部报告的规则，而是根据内部使用者的特定需要来设计。

[4] Internal controls are procedures set up to protect company property and equipment, ensure reliable accounting reports, promote efficiency, and encourage adherence to company policies. 内部控制是为了保护公司财产和设备、确保会计报告的可靠性、提高效率、鼓励遵守公司政策而设立的程序。

1.3 Accounting Assumptions
会计假设

A conversation between A—an accountant and S—a freshman majoring in accounting.

S: How many accounting assumptions are there?

A: There are four fundamental assumptions: economic entity assumption, going concern assumption, monetary unit assumption, and time period assumption.

S: Does the accounting entity refer to an organization accounting serves?

A: Yes. Accounting for every entity should be independent.

S: I guess the time period refers to a time period like a year or a month, right?

A: Right. We divide the life of a business into time periods of equal length, like a year, a quarter or a month.

S: Then what does monetary unit assumption refer to?

A: It requires that money be used as the basic measuring unit for financial reporting.

S: Does the going concern assumption mean the business won't be closed for ever?

A: Yes. It assumes that the business will continue in operation indefinitely.

The most fundamental concepts or assumptions underlying the accounting structure are (1) **economic entity assumption**, (2) **going concern assumption**, (3) **monetary unit assumption**, and (4) **time period assumption**.

Economic Entity Assumption

Financial records must be separately maintained for each economic entity. Economic entities include businesses, governments, schools, and other social organizations. The economic entity can be identified with a particular unit of **accountability**. Although accounting information from many different entities may be combined for financial reporting purposes, every economic event must be associated with and recorded by a specific entity. [1] In addition, the business is separate and distinct from its owners. Entity's assets and other financial elements are not **commingled** with those of the owners. The economic entity assumption is an accounting concept, and not a legal construct.

Going Concern Assumption

Unless otherwise noted, the business is assumed to continue **indefinitely** unless **terminated** by owners. And financial statements are prepared under the assumption that the company will remain in business indefinitely. Therefore, it is assumed that the entity will realize its assets and settle its obligations in the normal course of the business.

Monetary Unit Assumption

An economic entity's accounting records include only quantifiable transactions. Certain economic events that affect a company, such as hiring a new **chief executive officer (CEO)** or introducing a new product, cannot be easily quantified in monetary units and, therefore, do not appear in the company's accounting records. Transactions are recorded based on a common **currency** and not adjusted for changes in value.

Time Period Assumption

The time period assumption presumes that the life of a company can be divided into time periods, such as a year, and that useful reports can be prepared for those periods. Although businesses intend to continue in long term, it is always helpful to account for their performance and position based on certain time periods because it provides timely **feedback** and helps in making timely decisions. [2]

Vocabulary

economic entity assumption	会计主体假设；经济主体假设
going concern assumption	持续经营假设
monetary unit assumption	货币计量假设；货币单位假设
time period assumption	会计分期假设；会计期间假设
accountability	*n.* 会计责任
commingle	*vt. & vi.* 混合，掺和，合并
indefinitely	*adv.* 无限期地；不定期地；不明确地
terminate	*vt. & vi.* 结束；使终结；解雇；到达终点站
chief executive officer (CEO)	执行长，首席执行官
currency	*n.* 货币
feedback	*n.* 反馈

Notes

[1] Although accounting information from many different entities may be combined for financial reporting purposes, every economic event must be associated with and recorded by a specific entity.　尽管为了财务报告目的可以把许多不同主体的会计信息合并，但是每一个经济事项必须被相应记录到一个特定主体。

[2] Although businesses intend to continue in long term, it is always helpful to account for their performance and position based on certain time periods because it provides timely feedback and helps in making timely decisions.　虽然企业打算长期经营下去，但是根据特定的时间期限簿记企业的经营绩效和经营状况总是有益的，因为这提供了及时的反馈，并有助于做出及时的决策。

1.4 Qualitative Characteristics of Accounting Information
会计信息质量特征

A conversation between A—an accountant and S—a freshman majoring in accounting.

S: Have you ever heard of the abbreviation of GAAP?

A: Yes, GAAP are the initials of "generally accepted accounting principles". We can translate GAAP into Chinese as "公认会计准则". When we say GAAP, we usually mean the US GAAP. Many countries have their own GAAP, like Australia GAAP, India GAAP and so on, but the US GAAP remains the most influential.

S: If only all countries could follow the same rules.

A: An organization named International Accounting Standards Board (国际会计准则委员会) has established International Financial Reporting Standards, which have been accepted by many countries. The Chinese Accounting Standards, which have been implemented since 2007, are substantially in line with the international standards, though a few exceptions are noted.

S: Are there any qualitative characteristics of accounting information in the US GAAP?

A: Of course. Such as relevance, reliability, timeliness, comparability and materiality. Accounting fundamentals are similar all over the world.

In China, on 15 February 2006, the Ministry of Finance of the People's Republic of China announced that it had adopted a new basic standard and 38 new Chinese Accounting Standards. In the second chapter of the basic standard, it indicates 8 qualitative characteristics (requirements) of accounting information, including **reliability**, **relevance**, **understandability**, **comparability**, **substance over form**, **materiality**, **conservatism** and **timeliness**.

 Reliability

Information is reliable if a user can depend upon it to be materially accurate and <u>if it faithfully represents the information that it purports to present</u>[1]. To be useful, information must be reliable as well as relevant. Degrees of reliability must be recognized. It is hardly ever a question of black or white, but rather of more reliability or less. Reliability rests upon the extent to which the accounting description or **measurement** is **verifiable** and representationally faithful. **Neutrality** of information also interacts with those two components of reliability to affect the usefulness of the information.

Relevance

Information is relevant if it helps users of the financial statements in predicting future trends of the business or confirming or correcting any past **predictions** they have made. <u>Information can make a difference to decisions by improving decision makers' capacities to predict or by</u>

providing feedback on earlier expectations. [2] Usually, information does both at once, because knowledge about the outcomes of actions already taken will generally improve decision makers' abilities to predict the results of similar future actions. Without knowledge of the past, the basis for a prediction will usually be lacking. Without an interest in the future, knowledge of the past is **sterile**.

 Understandability

Transactions and events must be accounted for and presented in the financial statements in a manner that is easily understandable by a user who possesses a reasonable level of knowledge of the business, economic activities and accounting in general. Understandability of the information contained in financial statements is essential for its relevance to the users.

Comparability

Information about a particular enterprise gains greatly in usefulness if it can be compared with similar information about other enterprises and with similar information about the same enterprise for some other period or some other point in time. Comparability between enterprises and **consistency** in the application of methods over time increases the informational value of comparisons of relative economic opportunities or performance.[3] The significance of information, especially quantitative information, depends to a great extent on the user's ability to relate it to some benchmark.

Substance over Form

Substance over form is an accounting principle used to ensure that financial statements give a complete, relevant, and accurate picture of transactions and events [4]. If an entity practices the substance over form concept, then the financial statements will show the overall financial reality of the entity (substance), rather than the legal form of transactions (form). In accounting for business transactions and other events, the measurement and reporting is for the economic impact of an event, instead of its legal form. Substance over form is critical for reliable financial reporting. It is particularly relevant in the case of revenue recognition, sale and purchase agreements, etc.

Materiality

Materiality is a pervasive concept that relates to the qualitative characteristics, especially relevance and reliability. Materiality and relevance are both defined in terms of what influences or makes a difference to a decision maker, but the two terms can be distinguished. A decision not to disclose certain information may be made, because investors have no need for that kind of information (it is not relevant) or because the amounts involved are too small to make a difference (they are not material).

Conservatism

Conservatism is the general concept of recognizing expenses and liabilities as soon as possible when there is uncertainty about the outcome, but only to recognize revenues and assets when they are assured of being received. Thus, when given a choice between several outcomes where the probabilities of occurrence are equally likely, the accountant should recognize that transaction resulting in the lower amount of profit, or at least the **deferral** of a profit. Similarly, if a choice of outcomes with similar probabilities of occurrence will impact the value of an asset, recognize the transaction resulting in a lower recorded asset valuation.

Timeliness

Timeliness, that is, having information available to decision makers before it loses its capacity to influence decisions, is <u>an ancillary aspect of relevance</u>[5]. If information is not available when it is needed or becomes available so long after the reported events that it has no value for future action, it lacks relevance and is of little or no use. Timeliness alone cannot make information relevant, but a lack of timeliness can rob information of relevance it might otherwise have had.

Vocabulary

reliability	*n.* 可靠性
relevance	*n.* 相关性
understandability	*n.* 可理解性
comparability	*n.* 可比性
substance over form	实质重于形式
materiality	*n.* 重要性
conservatism	*n.* 谨慎性；保守主义
timeliness	*n.* 及时性
measurement	*n.* 计量；量度
verifiable	*adj.* 能作证的，能证实的
neutrality	*n.* 中立，中立地位
prediction	*n.* 预测，预报
sterile	*adj.* 不毛的，贫瘠的；无效果的
consistency	*n.* 一贯性；一致性
deferral	*n.* 递延，延期

Notes

[1] if it faithfully represents the information that it purports to present　如果它忠实地表述了它意图要陈述的信息

[2] Information can make a difference to decisions by improving decision makers' capacities to predict or by providing feedback on earlier expectations.　通过提高决策者的预测能力或对早期的预期提供反馈，信息就可以影响决策。

[3] Comparability between enterprises and consistency in the application of methods over time increases the informational value of comparisons of relative economic opportunities or performance.　企业之间的可比性和一段时间内方法应用的一致性，增加了对于相关经济机会或绩效比较的信息价值。

[4] a complete, relevant, and accurate picture of transactions and events　关于交易和事项的完整的、相关的和准确的图片

[5] an ancillary aspect of relevance　相关性的补充方面

1.5　Accounting Elements
会计要素

A conversation between A—an accountant and S—a freshman majoring in accounting.

S: Every time I see financial statements, I get confused, for there always seem to be too many items in the statement.

A: I believe you won't find them difficult as long as you understand their major elements.

S: What are the elements then?

A: Elements can be categorized into six groups according to Chinese Accounting Standards, and they are assets, liabilities, owner's equity, revenues, expenses, and profits. Assets are economic resources that are owned by the business. Liabilities represent the debts owed to others. Owners' equity represents the portion of the assets that belongs to the owner of the business.

S: Sorry, I'm still confused.

In China, it is said that the basics of accounting involve six fundamental elements: **assets, liabilities, owner's equity**, **revenues**, **expenses**, and **profits**. The first three are the basic accounting elements that describe the amounts of resources and claims to resources at a specific time, which make up the basic **accounting equation**. The last three accounting elements describe events that affect a business' gains and losses during a period of time and make up the expanded accounting equation. We will discuss the accounting equation later in detail.

 Assets

Assets are probable future economic benefits obtained or controlled by a particular entity as a result of past transactions or events.[1] An asset has three essential characteristics: (1) it **embodies** a probable future benefit that involves a capacity, singly or in combination with other assets, to contribute directly or indirectly to future net cash inflows; (2) a particular entity can obtain the benefit and control others' access to it; and (3) the transactions or other events giving

rise to the entity's right to or control of the benefit have already occurred.

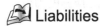 Liabilities

Liabilities are probable future sacrifices of economic benefits arising from present obligations of a particular entity to transfer assets or provide services to other entities in the future as a result of past transactions or events.[2] A liability has three essential characteristics: (1) it embodies a present duty or responsibility to one or more other entities that entails settlement by probable future transfer or use of assets at a specified or determinable date, on occurrence of a specified event, or on demand; (2) the duty or responsibility obligates a particular entity, leaving it little or no discretion to avoid the future sacrifice; and (3) the transactions or other events obligating the entity have already happened.

Owner's Equity

Owner's equity is the residual interest in the assets of an entity that remains after deducting its liabilities. A major distinguishing characteristic of the equity of a business enterprise is that it may be increased through investments of assets by owners who also may, from time to time, receive **distributions** of assets from the entity. Owners invest in a business enterprise with the expectation of obtaining a return on their investment as a result of the enterprise's providing goods or services to customers at a profit. [3] Owners benefit if the enterprise is profitable but bear the risk that it may be unprofitable.

Revenues

Revenues are inflows of cash or other properties in exchange for goods or services provided to customers as part of central operations of the business. [4] Revenues represent actual or expected cash inflows (or the equivalent) that have occurred or will eventuate as a result of the entity's ongoing major or central operations. The assets increased by revenues may be of various kinds—for example, **cash**, **claims** against customers or clients, other goods or services received, or increased value of a product resulting from production.

Expenses

Expenses are decreases in economic benefits during an accounting period in the form of outflows or depletions of assets or incurrence of liabilities that result in decreases in equity, other than those relating to distributions to owners[5]. Expenses represent actual or expected cash outflows (or the equivalent) that have occurred or will eventuate as a result of the entity's ongoing major or central operations. The assets that flow out or are used or the liabilities that are incurred may be of various kinds—for example, units of product delivered or produced, employees' services used, kilowatt hours of electricity used to light an office building, or taxes on current income.

Profits

Profit, sometimes called comprehensive income, is <u>the residual amount that remains after expenses have been deducted from revenues</u> [6]. If revenues exceed expenses, there is a net income and the amount is a positive figure; if expenses **exceed** revenues, there is a net loss and the amount is a negative figure. It is important to note that profit (comprehensive income) is the change in equity of a business enterprise during a period from transactions and other events and circumstances from non-owner sources. It includes all changes in equity during a period except those resulting from investments by owners and distributions to owners.

Vocabulary

asset	*n.* 资产，财产
liability	*n.* 负债
owner's equity	所有者权益，业主权益
revenue	*n.* 收入，收益
expense	*n.* 费用
profit	*n.* 利润
accounting equation	会计等式
embody	*vt.* 表现，体现
distribution	*n.* 分配
cash	*n.* 现金；支付金额 & *vt.* 支付现款；兑现 & *adj.* 现金的
claim	*n.* (根据权利而提出的)要求
exceed	*vt.* 超过；超越

Notes

[1] Assets are probable future economic benefits obtained or controlled by a particular entity as a result of past transactions or events.   资产是指由过去的交易或事项形成的，并由特定主体企业拥有或控制的资源，该资源预期未来可能带来经济利益。

[2] Liabilities are probable future sacrifices of economic benefits arising from present obligations of a particular entity to transfer assets or provide services to other entities in the future as a result of past transactions or events.   负债是指过去的交易或事项形成的现实义务，履行该义务预期会导致经济利益流出企业。现实义务是指企业在现行条件下已承担的义务。

[3] Owners invest in a business enterprise with the expectation of obtaining a return on their investment as a result of the enterprise's providing goods or services to customers at a profit.   所有者向企业投资期望获得投资回报，而回报来自企业为客户提供商品或服务所得的获利。

[4] Revenues are inflows of cash or other properties in exchange for goods or services provided to customers as part of central operations of the business.   收入是企业在日常(重要经营)活动中向客户提供商品或服务交换来的现金或其他资产的流入。

[5] other than those relating to distributions to owners   而不是与所有者分配相关的那些

[6] the residual amount that remains after expenses have been deducted from revenues 从收入中扣除费用后留下的余额

1.6 Accounting Equation
会计等式

A conversation between A—an accountant and S—a freshman majoring in accounting.

A: Do you know anything about the accounting equation?

S: Yes. The amount of assets is equal to the sum of liabilities and owners' equity.

A: Very good. In fact, they are two sides of the same business resources. Assets tell us what resources the business owns and how much it owns. Liabilities and owners' equity tell us who supplied these resources and how much they supplied.

S: In other words, everything the business owns has been supplied by the creditors and the owners, hasn't it?

A: Yes. According to the law, if the business goes bankrupt, liabilities should be given priority over owners' equity.

What is Accounting Equation

The basic accounting equation, also called <u>the balance sheet equation</u>[1], represents the relationship between the above first three accounting elements. It can be expressed as:

$$\text{Assets} = \text{Liabilities} + \text{Owner's Equity}$$

A business transaction is an exchange of goods or services that affects this equation. It is essential to understand the effects of transactions on the accounting equation in order to understand the accounting function.

We have learned the relationship between revenue and expense:

$$\text{Net income (Net loss)} = \text{Revenues} - \text{Expenses}$$

Next net income or net loss will be **closed** to owner's equity. And we can have the following presentation of accounting equation:

$$\text{Assets} = \text{Liabilities} + [\text{Owner's equity} + (\text{Revenues} - \text{Expenses})]$$

Effects of Transactions on the Accounting Equation

All business transactions, from the simplest to the most complex, can be **stated** in terms of the resulting change in the five basic elements of the accounting equation. <u>The accounting equation **applies** to all economic and legal entities—from **sole proprietorship** to large corporations.</u>[2] Various transactions that affect the accounting equation are introduced in the following Table 1-1.

Table 1-1　Accounting Equation Affected by Various Transactions

Explanation	Assets		Expenses		Liabilities		Owner's equity		Revenues	
Cash or other assets from owner's investment	+	6,000					+	6,000		
Selling assets on credit	+	900	+	1,100					+	2,000
Buying assets on credit	+	1,000			+	1,000				
Paying expenses (e.g. rent or professional fees) or dividends	−	200	+	200						
Recording expenses, but not paying them at the moment			+	100	+	100				
Paying a debt that you owe	−	500			−	500				
Receiving cash for sale of an asset: one asset is exchanged for another; no change in assets or liabilities		0		0		0		0		0

One of the direct effects of the accounting equation illustrated above is the **double-entry system** of recording, which simply means that both sides of a business transaction are recorded. And when you record both sides of a business transaction, you are keeping the books in balance. For example, if supplies were purchased for $1,000 from a supplier on credit, a business would own supplies costing $1,000 and owe the creditor $1,000 for the purchase on account. Both sides of the transaction would be recorded, and that results in an increase in the supplies (asset) and an increase in the accounts payable (liability) for the purchase, and eventually a balance in books.

Vocabulary

accounting equation	会计等式
close	*vt.* 结转，结清
state	*vt.* 规定；陈述，声明
apply	*vt.* 应用，运用
sole proprietorship	独资企业；独资(经营)
double-entry system	复式会计制度

Notes

[1] the balance sheet equation　资产负债表等式

[2] The accounting equation applies to all economic and legal entities — from sole proprietorship to large corporations.　会计等式适用于所有的经济和法律个体，不管是独资企业还是大型公司。

Exercises

I. Discuss the following questions in English.

1.   What is the relationship between accounting and bookkeeping?

2.   What is the purpose of accounting?

3.   Describe various career opportunities in accounting.

4.   Who are the internal and external users of accounting information?

5.   What are the basic assumptions of accounting?

6.   Identify the qualitative characteristics of accounting information.

7.   Choose two principal qualitative characteristics of accounting information and explain why.

8.   Describe the elements of accounting.

9.   What is the difference between revenue and profit?

10.   What is the accounting equation? What is the expanded accounting equation?

11.   What are the advantages of double-entry system of accounting?

II. Choose the best word or phrase that fits the sentence.

1.   Accounting also identifies and communicates information on transactions and events, and it includes the _____ processes of analysis and interpretation.

      A. essential   B. important

      C. crucial   D. necessary

2.   Public accountants work for many clients and offer auditing, tax and _____ services.

      A. management advisory   B. internal control

      C. regulation   D. financing

3.   _____ is the area of accounting aimed at serving external users by providing them with general-purpose financial statements.

      A. Managerial accounting   B. Financial accounting

      C. Social accounting   D. Budget accounting

4.   _____ managers depend on information to monitor costs and ensure quality.

      A. Research and development   B. Marketing

      C. Purchasing   D. Production

5.   The assumption that holds that an entity will remain in operation for the foreseeable future is the_____.

      A. economic entity assumption   B. going concern assumption

      C. monetary unit assumption   D. time period assumption

6.   An economic entity's accounting records include only _____ transactions.

      A. valuable   B. marketable

C. quantifiable   D. serviceable

7. Relevant accounting information is capable of making a _____ in a decision.

   A. choice   B. difference

   C. selection   D. point

8. Timeliness is an ancillary aspect of _____.

   A. relevance   B. reliability

   C. comparability   D. materiality

9. _____ are probable future economic benefits obtained or controlled by a particular entity as a result of past transactions or events.

   A. Properties   B. Capital

   C. Assets   D. Wealth

10. _____ are probable future sacrifices of economic benefits arising from present obligations of a particular entity to transfer assets or provide services to other entities in the future as a result of past transactions or events.

   A. Liabilities   B. Debts

   C. Obligations   D. Responsibilities

11. One of the direct effects of the accounting equation is _____.

   A. the actual accounting   B. the double-entry system of recording

   C. the cash accounting   D. the budget accounting

III. Match each word on the left with its corresponding meaning on the right.

A	B
1. essential	(a) including all or everything
2. entity	(b) the quality of nearness to the truth or the true value
3. crucial	(c) spread throughout
4. categorize	(d) something that exists as a single and complete unit
5. accuracy	(e) of extreme importance
6. possess	(f) absolutely necessary; vitally necessary
7. distribution	(g) place into or assign to a group
8. pervasive	(h) something that results
9. comprehensive	(i) the act of distributing or spreading
10. outcome	(j) to own or have something

IV. Fill in the blanks with words or phrases from the list below.

A.	casting	B.	continuing	C.	trusted	D.	direct
E.	donations	F.	ethical	G.	figures	H.	beliefs
I.	senior	J.	success	K.	wages	L.	prepare
M.	refers to	N.	suppliers	O.	pay	P.	large

The goal of accounting is to provide useful information for decisions. For information to be useful, it must be (1)____ . This demands ethics in accounting. Ethics are (2)____ that distinguish right from wrong. They are accepted standards of good and bad behavior.

Identifying the (3)____ path is sometimes difficult. The preferred path is a course of action that avoids (4)____ doubt on one's decisions. For example, accounting users are less likely to trust an audit report if the auditor's (5)____ depends on the success of the client's business. To avoid such concerns, ethics rules are often set. For example, auditors are banned from (6)____ investment in their clients and cannot accept pay that depends on (7)____ in the clients' reports.

Providers of accounting information often face ethical choices as they (8)____ financial reports. These choices can affect the price a buyer pays and the (9)____ paid to workers. They can even affect the (10)____ of products and services. Misleading information can lead to a wrongful closing of a division that harms workers, customers, and (11)____ . There is an old saying: *Good ethics are good businesses.*

Some people extend ethics to social responsibility, which (12)____ a concern for the impact of actions on society. An organization's social responsibility can include (13)____ to hospitals, colleges, community programs, and law enforcement. It can also include programs to reduce pollution, increase product safety, improve worker conditions, and support (14)____ education. These programs are not limited to (15)____ companies. For example, many small businesses offer discounts to students and (16)____ citizens. Still others help sponsor events such as the Special Olympics and summer reading programs.

V. Translate the following sentences into Chinese.

1. Accounting provides the techniques for accumulating and the language for communicating economic data to various individuals and institutions.

2. Accounting has evolved through time, changing with the needs of the society.

3. Accountants use numbers to portray the reality of an entity in financial terms.

4. Businesses all over the world need to keep records of their finances in order to satisfy investors and legislators.

5. An asset is anything of value that is owned by a business or an individual, the value of which is determined by the acquisition price, or historical cost of the item.

6. Expenses are often referred to as "the cost of doing business", which decrease the net asset in the business.

VI. Translate the following sentences into English.

1. 会计是以货币为主要计量单位，反映和监督一个单位经济活动的一种经济管理工作。
2. 会计信息的价值在于帮助所有者或其他利益相关方作出合理的经济决策。
3. 会计为了满足不同用户的信息需要，形成了财务会计和管理会计两大分支。
4. 会计要素是根据交易或者事项的经济特征所确定的财务会计对象的基本分类。
5. 企业收入的来源渠道多种多样，例如销售商品、提供劳务、让渡资产使用权等。
6. 会计等式是建立各种会计核算专门方法的理论基础。

Reading Material 1

Accounting Evolution

People in all civilizations have maintained various types of records of business activities. The oldest known are clay tablet records of the payment of wages in Babylonia around 3600 B.C. There are numerous evidences of record keeping and systems of accounting control in ancient Egypt and in the Greek city-states.

The evolution of the system of record keeping which came to be called "double entry" was strongly influenced by Venetian merchants. The first known description of the system was published in Italy in 1494. The author, a Franciscan monk by the name of Luca Pacioli, was a mathematician who taught in various universities in Perugia, Naples, Pisa, and Florence. Goethe, a German poet, novelist, scientist, and universal genius, wrote about double entry as follows: "It is one of the most beautiful inventions of the human spirit, and every good businessman should use it in his economic undertakings." In spite of the tremendous development of business operations since 1494, and the ever increasing complexities of business and governmental organizations, the basic elements of the double-entry system have continued virtually unchanged.

The Industrial Revolution, which occurred in England from the mid-eighteenth to mid-nineteenth century, brought many social and economic changes, notably a change from the handicraft method of producing marketable goods to the factory system. The use of machinery in turning out many identical products gave rise to the need to determine the cost of a large volume of machine-made products instead of the cost of a relatively small number of individually hand-crafted products. The specialized field of cost accounting emerged to meet the need for the analysis of various costs and for recording techniques.

In the early days of manufacturing operations, when business enterprises were relatively small and often isolated geographically, competition was frequently not very keen. Cost accounting was primitive and focused primarily on providing management with records of reports on past operations. As manufacturing enterprises became larger and more complex and as competition among manufacturers increased, the "scientific management concept" evolved. This concept emphasized a systematic approach to the solution of management problems. Paralleling this trend was the development of more sophisticated cost accounting concepts to supply management with analytical techniques for measuring the efficiency of current operations and in planning for future operations. This trend was accelerated in the twentieth century by the advent of the electronic computer with its capacity for manipulating large masses of data and its ability to determine the potential effect of alternative courses of action.

The expanded business operations initiated by the Industrial Revolution required increasingly large amounts of money to build factories and purchase machinery. This need for large amounts of capital resulted in the development of the corporate form of organization, which was first legally established in England in 1845. The Industrial Revolution spread rapidly to the United States, which became one of the world's leading industrial nations shortly after the Civil War. The accumulation of large amounts of capital was essential for establishment of new businesses in industries such as manufacturing, transportation, mining, electronic power, and communications. In the United States, as in England, the corporation was the form of organization that facilitated the accumulation of the substantial amounts of capital needed.

Almost all large American business enterprises, and many small ones, are organized as corporations largely because ownership is evidenced by readily transferable shares of stock. The shareholders of a corporation control the management of corporate affairs only indirectly. They elect a board of directors, which establishes general policies and selects officers who actively manage the corporation. The development of a class of owners far removed from active participation in the management of the business created an additional dimension for accounting. Accounting information was needed not only by management in directing the affairs of the corporation but also by the shareholders, who required periodic financial statements in order to appraise management's performance.

Nowadays, a number of specialized fields in accounting, apart from financial accounting and managerial accounting, have evolved as a result of rapid technological advances and accelerated economic growth. These specialized accounting areas include cost accounting, taxation accounting, budgetary accounting, auditing, social accounting, international accounting, human resource accounting, environmental accounting and so forth.

Answers:

II.	1	C	2	A	3	B	4	D	5	B	6	C	7	B	8	A
	9	C	10	A	11	B										

III.	1	f	2	d	3	e	4	g	5	b	6	j	7	i	8	c
	9	a	10	h												

IV.	1	C	2	H	3	F	4	A	5	O	6	D	7	G	8	L
	9	K	10	J	11	N	12	M	13	E	14	B	15	P	16	I

 **知识扩展**

1. 一般公认会计原则

一般公认会计原则(GAAP)是指被会计职业界采纳的用于指导报告企业经济活动的原则，包含一般原则(broad principles)和特定原则(specific principles)。一般原则来自长期采纳的会计实务，特定原则主要由规则制定者建立和发布。会计准则是 GAAP 的主要组成部分。

2. 会计信息的局限性

虽然会计信息为内外部使用者提供了大量对决策有用的信息，但是使用者仍然需要其他方面的信息。例如，潜在投资者除了研究公司的财务报告以外，还需要其他来源的信息，例如该公司的市场份额、上市时间、公司未来发展战略、行业信息等。会计信息的局限性还表现在：(1)一般只提供财务信息，即那些可以用货币量化的信息；(2)披露时间滞后，会计年度结束到年度报告对外公布一般需要 2~4 个月；(3)财务信息主要基于历史信息，而使用者的决策主要面向未来；(4)会计信息制作过程有很多主观判断因素，例如固定资产使用年限、残值等，并且存在会计政策选择问题，例如存货发出的计价可以采用先进先出法或者加权平均法。

3. 中国会计准则

中国会计准则(China's Accounting Standards, CAS)是由中华人民共和国财政部基于中国的国情并广泛征求意见，于 1997 年开始陆续出台的具体准则。至 2017 年，中国的企业会计准则增加到 43 项，其中基本准则 1 项，具体准则 42 项，是我国会计人员从事会计工作必须遵循的基本原则，是会计核算工作的规范。它大致包括三个层次：(1)基本会计准则，明确了财务报告的目标是向财务报告使用者提供决策有用的信息，并反映企业管理层受托责任的履行情况，强调了企业会计确认、计量和报告应该以会计主体、持续经营、会计分期和货币计量为会计基础假设；(2)具体准则，是在基本准则的指导下，处理具体业务标准的规范，具体内容可以分为一般业务准则、特殊行业和特殊业务准则、财务报告准则三大类；(3)应用指南，是从不同角度对企业具体准则进行强化，解决实务操作，包括具体准则解释部分、会计科目和财务报表部分。

Chapter 2　Accounting Cycle
会计循环

Learning Objectives

- Understand the basic phases of accounting cycle　理解会计循环的基本阶段
- Understand economic transactions and source documents 理解交易和原始凭证
- Understand T-accounts and the rules of debit and credit　理解 T 账户以及借方和贷方的规则
- Understand the preparation of entries and posting to the ledger, and know the practices in China　了解分录的准备和分类账的过账，以及其在中国的做法
- Understand the preparation of trial balance　理解试算表的编制
- Understand accrual basis of accounting　理解会计权责发生制
- Understand adjusting accounts　理解账项调整
- Understand the use of worksheet　理解如何使用工作表
- Know the preparation of the financial statements　知道如何编制财务报表
- Understand the closing procedures　理解如何结账

Chapter 2 English
Listening.mp3

Listening Practice　听力练习

第 2 章听写原文翻译和答案的音频见右侧二维码。

Dictation: *Listen and complete the passage with the words or phrases according to what you've heard from the speaker.*

Generally speaking, the accounting process is composed of _____1_____ major phases: analyzing, recording, classifying, summarizing, _____2_____and interpreting. It is highly necessary for us to know that accounting is more than just_____3_____ in the accounting reports. It is quite important to understand the _____4_____ concepts behind the numbers. Without them to provide some meanings, the_____5_____ numbers would make no sense.

Wisdom　至理名言

From eyeball economy to experience economy to fan economy, whoever masters the use of tools can win the future!　从眼球经济到体验经济再到粉丝经济，谁掌握工具的运用，谁就可以赢得未来！

 微型案例

For one year and a half Scarlett has gained every success in her operations of the bar. Figures looked good all the time. One day at the end of July 2008, she talked with her accountant over the business operations. Her accountant showed her the operational diary and source documents that evidenced as follows (partial):

July 1 Sold to Peter Clark $750 invoice number 262, terms 2/10, n/30.

2 Bought for cash 10 cases of whisky costing $2,600 from Timor, Check No. 112.

4 Collected $1,300 from Paul Roth, Invoice No. 245.

5 Sold to Jason Henry $500 invoice number 263, terms 2/10, n/30.

7 Purchased coffee beans from Aloez Co. on account/on credit, $430.

8 Sold to Maxwell Moore $355 invoice number 264, terms 2/10, n/30.

…

2.1   Analyzing Transactions 分析交易

A conversation between A—an accountant and S—a freshman majoring in accounting.

S: When a transaction occurs, how should we make an accounting record of it?

A: First, you should analyze the transaction, and decide which ledger account to debit and which ledger account to credit. Then you can record the transaction in the accounting voucher.

S: Does debit always mean increase and credit always mean decrease?

A: No. Debit and credit both can mean increase or decrease. The particular meaning in a circumstance depends on the nature of the accounts. A debit increases the balance of asset and expense accounts, but it decreases the balance of liabilities, owners' equity and revenue accounts.

S: For example, a retailer purchases $5,000 of goods on credit. We should record it like this: Debit the Inventory account for $5,000, credit the Accounts Payable for $5,000. Is that right?

A: Right. You've got it.

Transactions and Business Documents

Some activities or the day-to-day events of a business are known as transactions. Every business will usually have financial transactions as well as non-financial ones. From an accounting standpoint, we are only concerned with the financial transactions of the business, which involve the performance of a service or the sale of a product to a customer, or the acquisition of service or materials from a **creditor**. [1] However, not all events that have an effect on the organization are recorded as transactions. For example, changes in market interest rate [2]

Source documents, also known as business papers, identify and describe transactions and events entering the accounting process. Some types of source documents, such as a sales **invoice**, **purchase order**, or **check**, is prepared for every transaction entered into by a business.

The Account and Its Analysis

Each transaction recorded results in an increase or decrease in one or more asset, liability, owner's equity, revenue, or expense items. A part of the accounting function is to classify the effects of transactions into meaningful categories and to summarize the results in the firm's financial statements. [3] To **facilitate** accumulating financial statement data, transactions are recorded in accounts. An **account** is a business document used to record and retain monetary information about a company's transaction. Separate accounts are used for each type of asset, liability and owner's equity. The company's full set of accounts are kept in a general ledger and accounts are sometimes called **general ledger** accounts. The general ledger, or simply ledger, is a record containing all accounts used by a company.

An account may have different forms, but in every case the account will have a left side and a right side which are called **debit** side and **credit** side respectively. One simplified format, called a T-account because of its similarity to the letter T, is shown in Figure 2-1.

<table>
<tr><td colspan="2" align="center">Account Title</td></tr>
<tr><td>Left side or debit side
(Abbreviation-Dr.)</td><td>Right side or credit side
(Abbreviation-Cr.)</td></tr>
</table>

Figure 2-1　T-Account

A debit **entry** is an amount recorded in the left side of the account; a credit entry is an amount recorded in the right side of the account. It can be called "debited to" and "credited to" respectively. The debit and credit rules state that:

(1) Accounts on the left side of the accounting equation (asset accounts) are increased by debit entries and decreased by credit entries;

(2) Accounts on the right side of the accounting equation (liability and capital accounts) are increased by credit entries and decreased by debit entries.

The **balance** of an account is the difference between the total increases and decreases recorded in the account. [4] An asset account normally has a debit balance. Liability and owners' equity accounts normally have credit balances. The double entry rule requires that when a transaction is recorded in the accounts, the total amount of the debit entries must always be equal to the total amount of the credit entries.

 Vocabulary

creditor	*n.* 债权人，债主
source document	原始凭证
invoice	*n.* 发票；发货单

purchase order	*n.* 定单
check	*n.* <美>支票
facilitate	*vt.* 促进，助长；使容易；帮助
account	*n.* 账，账目，账户
general ledger	总分类账
debit	*n.* 借方；借方账目 & *vt.* 记入借方
credit	*n.* 贷方；贷方账目，信用 & *vt.* 记入贷方
entry	*n.* 分录；进入；登记
balance	*n.* 余额；平衡

✒ Notes

[1] From an accounting standpoint, we are only concerned with the financial transactions of the business, which involve the performance of a service or the sale of a product to a customer, or the acquisition of service or materials from a creditor.　从会计的角度看，我们仅仅关注企业的财务性交易，包括向顾客提供服务或销售产品，或者从债权人那里获得服务或材料。

[2] Changes in market interest rate　市场利率的变化

[3] A part of the accounting function is to classify the effects of transactions into meaningful categories and to summarize the results in the firm's financial statements.　会计职能的一个组成部分是将各项交易的影响按有意义的类别进行归类，并在公司财务报表中总结成果。

[4] The balance of an account is the difference between the total increases and decreases recorded in the account.　账户余额是记录在账户中总增加与总减少的差额。

2.2   Recording Transactions and Posting
记录交易并过账

A conversation between A—an accountant and S—a freshman majoring in accounting.

S: What does posting mean?

A: Posting is the process of transferring the debit and credit information recorded in each journal entry to the proper accounts in the ledger.

S: It's a piece of cake, since we have decided which account to be debited for what amount and which account to be credited for what amount.

A: But we are more likely to make mistakes with easy things. The ledger consists of many accounts, which are created on the basis of the items of financial statements. So careful accountants follow certain rules in posting.

S: How to test the accuracy of the posting?

A: We can prepare a trial balance to see whether the debit and credit balances of all the accounts are equal in the ledger. But you shouldn't believe in the trial balance completely, because it can't reveal all problems.

Journalizing Transactions

The first step of accounting procedures is analyzing transactions, and the next step is recording the transactions by a journal entry. The **journal**, or the book of original entry, is a chronological record, showing for each transaction the debit and credit changes in specific ledger accounts.[1] While companies can use various journals, every company uses a general journal.

In China, journal entries are first made in vouchers. There are three types of vouchers — **receipt voucher**, **payment voucher** and **transfer voucher**—their formats shown in Figure 2-2. If we receive cash or cash in bank, receipt vouchers are used. We have the fixed debit account, so only credit account title and amount will be **entered**. If we pay cash or cash in bank, payment vouchers are used. We have the fixed credit account, so only debit account title and amount will be entered. Cash journal and cash in bank journal are recorded by the receipt vouchers and payment vouchers. Transactions excluded receipts and payments will be entered in the transfer voucher.

Receipt Voucher

Debit Account:		Date		No.
	Credit Account			
Explanation	General Ledger Account	**Subsidiary Ledger** Account	PR	Amount
Total				

Payment Voucher

Credit Account:		Date		No.
	Debit Account			
Explanation	General Ledger Account	Subsidiary Ledger Account	PR	Amount
Total				

Transfer Voucher

		Date			No.
Explanation	General Ledger Account	Subsidiary Ledger Account	PR	Debit Amount	Credit Amount
Total					

Figure 2-2   Chinese Format of Vouchers

The process of recording transactions in the voucher usually follows these five steps:

(1) Identify the transactions from source documents;

(2) Specify each account affected by the transaction;

(3) Determine whether each account is increased or decreased by the transaction;

(4) <u>Use the rules of debit and credit, determine whether to debit or credit the account to record its increase or decrease;</u> [2]

(5) Enter the transaction based on the double-entry accounting including a brief explanation for the journal entry.

 Posting

Posting <u>is the process of transferring the debit and credit information recorded in each journal entry to the proper accounts in the ledger.</u> [3] The updated ledger accounts will serve as a basis from which the balance sheet and other financial statements are **prepared**. To help in posting, each account is assigned a number. The list of all the accounts and their numbers is called a chart of accounts.

In **International Accounting Standards (IAS)** and **Generally Accepted Accounting Principles (GAAP)**, there is no specific regulation as to how a chart of accounts is established. Nevertheless, in the Application Guidelines of Chinese Accounting Standards for Business Enterprises 2006, there is a uniform chart of 156 accounts. Table 2-1 is partial chart of accounts of Chinese Accounting Standards and their reference translations.

Table 2-1　Chart of Accounts of Chinese Accounting Standards (Partial)

Account Number	会计科目名称	Account Title
I. Assets		
1001	库存现金	Cash on Hand
1002	银行存款	Cash in Bank
1101	交易性金融资产	Marketable Financial Assets
1121	应收票据	Notes Receivable
1122	应收账款	Accounts Receivable
1123	预付账款	Advance to Suppliers
1131	应收股利	Dividends Receivable
1231	其他应收款	Other Receivables
1241	坏账准备	Allowance for Doubtful Accounts
1406	库存商品	Commodity Stocks
1461	存货跌价准备	Provision for Decline in Value of Inventory
1501	待摊费用	Prepaid Expenses
1521	持有至到期投资	Held-to-Maturity Investment

Table 2-1(Continued)

Account Number	会计科目名称	Account Title
1523	可供出售金融资产	Available-for-Sale Financial Assets
1524	长期股权投资	Long-Term Equity Investments
1526	投资性房地产	Investment Real Estate
1531	长期应收款	Long-Term Receivables
1601	固定资产	Fixed Assets
1602	累计折旧	Accumulative Depreciation
1603	固定资产减值准备	Provision for Fixed Assets Impairment
1604	在建工程	Construction in Progress
1606	固定资产清理	Fixed Assets Pending Disposal
1701	无形资产	Intangible Assets
1702	累计摊销	Accumulated Amortization
1703	无形资产减值准备	Provision for Intangible Assets Impairment
1811	递延所得税资产	Deferred Income Tax Assets
1901	待处理财产损溢	Unsettled Assets Profit and Loss

Ⅱ. Liabilities

2001	短期借款	Short-Term Loans
2101	交易性金融负债	Marketable Financial Liabilities
2201	应付票据	Notes Payable
2202	应付账款	Accounts Payable
2205	预收客户款	Advance from Customers
2211	应付职工薪酬	Payroll Payable
2221	应交税费	Taxes Payable
2231	应付股利	Dividends Payable
2232	应付利息	Interest Payable
2241	其他应付款	Other Payables
2601	长期借款	Long-Term Loans
2602	长期债券	Long-Term Bonds
2801	长期应付款	Long-Term Payable
2802	未确认融资费用	Unrecognized Financing Charges

Ⅲ. Common Classes

3101	衍生工具	Derivative Instruments
3201	套期工具	Arbitrage Instruments
3202	被套期项目	Arbitraged Items

Table 2-1(Continued)

Account Number	会计科目名称	Account Title
IV. Owner's Equity		
4001	实收资本	Paid-in Capital
4002	资本公积	Capital Surplus
4101	盈余公积	Earnings Surplus
4103	本年利润	Current Profit
4104	利润分配	Profit Distribution
4201	库存股	Treasury Stock
V. Costs		
5001	生产成本	Production Costs
5101	制造费用	Manufacturing Expenses
VI. Profit and Loss		
6001	主营业务收入	Prime Operating Revenues
6051	其他业务收入	Other Operating Revenues
6101	公允价值变动损益	Profit and Loss from Fair Value Changes
6111	投资收益	Income from Investments
6301	营业外收入	Non-Operating Revenues
6401	主营业务成本	Prime Operating Costs
6402	其他业务成本	Other Operational Costs
6405	营业税金及附加	Sales Tax and Extra Charges
6601	销售费用	Selling Expenses
6602	管理费用	Administrative Expenses
6603	财务费用	Financial Expenses
6711	营业外支出	Non-Operating Expenses
6801	所得税	Income Tax
6901	以前年度损益调整	Profit and Loss Adjustment of Prior Years

At appropriate intervals, the debit and credit entries recorded in the vouchers are transferred to the accounts in the ledger. When a transaction is first recorded, the posting reference (PR) column is left blank (in a manual system). Later, when posting entries, the identification numbers of the individual ledger accounts are entered in the PR column. Notice that there is also a PR column in the ledger that is used to indicate which the posted entries came from.

There is a common format for the general ledger in Figure 2-3.

The posting of journal entry to ledger can be performed in the following steps:

(1) Record the date and the amount of the entry in the account;

(2) Insert the number of the voucher in the PR column of the account;

(3) Insert the ledger account number in the PR column of the voucher.

Account Title				Account No.	
Date	PR	Explanation	Debit	Credit	Balance

Figure 2-3 The Common Format of a General Ledger

 Trial Balance

In a manual accounting system, a **trial balance** may be prepared at any time to test the equality of debits and credits in the ledger. A trial balance is a list of all accounts with their balances. It provides a check on accuracy by showing whether the total debits equal the total credits.

The trial balance is prepared using the following procedures:

(1) Determine the balance of each account in the ledger;

(2) List each account and place its balance beside it;

(3) Compute the total of debit balances and credit balances;

(4) Verify total debit balances equal total credit balances.

Some errors may not be revealed by the trial balance. <u>For example, one of the columns of the trial balance was incorrectly added, or an erroneous amount was posted to the account.</u> [4] If the trial balance is in balance, there are some indications of recording accuracy. However, errors can still be made.

Do not confuse the trial balance with the balance sheet. Accountants prepare a trial balance for their internal records. The company reports its financial position—both inside and outside the business—on the balance sheet, a formal financial statement.

Vocabulary

journal	*n.* 日记账
receipt voucher	收款凭证
payment voucher	付款凭证
transfer voucher	转账凭证
enter	*vt. & vi.* 登记；进入
subsidiary ledger	明细分类账
PR (posting reference)	过账索引
post	*vt.* 过账
prepare	*vt.* 编制；准备
International Accounting Standards (IAS)	国际会计准则
Generally Accepted Accounting Principles (GAAP)	(美国)公认会计准则
trial balance	试算表

Notes

[1] The journal, or the book of original entry, is a chronological record, showing for each transaction the debit and credit changes in specific ledger accounts. 日记账(原始分录账簿)是在特定分类账户内按借贷交易时间先后顺序逐日逐笔进行登记的账簿，又称序时账。

[2] Use the rules of debit and credit, determine whether to debit or credit the account to record its increase or decrease. 根据借贷规则，确定该账户借贷往来记录的增加或减少。

[3] Posting is the process of transferring the debit and credit information recorded in each journal entry to the proper accounts in the ledger. 过账是把每一个记录在日记账分录中的借贷信息过入适当的分类账户的过程。

[4] For example, one of the columns of the trial balance was incorrectly added, or an erroneous amount was posted to the account. 例如，试算表的一列加总错误，或过账金额错误。

2.3 Adjusting Accounts
账项调整

A conversation between A—an accountant and S—a freshman majoring in accounting.

A: Adjusting entries are usually made at the end of the accounting period.

S: Why should adjusting entries be made?

A: Some revenues and expenses affect more than one accounting period, and according to the accrual basis of accounting we should adjust them.

S: Do you mean to say that only revenues and expenses are adjusted?

A: Yes. But adjusting revenue and expense usually leads to the change of owners' equity. Therefore, every adjusting entry affects both an income statement account and a balance sheet account.

S: Would you please detail how the adjustment is made?

A: For instance, a business prepays $6,000 for one-year magazine subscriptions, so every month $500 should be apportioned. One should debit an expense account and credit an asset account for $500.

S: An expense increases, and an asset decreases. Is that right?

A: Right. The depreciation of a fixed asset is a typical example of the end-of-period adjustment.

Accrual Basis of Accounting

The easiest way to keep a record of business transactions is to record them when there is an exchange of cash. This is the cash system, or the **cash basis of accounting**. For example, when a business performs services to customers, the revenue earned would be recorded when cash is

actually received. <u>Therefore, only cash sales would be recorded as the revenue earned for a period, whereas sales on account or charge sales would not be recognized until the customers paid the account.</u> [1]

A more meaningful method used by most businesses is called the accrual system, or the **accrual basis of accounting**, which recognizesa revenues earned regardless of whether the cash is received. A sale on account is recorded as a revenue earned though the cash has not been received. Expenses for the period are recognized when they are incurred even if they have not been paid.

The accounting principles require that a business must use the accrual basis. This is because accrual basis of accounting provides more complete information than cash basis, which is very important for decision-makers.

In accrual accounting, the **revenue recognition principle** states that revenues are recorded when earned, and the **matching principle** states that expenses should be recorded during the period in which they are incurred, regardless of when the transfer of cash occurs. <u>Since many of the business transactions affect the net income of more than one period, all revenues earned during the period and all expenses incurred must be fully presented if a realistic net income figure is to be portrayed.</u> [2] Therefore, it is often necessary to **adjust** some account balances at the end of each accounting period to achieve a proper matching of costs and expenses with revenues.

 Which Accounts Need to Be Adjusted

The trial balance lists the accounts and their balances after the periods transactions have been recorded. These trial balance amounts are incomplete because they do not reflect certain revenue and expense transactions that affect more than one accounting period. Adjustments are necessary to record internal economic events such as the expiration of costs. These transactions are typically not evidenced by any source documents. Note that adjustments are not corrections of errors.

Before financial statements are prepared at the end of an accounting period, it is necessary to adjust the account balances that are not **up-to-date**. The purpose of making adjustments is to ensure that the information on accounting statements is comparable from period to period.

Accounting adjustments fall into three basic categories: deferrals, **depreciation**, and **accruals**.

Deferrals

A deferral is an adjustment for an item that the business paid or received cash **in advance**. It can be further divided into deferred (prepaid) expenses and deferred (unearned) revenues.

Prepaid expense is an expense paid in advance, such as the prepaid rent. Therefore, prepaid expenses are assets because they provide a future benefit for the owner. When these assets are used, their costs become expenses. Adjusting entries involve increasing an expenses and decreasing assets, as follows:

Expense

Asset

Unearned revenue refers to cash received in advance of providing products and services. Therefore, unearned revenues are liabilities because the business owes the customer products or services. As products or services are provided, the unearned revenues become earned revenue. Adjusting entries for unearned revenues involve increasing revenue and decrease liabilities, as follows:

> Liability
>
>> Revenue

 Depreciation

Fixed assets are long-lived tangible assets, such as buildings, furniture, and equipment. Sometimes you may see them referred to as **property, plant and equipment (PPE)** or **plant assets**. All fixed assets decline in usefulness and this decline is an expense. Accountants **allocate** the cost to expense for fixed assets. The general format of the entry to record depreciation expense of a fixed asset is shown as follows:

> Expense
>
>> Accumulated Depreciation

The **accumulated depreciation** account is a **contra asset** account on the balance sheet. A contra account has two distinguishing characteristics:

(1) It always has an associated account;

(2) Its normal balance is opposite that of the associated account.

The contra fixed asset account, accumulated depreciation, is used to reflect the total decline in usefulness of the asset. <u>The balance in a contra account is subtracted from the balance of its associated account when preparing financial statements.</u> [3] The net amount of a fixed asset (cost minus accumulated depreciation) is called that asset's **book value**, or **carrying amount**. The purpose of accumulated depreciation in a contra asset account is to keep track of the original cost of an asset separately from the amount of depreciation that has been charged to expense.

 Accrual

An accrual is the opposite of a deferral. Businesses incur expenses before they pay cash. The term **accrued expense** refers to a liability that arises from an expense that has yet been paid. Some businesses collect cash from customers before earning the revenue. A revenue that has been earned but not yet collected is called an **accrued revenue**.

<u>Accrued expenses refer to costs that are incurred in a period but are both unpaid and unrecorded.</u> [4] Accrued expenses must be reported on the income statement of the period when incurred. Consider an employee's salary and interest expense to a note payable. Adjusting entries for accrued expenses involve increasing expenses and increasing liabilities, as follows:

> Expense
>
>> Liability

Accrued revenues refer to revenues earned in a period that are both unrecorded and not yet received in cash. Accrued revenues are not recorded until adjusting entries are made at the end of the accounting period. An example is a technician who bills customers only when the job is done. Adjusting entries for accrued revenues involve increasing assets and increasing revenues, as follows:

> Asset
>
> > Revenue

Vocabulary

cash basis of accounting	收付实现制会计
accrual basis of accounting	权责发生制会计
revenue recognition principle	收入确认原则
matching principle	配比原则
adjust	*vt. & vi.* 调整；(改变……以)适应
up-to-date	*adj.* 现代的，最新的；最近的
depreciation	*n.* (资产等)折旧
accrual	*n.* 应计项目
in advance	预先，事先；提前
prepaid expense	预付费用；待摊费用
unearned revenue	预收收入
fixed asset	固定资产
property, plant and equipment (PPE)	固定资产；财产、厂房和设备
plant asset	固定资产，厂房资产
allocate	*vt.* 分配，分派；把……拨给
accumulated depreciation	累积折旧
contra asset	备抵账户
book value	账面价值
carrying amount	账面金额
accrued expense	应计费用，预提费用
accrued revenue	应计收入

Notes

[1] Therefore, only cash sales would be recorded as the revenue earned for a period, whereas sales on account or charge sales would not be recognized until the customers paid the account. 因此，只有现销才可记作某一期间赚取的收入，而赊销则要等到顾客付清账款时方予确认。

[2] Since many of the business transactions affect the net income of more than one period, all revenues earned during the period and all expenses incurred must be fully presented if a realistic net income figure is to be portrayed. 由于许多企业交易会对一个以上期间的净收益产生影

响，如果要展示真实的净收益数字，就必须全面地表述某一期间赚取的所有收入和发生的所有费用。

[3] The balance in a contra account is subtracted from the balance of its associated account when preparing financial statements.　当编制财务报表时，从相关账户余额中减去备抵账户余额。

[4] Accrued expenses refer to costs that are incurred in a period but are both unpaid and unrecorded.　应计费用是指在某一会计期间内已经发生，但仍未支付和记录的成本。

2.4　Preparation of Financial Statements
编制财务报表

A conversation between A—an accountant and S—a freshman majoring in accounting.

S: I find the preparation of financial statements is not an easy job. Do accountants prepare the statements every month?

A: Not necessarily. Some businesses require that the accountants prepare a complete set of financial statements every month, but some businesses require a set every quarter, and the usual accounting period is one year.

S: Do you have any method that can facilitate the preparation?

A: You can use a worksheet, which is a working paper used to organize accounting information for preparing the financial statements and adjusting entries.

S: A worksheet? Please tell me more about it.

A: It's an informal document for the accountant's use only, and enables the accountants to see the entire accounting process from the beginning to the end. On the worksheet, account titles are listed in the first column, followed by five sets of money columns provided for (1) unadjusted trial balance, (2) adjusting entries, (3) adjusted trial balance, (4) income statement, and (5) balance sheet.

Adjusted Trial Balance and Worksheet

With the adjusting entries having been journalized and posted, adjusted trial balance is usually taken to verify the equality of debits and credits in the accounts. It lists all the accounts and their final balances in a single place.

Once the appropriate adjusting entries have been made and posted to the ledger accounts, an income statement and a balance sheet can be prepared directly from the account balances. In a manual system, however, many accountants find that drawing up a **worksheet** first facilitates the preparation of the financial statements.

A worksheet is a form designed to bring together in one place the information needed to prepare formal financial statements and to record the adjusting and closing entries. [1] It replaces neither the financial statements nor the necessity to journalize and post the adjusting and closing entries; it is simply a tool used to gather and organize the information needed to complete these steps of the accounting cycle. The worksheet as is presented in Table 2-2 is prepared after all transactions for 2013 have been recorded in vouchers and posted to the ledger accounts of a grocery store owned by John.

Table 2-2 The Worksheet of John's Grocery Store

John's Grocery Store
Worksheet
For the Month of December 2013

Title	Trial Balance		Adjustments		Adjusted Trial Balance		Balance Sheet		Income Statement	
	Debit	Credit	Debit	Credit	Debit	Credit	Debit	Credit	Debit	Credit
Cash	3,267				3,267		3,267			
Accounts receivable	200				200		200			
Goods available for sale	14,257				14,257		14,257			
Fixed assets	8,000				8,000		8,000			
Accumulated depreciation				300		300		300		
Accounts payable		4,300				4,300		4,300		
Payroll payable				1,500		1,500		1,500		
Capital		15,300				15,300		15,300		
Withdrawals	3,200				3,200		3,200			
Sales revenue		28,724				28,724				28,724
Cost of goods sold	17,000				17,000				17,000	
Utilities expense	400				400				400	
Salary expense			1,500		1,500				1,500	
Depreciation expense			300		300				300	
Rent expense	2,000				2,000				2,000	
Total	48,324	48,324			50,124	50,124	28,924	21,400	21,200	28,724
Net income								7,524	7,524	
								28,924	28,724	

The worksheet does not eliminate the need to journalize and post the adjusting journal entries.

Preparation of Financial Statements

If the worksheet is not used, we should prepare the income statement first, followed by the balance sheet. The heading of the statement includes: the name of the entity, the title of the statement, and the date or period covered by the statement.

The **income statement** for the month then ended and the **balance sheet** of John's Grocery Store on December 31, 2013 are shown respectively in Table 2-3 and Table 2-4.

Table 2-3   The Income Statement of John's Grocery Store

John's Grocery Store		
Income Statement		
For the month ended December 31, 2013		
Sales revenue		$28,724
Cost of goods sold	$17,000	
Utilities expense	400	
Salary expense	1,500	
Depreciation expense	300	
Rent expense	2,000	
Total expenses		21,200
Net income		$7,524

Table 2-4   The Balance Sheet of John's Grocery Store

John's Grocery Store			
Balance Sheet			
December 31, 2013			
Assets		Liabilities	
Cash	$3,267	Accounts payable	$4,300
Accounts receivable	200	Payroll payable	1,500
Goods available for sale	14,257	Total liabilities	5,800
Fixed assets	8,000		
Less: accumulated depreciation	(300)	Capital	19,624
Total assets	$25,424	Total liabilities and capital	$25,424

The basic financial statements of an enterprise include balance sheet, income statement, **statement of cash flows** and **statement of changes in owners' equity**. We will discuss all of them in detail in the next chapter.

 Vocabulary

worksheet	*n.* 工作底稿；工作表
income statement	损益表；利润表

balance sheet	资产负债表
statement of cash flows	现金流量表
statement of changes in owners' equity	所有者权益变动表

✎ Notes

A worksheet is a form designed to bring together in one place the information needed to prepare formal financial statements and to record the adjusting and closing entries. 工作表是把用来编制正式财务报表所需的资料集中于一处，并登记调整及结账分录的一种表格。

2.5　Closing Procedures
结账

A conversation between A—an accountant and S—a freshman majoring in accounting.

S: Why are income statement accounts called temporary accounts?

A: Because revenue and expense accounts are closed at the end of the accounting period. The accounts for each accounting period begin with a zero balance.

S: Oh, I see. But what is the purpose?

A: The purpose of closing the accounts is to know whether the company has gained a profit or incurred a loss for the current year.

S: How should the revenue account be closed?

A: The revenue account usually has a credit balance, and you can close it by transferring the balance into the income summary account.

S: How should the relative entry be made?

A: Debit the revenue account and credit the income summary account for an amount equal to the credit balance of the revenue account. Now, maybe you can tell me how to close the expense account.

📖 Temporary Accounts and Permanent Accounts

Revenues and expenses are accumulated and reported by a period, either monthly, quarterly, or yearly. To prevent them not being added to or comingled with revenues and expenses of another period, they need to be closed out—that is, given zero balances—at the end of each period. Their net balances, which represent the income or loss for the period, are transferred into owners' equity. Because these account's balances relate to a particular accounting period and are therefore closed at the end of the period, the revenue and expense accounts are called **temporary (nominal) accounts**.[1]

Once revenue and expense accounts are closed, the only accounts that have balances are the asset, liability, and owners' equity accounts. The **permanent (real) accounts** are continuous accounts, and their balances are carried forward to the next period. Consider cash, supplies, buildings, accounts payable, notes payable, and capital. These accounts do not represent which relate increases and decreases for a single period as do revenues and expenses, which related only to one accounting period. Instead the permanent accounts represent assets, liabilities, and capital that are on hand at a specific time.

Accounts are either temporary (nominal) or permanent (real). The income statement accounts are temporary accounts, and while the balance sheet accounts are permanent accounts.

 Closing Entries

When interim (monthly or quarterly) financial statements are being prepared, the adjustments are only made on the worksheet directly and will not be recorded in the journals and posted to the ledger accounts. Then, the adjusted balances are extended into the income statement and balance sheet columns, providing the necessary data for formal financial statements. At the close of the **fiscal year**, however, the necessary adjusting entries must be recorded in the general journal and posted to the ledger accounts in order to accomplish the proper closing procedures.

Once the income statement has been prepared for the **current year**, their balances are closed or cleared (reduced to a zero balance) by transferring their balances to another account. This step in the accounting cycle is referred to as **closing entries**, where a new temporary account called the income summary [2] account is established to summarize the balances in the revenue and expense accounts.

Closing entries are generally made in the following sequence:

(1) Closing the Revenue Accounts

To achieve this, a revenue account must be debited for an amount equal to its credit balances. The offsetting credit is made to the income summary account. The journal entry to close the revenue account is:

Sales revenue	28,724	
Income summary		28,724

(2) Closing the Expense Accounts

Since expense accounts normally have debit balances, each expense account is therefore credited for an amount equal to its balance, and the income summary account is debited for the sum of the individual balances. [3] The **compound journal entry** is:

Income Summary	21,200	
Cost of goods sold		17,000
Utilities expense		400
Salary expense		1,500
Depreciation expense		300
Rent expense		2,000

(3) Closing the Income Summary Account

After the first two closing entries are posted, the balances formerly reported in the individual

revenue and expense accounts are summarized in the income summary account. <u>A net income is earned and the income summary account will contain a credit balance if revenues exceed expenses, whereas a net loss is indicated and the account will have a debit balance if expenses exceed revenues.</u> [4] In our John Grocery Store illustration, a net income earned, the credit balance of $7,524 in the income summary account, is closed as follows:

Income summary	7,524
Capital	7,524

(4) Closing the **Withdrawal** Account

The debit balance in the withdrawal account of a sole proprietorship or a **partnership** reflects the decrease in the owner's interest during the period from the withdrawal of cash and/or other assets for personal use. The balance in the account is transferred directly to the owner's capital account by the following entry:

Capital	3,200
Withdrawals	3,200

After the closing entries have been posted, all the revenue, expense, and withdrawal accounts have zero balances and are ready for recording transactions of next period. <u>The balances in the balance sheet accounts, the only accounts which have a balance, are carried forward to the next period and the equality of their debits and credits can be verified by preparing a post-closing trial balance.</u> [5]

Vocabulary

temporary (nominal)　accounts	临时(虚)账户
permanent (real)　accounts	永久(实)账户
fiscal year	财务年度，财政年度
current year	本年，当年
closing entry	结账分录
compound journal entry	复合分录；贷借方多项分录；复合日记账分录
withdrawal	*n*. 提款，撤资
partnership	*n*. 合伙企业；合作关系

Notes

[1] Because these account's balances relate to a particular accounting period and are therefore closed at the end of the period, the revenue and expense accounts are called temporary (nominal) accounts. 由于收入和费用账户只在特定会计期间内有效且在期末结清，所以这些账户被称为临时(虚)账户。

[2] income summary 收益汇总，在中国，收入和费用被汇总至"本年利润"账户，参考翻译为"current year profit"或"current profit"。

[3] Since expense accounts normally have debit balances, each expense account is therefore

credited for an amount equal to its balance, and the income summary account is debited for the sum of the individual balances.　由于费用账户通常有借方余额，因此要贷记各费用账户余额相等金额，同时把各个余额的合计数借记"收益汇总"账户。

[4] A net income is earned and the income summary account will contain a credit balance if revenues exceed expenses, whereas a net loss is indicated and the account will have a debit balance if expenses exceed revenues.　如果收入超出费用，便赚得净收益，"收益汇总"账户会有贷方余额；如果费用超过收入，则显示为净亏损，"收益汇总"账户会有借方余额。

[5] The balances in the balance sheet accounts, the only accounts which have a balance, are carried forward to the next period and the equality of their debits and credits can be verified by preparing a post-closing trial balance.　资产负债账户的余额(仅仅这类账户会有余额)将转入下一期间，同时，可以通过编制一张结账后的试算平衡表来验证其借项和贷项是否相等。

Exercises

I. Discuss the following questions in English.

1.　What kinds of transactions can be recorded in the accounting system?

2.　If assets are valuable resources and asset accounts have debit balances, why do expense accounts also have debit balances?

3.　What is an account? What is a ledger?

4.　Why is a trial balance prepared?

5.　What are the differences between accrual basis of accounting and cash basis?

6.　What is the purpose of making adjustments?

7.　What is a contra account? Explain its purpose.

8.　Why is a prepaid expense an asset? Give some examples.

9.　Why are revenue and expense accounts called temporary?

10.　What accounts are listed on the post-closing trial balance?

11.　Why do companies prepare interim financial statements?

12.　What are the major steps in preparing closing entries?

II. Choose the best word or phrase that fits the sentence.

1.　To _____ accumulating financial statement data, transactions are recorded in accounts.

　　　A. promote　　　　　　　　　　B. facilitate

　　　C. assist　　　　　　　　　　　D. help

2.　Accounts on the left side of the accounting equation are increased by _____ entries.

　　　A. negative　　　　　　　　　　B. positive

　　　C. credit　　　　　　　　　　　D. debit

3.　There are three types of vouchers — _____ voucher, payment voucher and transfer voucher.

         A. collection   B. receiving

         C. receipt   D. acquisition

4.   A trial balance may be prepared at any time to test the equality of debits and credits in the _____.

         A. ledger   B. journal

         C. accounts   D. vouchers

5.   In accrual accounting, _____ states that revenues are recorded when earned.

         A. the matching principle   B. the revenue recognition principle

         C. historical cost principle   D. time period assumption

6.   _____ refers to cash received in advance of providing products and services.

         A. Unearned revenue   B. Prepaid expense

         C. Accrued revenue   D. Accrued expense

7.   Accountants _____ the cost to expense for fixed assets.

         A. distribute   B. allocate

         C. appropriate   D. apportion

8.   The term _____ refers to a liability that arises from an expense that has yet been paid.

         A. deferred revenue   B. deferred expense

         C. accrued revenue   D. accrued expense

9.   Preparing a(n) _____ is an optional procedure in the accounting cycle.

         A. balance sheet   B. income statement

         C. worksheet   D. cash flow statement

10.   The net balances of temporary accounts are finally transferred into _____.

         A. assets   B. owners' equity

         C. liabilities   D. profits

11.   A _____ journal entry is an entry that includes debits or credits to more than one account, and it is an easy and time-saving method of closing the accounts.

         A. mixture   B. compound

         C. combination   D. multiple

III. Match each word on the left with its corresponding meaning on the right.

A	B
1. firm	(a) involving using the hands or physical strength
2. associate	(b) writing that provides information
3. accrue	(c) a book which commercial accounts are recorded
4. illustrate	(d) decide upon or fix definitely
5. match	(e) a company business or company, especially a small one
6. ledger	(f) to increase over a period of time

7. interval (g) to make the meaning of sth. clearer by using examples, pictures, etc.

8. specify (h) make correspond or harmonize

9. document (i) make a connection

10. manual (j) a period of time between two events

IV. Fill in the blanks with words or phrases from the list below.

A.	partner	B.	consists of	C.	high-quality	D.	centralized
E.	spot	F.	tightly	G.	worldwide	H.	chain
I.	supervisors	J.	INTERNET	K.	appropriately	L.	accounting
M.	staff	N.	globalization	O.	accounts receivable	P.	forces

An (1) accounting system, where transactions are entered on the (2) and business data created by transactions are distributed to appropriate (3) of the company, becomes more important for companies operating (4) . The Internet accounting system (5) a three-level structure: Web, application and database servers. The accounting system provides complete accounting functions including general ledger, accounts payable, (6) , purchase order, sales order, inventory management, fixed assets, temporary payment, multi-users, multi-currencies, multi-companies and multi-languages allowing customer relation management, (7) relation management, supply (8) management and performance analysis. A prototype system has been completed and a full-scale system is now under development. Globalization (9) every level of companies to operate worldwide. The traditional (10) accounting system, where officers of the accounting department mainly operate the system at the head office, does not (11) function in the globalization environment. An Internet accounting system is strongly required in worldwide operating companies, while providing (12) enterprise resource planning (ERP) and customer relation management (CRM). Transactions occurring at each branch office (13) related to customers are entered on-site into the system through a website. Transactions sent to the main office are used to provide ERP and CRM information for top executives and (14) .

V. Translate the following sentences into Chinese.

1. Transactions are analyzed on the basis of the business documents known as source documents and are recorded in the vouchers.

2. An account is debited when an amount is entered on the left-hand side, and credited when an amount is entered on the right-hand side.

3. A chart of accounts is a list of all accounts used in a company.

4. When more than two accounts are affected, it is called a compound journal entry.

5. Depreciation is a method of cost allocation, not asset valuation.

6. An accrued liability may exist for interest, wages, taxes, or other expenses that have been incurred in the accounting period but have not been paid by the period end.

7. Temporary or nominal accounts are maintained to facilitate the preparation of income

statement.

VI. Translate the following sentences into English.

1. 原始凭证是在经济业务发生时取得或填制的，记录经济业务的执行和完成情况，明确经济责任的凭证。

2. 根据复式记账法的要求，每一笔交易至少会对两个账户产生影响，因此需要在两个账户中分别记录。

3. 会计分录是分析和描述各种经济业务对企业影响的工具。

4. 总分类账户是指对会计要素的具体内容进行总括反映的账户。

5. 由于每笔经济业务都用相等的借贷金额记录，因此分类账中借方合计数等于贷方合计数。

6. 对于跨期进行的交易和事项，账项调整是必不可少的一个步骤。

7. 资产负债表是根据资产、负债与权益资本的余额来编制的。

8. 完成结账过程以后，收入和费用账户余额为零。

Reading Material 2

Computerized Accounting Systems

In today's rapid development of information technology, the network and computer have applied to all areas of society, work and life. The reform of corporate accounting system is a necessary and inevitable step in the development of economy. Computerized accounting systems have become more widely used as the cost of computer hardware and software has declined. In a computerized system all the multiple steps of a manual system are collapsed into one entry. For example, when you create a check there is an automatic and simultaneous posting to a register and to the general ledger accounts. Financial statements can be created at any time and as often as needed.

There are three main advantages about the computerized accounting system. First, computerized accounting systems simplify the record-keeping process. The transactions are simultaneously recorded in journals and posted electronically to general and subsidiary ledger accounts in a computerized accounting system. The posting process is done, since the original transitions include the required information for posting to the ledger. Second, computerized accounting systems will not make common mistakes, such as math errors, posting errors, and journal recording errors. Third, computerized systems provide the management current account balance information, since account balances are posted as the transitions occur. Thus, a computerized accounting system provides management more current information to support design making.

Despite their many advantages, computer-based systems are not without their problems. Firstly, if the initial input to the computer is made by a person, an error made by that person may not be detected. For example, if a check is supposed to be for $897 and the bookkeeper keys in $879, the computer may not detect the error. Secondly, although a small company can purchase "of-the-shelf" software and have its system set up and run in a few days, system development and installation in a larger, more complex organization may take many months and cost miuions of dollars. Such systems usually require an outside consultant for their design and implementation. Moreover, technological advances make existing systems obsolete within a few years, and much time and money must be spent to update them. Thirdly, unlike a manual system, a computer-based system does not leave a paper trail that can be readily audited. In a few spectacular instances the lack of internal controls has resulted in business frauds and resultant failure. Finally, a computer-based system will not be fully effective until its developers learn to design reports that the system's users need and can understand. If it is not done properly the system will spew out reports that no one uses, and the potential users will not appreciate the information that they could receive if only they know how to ask for it.

Answers:

II.	1	B	2	D	3	C	4	A	5	B	6	A	7	B	8	D
	9	C	10	B	11	B										
III.	1	e	2	i	3	f	4	g	5	h	6	c	7	j	8	d
	9	b	10	a												
IV.	1	J	2	E	3	M	4	G	5	B	6	O	7	A	8	H
	9	P	10	D	11	K	12	C	13	F	14	I				

 知识扩展

我国常用的账务处理程序

我国常用的账务处理程序主要有：记账凭证账务处理程序、汇总记账凭证账务处理程序、科目汇总表账务处理程序等。

1. 记账凭证账务处理程序

记账凭证账务处理程序是指对发生的经济业务事项，都要根据原始凭证或汇总原始凭证编制记账凭证，然后直接根据记账凭证逐笔登记总分类账的一种账务处理程序。它是基本的账务处理程序，其一般程序是：

①根据原始凭证编制汇总原始凭证；②根据原始凭证或汇总原始凭证，编制记账凭证；③根据收款凭证、付款凭证逐笔登记现金日记账和银行存款日记账；④根据原始凭证、汇总原始凭证和记账凭证，登记各种明细分类账；⑤根据记账凭证逐笔登记总分类账；⑥期末，现金日记账、银行存款日记账和明细分类账的余额同有关总分类账的余额核对相符；⑦期末，根据总分类账和明细分类账的记录，编制会计报表。

记账凭证账务处理程序简单明了，易于理解，总分类账可以较详细地反映经济业务的

发生情况。其缺点是：登记总分类账的工作量较大。该财务处理程序适用于规模较小、经济业务量较少的单位。

2. 汇总记账凭证账务处理程序

汇总记账凭证账务处理程序是根据原始凭证或汇总原始凭证编制记账凭证，定期根据记账凭证分类编制汇总收款凭证、汇总付款凭证和汇总转账凭证，再根据汇总记账凭证登记总分类账的一种账务处理程序。其一般程序是：①根据原始凭证编制汇总原始凭证；②根据原始凭证或汇总原始凭证，编制记账凭证；③根据收款凭证、付款凭证逐笔登记现金日记账和银行存款日记账；④根据原始凭证、汇总原始凭证和记账凭证，登记各种明细分类账；⑤根据各种记账凭证编制有关汇总记账凭证；⑥根据各种汇总记账凭证登记总分类账；⑦期末，现金日记账、银行存款日记账和明细分类账的余额同有关总分类账的余额核对相符；⑧期末，根据总分类账和明细分类账的记录，编制会计报表。

汇总记账凭证账务处理程序减轻了登记总分类账的工作量，便于了解账户之间的对应关系。其缺点是：按每一贷方科目编制汇总转账凭证，不利于会计核算的日常分工，当转账凭证较多时，编制汇总转账凭证的工作量较大。该财务处理程序适用于规模较大、经济业务较多的单位。

3. 科目汇总表账务处理程序

科目汇总表账务处理程序又称记账凭证汇总表账务处理程序，它是根据记账凭证定期编制科目汇总表，再根据科目汇总表登记总分类账的一种账务处理程序。其一般程序是：①根据原始凭证编制汇总原始凭证；②根据原始凭证或汇总原始凭证编制记账凭证；③根据收款凭证、付款凭证逐笔登记现金日记账和银行存款日记账；④根据原始凭证、汇总原始凭证和记账凭证登记各种明细分类账；⑤根据各种记账凭证编制科目汇总表；⑥根据科目汇总表登记总分类账；⑦期末，现金日记账、银行存款日记账和明细分类账的余额同有关总分类账的余额核对相符；⑧期末，根据总分类账和明细分类账的记录，编制会计报表。

科目汇总表账务处理程序减轻了登记总分类账的工作量，并可做到试算平衡，简明易懂，方便易学。其缺点是：科目汇总表不能反映账户对应关系，不便于查对账目。它适用于经济业务较多的单位。

Chapter 3　Financial Statements
财务报表

 **Learning Objectives**

- Understand the uses of financial statements, including the balance sheet, the income statement, the statement of cash flows and the notes 学会使用财务报表，包括资产负债表、利润表、现金流量表和财务报表附注
- Identify the major classifications of the balance sheet, the income statement and the statement of cash flows 识别资产负债表、利润表和现金流量表的主要分类
- Discuss the format of the balance sheet, the income statement, the statement of cash flows and the statement of changes in owners' equity 讨论资产负债表、利润表、现金流量表和所有者权益变动表的格式
- Understand the notes to financial statements 学会使用财务报表附注

 **Listening Practice** 听力练习

Chapter 3 English Listening.mp3

第 3 章听写原文翻译和答案的音频见右侧二维码。

Dictation: *Listen and complete the passage with the words or phrases according to what you've heard from the speaker.*

Human Resource Accounting (HRA), a totally new ＿＿＿1＿＿＿ in accounting research, appeared in the 1960s ＿＿＿2＿＿＿ on the theory of Human Capital. It is defined as the process of identifying, measuring, and ＿＿＿3＿＿＿ information about human ＿＿＿4＿＿＿ to help effective management within an organization. HRA is not so widespread and rapidly applied as other accounting because of the inconvenience of human asset measurements. According to ＿＿＿5＿＿＿ measurements, HRA is presently divided into two branches: human resource cost accounting and human resource value accounting.

Wisdom 至理名言

science has a deep understanding of the way in which society operates. Economics is about exchange. 一门科学，对社会运转方式有深刻的见解。经济学是关于交换的研究。

Mini Case 微型案例

In early 2001, Enron appeared on the top of the world. The high-flying energy firm had a market capitalization of $60 billion, and its stock was trading at $80 a share. Wall Street analysts frequently touted its innovation and management success, and most strongly recommended the stock. Less than a year later, Enron had declared bankruptcy, its stock was basically worthless, and investors had lost billions of dollars. The dramatic and sudden collapse left many wondering how so much value could be destroyed in such a short period of time.

3.1   Balance Sheet
资产负债表

A conversation between A—an accountant and S—a freshman majoring in accounting.

S: Of financial statements, the balance sheet is perhaps the most familiar to most people.

A: Yes. Many people begin their accounting study with the understanding of the accounting equation. The three elements in the equation represent the three categories in the balance sheet.

S: I know it. But there are so many items in the balance sheet that I always get confused at a glance.

A: In fact, these items in the balance sheet are arranged in a certain order. There are two forms—account form and report form. In the account form, assets items are placed on the left, liabilities and owners' equity items on the right, and liability items are always above owners' equity item. In the report form, assets are at the top of the statement, and below it are liabilities and owners' equity in that order.

S: How are asset items arranged then?

A: Listed first are current assets and non-current assets follow them.

S: Are current assets you mentioned related to liquidity?

A: Yes. The order of assets and liabilities are listed in the order of their liquidity.

What is Balance Sheet

The balance sheet, also known as statement of financial position, reports major classes and amounts of assets (resources owned or controlled by the firm), liabilities (external claims on those assets), and owners' equity (owners' capital contributions and other internally generated sources of capital) and their interrelationships at specific points in time. The balance sheet presents a view of the business as a collection of resources or assets belonging to the company that is equal to the sources of or claims against those assets.[1] The sources consist of liabilities and owners' equity.

Assets reported on the balance sheet are either purchased by the firm or generated through operations; they are, directly or indirectly, **financed** by the creditors and shareholders of the firm. This fundamental accounting relationship provides the basis for recording all transactions in financial reporting and is expressed as the accounting equation which mentioned in Chapter 1. In its traditional format, a balance sheet lists assets on the left-hand side of the page and liabilities and owners' equity on the right-hand side. When the liabilities and owners' equity are added together, they will be equal to the assets. Therefore, the statement is said to "balance" because the left-hand column is equal to (i.e. balance with) the right-hand column.

The balance sheet provides information about the nature and amounts of investments in enterprise resources, obligations to creditors, and the owners' equity in net assets. But most are reported at historical cost. Furthermore, Companies use judgments and **estimates** to determine many of the items reported in the sheet. For example, estimates the amount of **bad debts** that will not collect and the useful life of its equipment.

Classification

The definitions of assets, liabilities and owners' equity have been discussed in Chapter 1. Assets and liabilities are classified according to **liquidity**, that is, their expected use in operations or **conversion** to cash in the case of assets and time to maturity for liabilities. Assets and liabilities list components in order of their liquidity.

Assets can be classified into **current assets** and **non-current assets**. Current assets are those assets that are in the form of cash or are expected to be turned into cash **in the short run**, usually within one year.[2] Among them are cash, marketable securities, accounts receivable, notes receivable and inventories. [3] Non-current assets are those **tangible or intangible assets** that are to be used in the conduct of the business rather than to be sold. They are usually divided into several categories such as long-term investment in equity, fixed assets and so forth.

Another category of balance sheet items is liabilities, which can be further classified into current liabilities and long-term liabilities. Current liabilities are debts that must be paid off within one year or the normal operating cycle, whichever is longer, such as accounts payable, notes payable, revenues collected in advance, etc. [4] Long-term liabilities usually consist of long-term loans and bonds, which are debts not due for at least one year.

Owners' equity is the difference between total assets and total liabilities. It represents a business enterprise's ownership interest, that is, the residual interest in the assets of the entity that remains after deducting its liabilities. Owners' equity lists components in order of their priority in **liquidation**. The most important change in a balance sheet between two periods of time is the change in owners' equity. It is important that the potential creditor or investor know not only the amount of this change, but also the principal factors that have contributed to it. [5]

Format of the Balance Sheet

One common arrangement that companies use in presenting a classified balance sheet is the

account form. It lists assets on the left side, and liabilities and owners' equity on the right side. The other is the **report form** that lists the assets at the top, followed by liabilities and owners' equity below.

Since US GAAP and **IFRS (International Financial Reporting Standards)** do not prescribe a fixed format for balance sheets, when we look at balance sheets of different companies in English, we will find the items and even the orders are quite different from one another. For example, there are many accounting terms for fixed assets, such as property, plant and equipment, plant assets, or equipment. The balance sheet in Table 3-1 illustrates a report format of an adapted company—ABC Company.

Table 3-1   The Balance Sheet of ABC Company

ABC Company Balance Sheet December 31, 2013 (in millions USD)	
Current Asset:	
Cash and cash equivalent	2,910
Accounts receivable and prepayments	807
Inventories	60
Other current assets	24
Total current assets	3,801
Non-Current Assets:	
Investment in associates and joint ventures	3,457
Property, plant and equipment	5,260
Intangible assts	4,365
Total non-current assets	13,082
Total assets	16,883
Current Liabilities:	
Accounts payable and accruals	872
Interest bearing loans and borrowings	483
Income tax liabilities	127
Total current liabilities	1,482
Non-Current Liabilities:	
Long-term note payable	6,054
Bonds payable	3,210
Total non-current liabilities	9,264
Shareholders' Equity:	
Share capital	4,202

Table 3-1(Continued)

ABC Company	
Balance Sheet	
December 31, 2013	
(in millions USD)	
Shareholders' Equity:	
Share eapital	4,202
Retained earnings	1,935
Total shareholders' equity	6,137
Total liabilities and shareholders' equity	16,883

In China, the balance sheet is usually presented in the format of Table 3-2, and the reference translation of the items lists on the right column.

Table 3-2　Bilingual items of the Balance Sheet

资　产	Assets
流动资产：	**Current assets:**
货币资金	Cash and cash equivalent
交易性金融资产	Marketable financial assets
应收票据	Notes receivable
应收账款	Accounts receivable
预付款项	Advances to suppliers /Prepayments
应收利息	Interest receivable
应收股利	Dividends receivable
其他应收款	Other receivables
存货	Inventories
其他流动资产	Other current assets
流动资产合计	Total current assets
非流动资产：	**Non-current assets:**
可供出售金融资产	Available-for-sale financial assets
持有至到期投资	Held-to-maturity investments
长期应收款	Long-term receivables
长期股权投资	Long-term equity investments
投资性房地产	Investment properties
固定资产	Fixed assets /Property, plant and equipment
在建工程	Construction in progress
工程物资	Construction materials
固定资产清理	Fixed assets pending disposal
生产性生物资产	Productive biological assets
油气资产	Oil and gas assets

Table 3-2(Continued)

资　产	Assets
无形资产	Intangible assets
开发支出	Development costs
商誉	Goodwill
长期待摊费用	Long-term prepaid expenses
递延所得税资产	Deferred income tax assets
其他非流动资产	Other non-current assets
非流动资产合计	Total non-current assets
资产总计	**Total assets**
负债及所有者权益	Liabilities and owners' equity
流动负债：	**Current liabilities:**
短期借款	Short-term loan
交易性金融负债	Marketable financial liabilities
应付票据	Notes payable
应付账款	Accounts payable
预收款项	Advances from customers
应付职工薪酬	Payroll Payable
应交税费	Taxes payable
应付利息	Interest payable
应付股利	Dividends payable
其他应收款	Other payables
其他流动负债	Other non-current liabilities
流动负债合计	Total current liabilities
非流动负债：	**Non-current liabilities:**
长期借款	Long-term borrowings
应付债券	Bonds payable
递延所得税负债	Deferred tax liabilities
其他非流动负债	Other non-current liabilities
非流动负债合计	Total non-current liabilities
负债合计	Total liabilities
所有者(股东)权益	Owners' (Shareholders') equity
实收资本	Paid-in capital
资本公积	Capital surplus
盈余公积	Earnings surplus
未分配利润	Undistributed profits
所有者权益合计	**Total owners' equity**
负债及所有者权益合计	**Total liabilities and owners' equity**

Vocabulary

finance	*vt.* 为……供给资金；筹资，融资
estimate	*n. & vt.* 估计，预测
bad debt	坏账，呆账
liquidity	*n.* 流动性；流动资金；资产流动性
conversion	*n.* 变换，转变
current asset	流动资产
non-current asset	非流动资产
in the short (long) run	在短(长)期内
tangible assets	有形资产
intangible assets	无形资产
liquidation	*n.* 清偿；结算；清算
account form	账户式(资产负债表)
report form	报告式(资产负债表)
IFRS (International Financial Reporting Standards)	国际财务报告准则

Notes

[1] The balance sheet presents a view of the business as a collection of resources or assets belonging to the company that is equal to the sources of or claims against those assets. 资产负债表表明企业在某一特定日期所拥有或控制的经济资源，所承担的现时义务和所有者对净资产的要求权。

[2] Current assets are those that are in the form of cash or are expected to be turned into cash in the short run, usually within one year. 流动资产是指那些以现金形式存在或者可望在短期内(通常在一年内)转换为现金的资产。

[3] Among them are cash, marketable securities, accounts receivable, notes receivable and inventories. 这类资产包括现金、有价证券、应收账款、应收票据以及存货。

[4] Current liabilities are debts that must be paid off within one year or the normal operating cycle, whichever is longer, such as accounts payable, notes payable, revenues collected in advance, etc. 流动负债是必须在一年或一个正常经营周期(视何者孰长)内偿付的债务，如应付账款、应付票据、预收收入等。

[5] It is important that the potential creditor or investor know not only the amount of this change, but also the principal factors that have contributed to it. 让可能成为债权者或投资者的人们不仅了解这一变动的金额，而且了解导致这一变化的主要因素是至关重要的。

3.2 Income Statement
利润表

A conversation between A—an accountant and S—a freshman majoring in accounting.

S: Of financial statements, which can reflect the profit or loss of the business directly? I think what investors are most interested in is the profitability of the business.

A: The income statement can directly reflect the profit or loss of the business for the current period. As you know, the profit is equal to revenues minus expenses.

S: The income statement consists of the balances of revenue and expense accounts, doesn't it?

A: In a sense, it does. The income statement consists of three parts — revenues, expenses, and profit.

S: All the expenses should be listed in the income statement directly, like the salary expense and advertising expense, right?

A: No. Usually salaries for sales staff are included in the selling expenses, salaries for office workers and executives are included in administrative expenses, and the advertising expense is included in the selling expenses.

What is Income Statement

Income statement, also known as statement of comprehensive income, is a financial statement that measures a company's financial performance over a specific accounting period. Financial performance is assessed by giving a summary of how the business incurred its revenues and expenses—due to both **operating** and **non-operating** activities. It also shows the net income or loss incurred over a specific accounting period, typically over a fiscal quarter or year.

The purpose of the income statement is to indicate how successful the business has been in meeting the objective of earning profits, which are of primary importance to the board of directors in evaluating the management of the company, to shareholders or potential shareholders in deciding on actions to be taken **with respect to** loans. [1] Other things being equal, a profitable company is a good company to invest in, lend money to, work for, and deal with in general. Many people consider income statement as the most important financial report because its purpose is to measure whether or not the business achieved the primary objective of earning an acceptable income. [2]

Classification

The definitions of revenues, expenses and profits have been discussed in Chapter 1. They are the elements which form the income statement. Revenues represent assets coming into the business from the performance of a service or the sales of a product to a customer for cash or on credit. [3] In some cases, however, realization of revenues may simply mean the **discharge** of a debt owed by the business. Expenses represent assets that are used, consumed, or **worn out** as a result of employing them in the business for the purpose of earning revenues. Expenses are often referred to as "the cost of doing business", which decrease the net asset in the business. Profits are the difference between revenues and expenses and should be calculated at the end of each accounting period.

In practice, the income statement is divided into two parts: the operating and non-operating sections. The portion of the income statement that deals with operating items is interesting to investors and analysts alike, because this section discloses information about revenues and expenses that are a direct result of the regular business operations. [4] For example, if a business creates sports equipment, then the operating items section would talk about the revenues and expenses involved with the production of sports equipment. In addition to its operating business, a firm may have income (loss) from other activities, such as gains or losses on sale or **disposal** of assets.

 Format of the Income Statement

Since US GAAP and IFRS do not specify the format of the income statement, actual formats vary across companies, especially in the reporting of the gains or losses on sale of the assets, equity in earnings of **affiliates**, and non-operating income and expenses. The income statement in Table 3-3 illustrates a generic format of an adapted company—ABC Company.

Table 3-3　The Income Statement of ABC Company

ABC Company	
Income Statement	
For year ended December 31, 2013	
(in millions USD)	
Net sales	2,999
Cost of sales	(2,064)
Gross profit	935
Operating expenses:	
Selling expenses	156
General expenses	127
Other operating expenses	53
Total operating expenses	(336)
Income from operations	599
Other income (expense)	98
Interest expenses	(356)
Tax expenses	(54)
Net income	287

In China, the income statement is usually presented in the format of Table 3-4, and the reference translation of the items lists on the right column.

Table 3-4　Bilingual Items of the Income Statement

项　目	ITEMS
一、营业收入	**Revenues from the sales of goods and services**
减：营业成本	Less: Cost of goods sold
营业税金及附加	Sales tax and extra charges
销售费用	Selling expenses
管理费用	Administrative expenses
财务费用	Financial expenses
资产减值损失	Asset impairment loss
加：公允价值变动收益	Add：Changes of fair value of assets
投资收益	Income from investments
其中：对联营企业和合营企业的投资收益	Include：Income from related parties
二、营业利润	**Operating profits**
加：营业外收入	Add：Non-operating revenues
减：营业外支出	Less：Non-operating expenses
其中：非流动资产处置损失	Include：Loss on disposal of non-current assets
三、利润总额	**Total profit**
减：所得税费用	Less：Income tax
四、净利润	**Net income/loss**
五、每股收益	**Earning per share**
(一)基本每股收益	Basic earnings per share
(二)稀释每股收益	Diluted earnings per share

Vocabulary

operating	*adj.* 业务上的，营运的；操作的
non-operating	非营业的，营业外的
with respect to	关于，(至于)谈到
discharge	*vt.* 免除(自己的义务、负担等)
wear out	文中被动语态 worn out，表示用坏；穿破；耗尽
disposal	*n.* 处置；清理
affiliate	*n.* 附属企业；分支机构

Notes

[1] The purpose of the income statement is to indicate how successful the business has been

in meeting the objective of earning profits, which are of primary importance to the board of directors in evaluating the management of the company, to shareholders or potential shareholders in deciding on actions to be taken with respect to loans.　利润表的目的在于表明企业在实现赚取利润这一目标方面所取得的经营成果(利润或亏损)，这对董事会评价公司的管理状况，股东和潜在股东做出投资决策，对银行和其他债权人决定就贷款事宜采取相应举措等，都具有重要意义。

[2] Many people consider income statement as the most important financial report because its purpose is to measure whether or not the business achieved the primary objective of earning an acceptable income.　许多人将利润表看作是最为重要的财务报表，因为利润表的目的在于衡量企业是否实现了"赚取一定(可接受)的利润"这一首要目标。

[3] Revenues represent assets coming into the business from the performance of a service or the sales of a product to a customer for cash or on credit.　收入表示向顾客提供服务或向顾客现销或赊销产品而流入企业的资产。

[4] The portion of the income statement that deals with operating items is interesting to investors and analysts alike, because this section discloses information about revenues and expenses that are a direct result of the regular business operations.　投资者、分析师等(诸如此类会计报表使用者)关注利润表中反映经营性事项的内容，因为这部分内容披露了关于收入和费用的相关信息，而这些信息直接反映了企业正常业务经营的成果。

3.3　Statement of Cash Flows
现金流量表

A conversation between A—an accountant and S—a freshman majoring in accounting.

S: Nowadays, when people discuss the issue of financial position, they often talk about the cash flow. The cash flow seems to be very important to the business.

A: Very important. In the past people didn't pay enough attention to the cash flow, but now people have recognized its significance. Judging from the balance sheet and the income statement, some businesses seemed to be performing well, but they went bankrupt in the end. The major cause is that they lacked sufficient positive cash flows.

S: Incredible! If the income statement indicates a good net income, then the business has sufficient cash flows, right?

A: Not necessarily. The income statement is prepared on the accrual basis of accounting, so some items are estimates like depreciation expenses and perhaps some accrued revenues can't be collected as expected. All these will lead to an insufficiency of cash receipts.

S: Of financial statements, which can reflect the cash flow of the business?

A: The statement of cash flows is based on the cash basis, and it only records the cash that has actually been paid or received.

What is the Statement of Cash Flows

The statement of cash flows reports all the cash inflows and outflows of the firm for a specified period.[1] Because the income statement is prepared under the accrual basis of accounting, the revenues reported may not have been collected. Similarly, the expenses reported on the income statement might not have been paid. You could review the balance sheet changes to determine the facts, but the cash flow statement already has **integrated** all that information. Therefore, cash flow data supplement the information provided by the income statement as both link consecutive balance sheets. The statement shows how changes in balance sheet and income accounts affect cash and **cash equivalents**. The statement of cash flow has been adopted as a standard financial statement because it eliminates allocations, which might **be derived from** different **accounting methods**, such as various **timeframes** for depreciating fixed assets [2].

Cash is a company's lifeblood. The money coming into the business is called cash inflow, and money going out from the business is called cash outflow. A company uses cash to pay bills, repay loans and make investments, allowing it to provide goods and services to customers. If all goes well, a company uses cash to generate even more cash as a result of higher profits. The statement of cash flows reports the company's sources and uses of cash and the beginning and ending values for cash each year. [3]

This statement is extremely valuable to management and investors because it is intended to:

(1) Provide information on a firm's liquidity and solvency and its ability to change cash flows in future circumstances;

(2) Provide additional information for evaluating changes in assets, liabilities, and equity;

(3) Improve the comparability of different firms' operating performance by eliminating the effects of different accounting methods;

(4) Indicate the amount, timing, and probability of future cash flows.

Classification

The cash flow statement reports cash inflows and outflows in three groups: operating activities, financing activities and investing activities.

Operating cash flow (cash flows from operations) measures the amount of cash generated by the firm as a result of its production and sales of goods and services. Although **deficits** or negative cash flows from operations are expected in some circumstances (e.g., rapid growth), for most firms positive operating cash flows are essential for long-run survival. Internally generated funds can be used to pay **dividends**, repay loans, replace existing capacity, or invest in other companies' shares and bonds. [4]

Investing cash flow reports the amount of cash used to acquire assets such as plant and equipment as well as investments and entire businesses. These outlays are necessary to maintain a firm's current operating capacity and to provide capacity for future growth. Investing cash flow also includes cash received from the sale or disposal of assets or affiliates of the business.

Financing cash flow contains the cash flow consequences of the firm's **capital structure** (debt and equity) decisions, including **proceeds** from the **issuance** of shares, returns to shareholders in the form of dividends, the incurrence and repayment of debt, etc. [5]

The statement of cash flows shows the cash receipts and payments related to the above three activities. The major classes of cash receipts and payments are shown in Table 3-5.

Table 3-5　Major Classes of Cash Receipts and Payments

Operating cash flow	Investing cash flow	Financing cash flow
Collections from customers	Receipts of interest and dividends	Payment of interest and dividends
Payments to suppliers	Sale and purchase of investments	Issuance of shares and bonds
Payments to employees	Sale and purchase of fixed assets	Proceeds of loans and borrowing
Payments of taxes	Making loans to others	Payment of debts
	Collections of loans from others	

In addition, firms with significant foreign operations separately report a fourth category, the effect of **exchange rate** changes on cash, which accumulates the effects of changes in exchange rates on the translation of foreign currencies. This segregation is essential to accurately report the cash flow consequences of operating, investing, and financing decisions, unaffected by the impact of changes in exchange rates.

 ## Format of the Statement of Cash Flows

The format of the statement of cash flows varies greatly across countries. You may see some companies' cash flow items not being categorized in the same way we have learnt. For example, interest paid usually categorized as an operating cash flow item in America, should be classified as financing cash flow item in China.

In China, the statement of cash flows is usually presented in the format of Table 3-6, and the reference translation of the items lists on the right column.

Table 3-6　Bilingual Items of the Statement of Cash Flows

项　目	ITEMS
一、经营活动产生的现金流量：	**1. Cash flows from operating activities:**
销售商品、提供劳务收到的现金	Cash received from sale of goods or rendering of services
收到的税费返还	Refund of tax and levies
收到的其他与经营活动有关的现金	Other cash received relating to operating activities
现金流入小计	Sub-total of cash inflows
购买商品、接受劳务支付的现金	Cash paid for goods and services
支付给职工以及为职工支付的现金	Cash paid to employees and for employees
支付的各项税费	Tax payments

Table 3-6(Continued)

项 目	ITEMS
支付的其他与经营活动有关的现金	Other cash paid relating to operating activities
现金流出小计	Sub-total of cash outflows
经营活动产生的现金流量净额	Net cash flows from operating activities
二、投资活动产生的现金流量：	**2. Cash flows from investing activities:**
收回投资所收到的现金	Cash received from disposal of investments
取得投资收益所收到的现金	Cash received from returns on investments
处置固定资产、无形资产和其他长期资产所收回的现金净额	Net cash received from disposal of fixed assets, intangible assets and other long-term assets
收到的其他与投资活动有关的现金	Other cash received relating to investing activities
现金流入小计	Sub-total of cash inflows
购建固定资产、无形资产和其他长期资产所支付的现金	Cash paid to acquire fixed assets, intangible assets and other long-term assets
投资所支付的现金	Cash paid to acquire investments
支付的其他与投资活动有关的现金	Other cash payments relating to investing activities
现金流出小计	Sub-total of cash outflows
投资活动产生的现金流量净额	Net cash flows from investing activities
三、筹资活动产生的现金流量：	**3. Cash flows from financial activities:**
吸收投资所收到的现金	Cash received from capital contribution
借款所收到的现金	Cash received from borrowings
收到的其他与筹资活动有关的现金	Other cash received relating to financing activities
现金流入小计	Sub-total of cash inflows
偿还债务所支付的现金	Cash repayments of amounts borrowed
分配股利、利润和偿付利息所支付的现金	Cash payments for interest expenses and distribution of dividends or profit
支付的其他与筹资活动有关的现金	Other cash payments relating to financing activities
现金流出小计	Sub-total of cash outflows
筹资活动产生的现金流量净额	Net cash flows from financing activities
四、汇率变动对现金的影响：	**4. Effect of foreign exchange rate changes on cash:**
五、现金及现金等价物净增加额：	**5. Net change in cash and cash equivalents:**
加：期初现金及现金等价物余额	Add: Beginning cash and cash equivalents balance
六、期末现金及现金等价物余额：	**6. The final cash and cash equivalents balance:**
补充资料	SUPPLEMENTARY INFORMATION
1. 将净利润调节为经营活动的现金流量	1. Reconciliation from net income to cash flow from operating activities
净利润	Net income
加：资产减值准备	Add：Provision for asset impairment

Table 3-6(Continued)

项 目	ITEMS
固定资产折旧、油气资产折耗、生产性生物资产折旧	Depreciation of fixed assets, depletion of oil and gas assets, and depreciation of productive biological assets
无形资产摊销	Amortization of intangible assets
长期待摊费用摊销	Amortization of long-term prepaid expenses
处理固定资产、无形资产和其他长期资产的损失	Loss of disposing fixed assets, intangible assets and other long-term assets
固定资产报废损失	Loss on retirement of fixed assets
公允价值变动损失	loss from the changes in the fair value
财务费用	Financial expenses
投资损失	Investment losses
递延所得税资产减少	Decrease in deferred income tax assets
递延所得税负债增加	Increase in deferred income tax liabilities
存货的减少	Decrease in inventory
经营性应收项目的减少	Decrease in operating receivables
经营性应付项目的增加	Increase in operating payables
其他	Others
经营活动产生的现金流量净额	Net cash flows from operating activities
2. 不涉及现金收支的投资和筹资活动	2. Investing and financing activities that do not involve cash receipts and payments
债务转为资本	Conversion of debt into capital
一年内到期的可转换公司债券	Convertible bond maturity within one year
融资租入固定资产	Fixed assets acquired under finance leasing
3. 现金及现金等价物净变动情况	3. Net changes in cash and cash equivalents
现金的期末余额	The ending balance of cash
减：现金的期初余额	Less: The beginning balance of cash
加：现金等价物的期末余额	Add: The ending balance of cash equivalents
减：现金等价物的期初余额	Less: The beginning balance of cash equivalents
现金及现金等价物的净增加额	Net increase of cash and cash equivalents

 Vocabulary

integrate	*vt. & vi.*	使一体化；使整合；使完整；合并
cash equivalent		准现金，现金等价物
be derived from		源自于，来源于
accounting methods		会计方法
timeframe	*n.*	时间表

operating cash flow	经营现金流
deficit	*n.* 不足额；赤字；亏损
dividend	*n.* 红利，股息，股利
investing cash flow	投资现金流
financing cash flow	筹资现金流
capital structure	资本结构
proceeds	*n.* (买卖等的)收入，收益
issuance	*n.* 发行，发布
exchange rate	*n.* 汇率，兑换率

Notes

[1] The statement of cash flows reports all the cash inflows and outflows of the firm for a specified period.　现金流量表报告了在特定期间内企业的现金流入和流出。

[2] because it eliminates allocations, which might be derived from different accounting methods, such as various timeframes for depreciating fixed assets.　是因为它(现金流量表)消除了源于不同会计方法而形成的分配，如固定资产折旧期限的差异。

[3] The statement of cash flows reports the company's sources and uses of cash and the beginning and ending values for cash each year.　现金流量表报告了每年公司的现金来源和使用以及期初、期末的现金值。

[4] Internally generated funds can be used to pay dividends, repay loans, replace existing capacity, or invest in other companies' shares and bonds.　内源资金可以被用来支付股利、偿还贷款、提升现有(生产)能力或投资其他公司的股票和债券。

[5] Financing cash flow contains the cash flow consequences of the firm's capital structure (debt and equity) decisions, including proceeds from the issuance of shares, returns to shareholders in the form of dividends, and the incurrence and repayment of debt, etc.　筹资现金流包含了由于公司资本结构(负债和权益)决策而产生的现金流，包括发行股票的收益、以股利形式给股东的回报、债务的举借以及偿还等。

3.4 Statement of Changes in Owners' Equity
所有者权益变动表

A conversation between A—an accountant and S—a freshman majoring in accounting.

A: The net income in the income statement has a direct effect on the owners' equity, so when accountants prepare the financial statements they, include the net income in the statement of changes in owners' equity.

S: The statement of changes in owners' equity? Besides the income statement, balance sheet and cash flow statement, we didn't expect that there is a statement of changes in owners' equity.

A: Income statement, balance sheet and cash flow statement are usually called the three primary financial statements, but the statement of changes in owners' equity is an essential part of the financial reporting system.

S: What does the statement of changes in owners' equity show?

A: It shows a company's transaction with its owners. Profits that a company generates ultimately belong to the owners of the company. After a company earns its net income, its board of directors decides if the company should pay a dividend to the owners. Sometimes you will also see companies issuing shares in their statement of changes in owners' equity.

What is the Statement of Changes in Owners' Equity

The statement of changes in owner' equity details changes to the equity portion of the balance sheet during a period of time. [1] It reports components of owners' equity or the investment of the owners in the firm, the earnings reinvested in the business, and various accounting adjustments that reflect selected market value changes in certain investments in securities, and certain **unrealized gains and losses** on cash flow **hedges**.

There are three forms of organizations—proprietorship, partnership and corporation. Although the financial statements are very similar for the three types of business organizations, there are some differences on the preparation of statement of changes in owners' equity. We will discuss it later in Chapter 7.

It is required by the law that a corporation's owners' equity be divided into two parts: capital stock, which is the amount, invested in the company; and **retained earnings**, which represent the **cumulative** earnings of the company less any distribution of these earning called dividends. Single proprietorships or partnerships, however, do not have to distinguish between amounts invested by the owners and any undistributed earnings. On the statement of changes in owners' equity, net income is added to the retained earnings balance to obtain the closing balance. This closing balance is then used in the owners' equity section on a corporate balance sheet.

Format of the Statement of Changes in Owners' Equity

In China, the statement of changes in owners' equity for a corporation is usually presented in the format of Table 3-7, and the reference translation of the items lists on the right in Table 3-8.

Table 3-7   Statement of Changes in Owners' Equity of Chinese Format

项　目	本年金额						上年金额					
	实收资本(或股本)	资本公积	减：库存股	盈余公积	未分配利润	所有者权益合计	实收资本(或股本)	资本公积	减：库存股	盈余公积	未分配利润	所有者权益合计
一、上年年末余额												
加：会计政策变更												
前期差错更正												

Table 3-7(Continued)

项 目	本年金额						上年金额					
	实收资本(或股本)	资本公积	减：库存股	盈余公积	未分配利润	所有者权益合计	实收资本(或股本)	资本公积	减：库存股	盈余公积	未分配利润	所有者权益合计
二、本年年初余额												
三、本年增减变动金额(减少以"-"号填列)												
四、本年年末余额												

Table 3-8　Bilingual Items of the Statement of Changes in Owners' Equity

项 目	ITEMS
实收资本	Paid-in capital
资本公积	Capital surplus
减：库存股	Less: Treasury stock
盈余公积	Earnings surplus
未分配利润	Undistributed profits
所有者权益总计	Total owners' equity
一、上年年末金额	1. Balance at the end of prior year
加：会计政策变更影响数	Add: Accounting policy changes
前期差错更正	Prior errors' correction
二、本年年初余额	2. Balance at the beginning of current year
三、本年增减变动金额	3. Increases/decreases in current year
(一)净利润	(1) Net income /loss
(二)直接计入所有者权益的利得或损失	(2) Gains or losses directly recorded into owners' equity
1. 可供出售金融资产公允价值变动净额	① Net changes in fair value of financial assets available for sale
2. 权益法下被投资单位所有者权益变动的影响	② Effect of owners' equity changes in the invested enterprise under equity method
3. 与计入所有者权益项目相关的所得税影响	③ Income tax effect related to items recorded in the owners' equity
4. 其他	④ Others
上述(一)和(二)小计	Sub-total of (1) & (2)

Table 3-8(Continued)

项 目	ITEMS
(三)所有者投入和减少资本	(3) Capital contributed by owners and capital decreases
1. 所有者投入	① Capital contributed by owners
2. 股份支付计入所有者权益的金额	② The amount of share-based payments recorded in owners' equity
3. 其他	③ Others
(四)利润分配	(4) Profit distribution
1. 提取盈余公积	① Appropriation of surplus reserve
2. 对所有者的分配	② Profit distributed to owners
3. 其他	③ Others
(五)所有者权益内部结转	(5) Transfers within the owners' equity
1. 资本公积转增资本	Capital transferred from capital surplus
2. 盈余公积转增资本	Capital transferred from earnings surplus
3. 盈余公积弥补亏损	Recovery of losses by earnings surplus
4. 其他	④ Others
四、本年年末余额	4. Balance at the end of the current year

 ## Vocabulary

unrealized gains and losses	未实现的利得和损失
hedge	*n.* 套期保值；保护手段； 防止损失(尤指金钱)的手段
retained earnings	留存收益
cumulative	*adj.* 累积的；渐增的；追加的

Notes

[1] The statement of changes in owner' equity details changes to the equity portion of the balance sheet during a period of time.   所有者权益变动表清晰地说明了一段期间内资产负债表权益部分的变化。

3.5   Notes to Financial Statements
财务报表附注

A conversation between A—an accountant and S—a freshman majoring in accounting.

S: What's the meaning of notes to financial statements?

A: Notes are additional information added to the end of financial statements, to help explain specific items in the financial statements as well as provide a more comprehensive assessment of a company's financial condition.

S: The preparation of notes is an optional part of financial statements, isn't it?

A: No. It's an essential part. These notes help company decision makers and shareholders understand the accounting methods and practices employed by the company, while preserving readability of the body of the document itself.

S: What kind of information should be disclosed in the notes?

A: For example, general information about the company, basis of preparation, significant accounting policies and accounting estimates, and contingencies.

S: Oh, I see. By the way, what is a contingency?

A: A contingency is something that might happen in the future, like a lawsuit.

Notes to financial statements (notes) are **additional** information added to the end of financial statements.

Information provided in the financial statements is **augmented** by notes and other **supplementary** disclosures. Notes are an integral part of the financial statements and provide data on such subjects as a **profile** of the company, basis of preparation, significant accounting policies and accounting estimates, **lawsuits** and other **loss contingencies**, and sales to **related parties**.[1] These data are required by either Chinese Accounting Standards or regulatory authorities (the **China Securities Regulatory Commission, abbreviated as CSRC**).

Notes provide information about the accounting methods, assumptions, and estimates used by management to develop the data reported in the financial statements. They are designed to allow users to improve assessments of the amounts, timing, and uncertainty of the estimates reported in the financial statements.

Vocabulary

additional	*adj.* 额外的,附加的,补充的
augment	*vt.* 增强,加强;(使)扩张,扩大
supplementary	*adj.* 增补的,追加的
profile	*n.* 侧面;轮廓;外形;剖面;简况
lawsuit	*n.* 诉讼;诉讼案件
loss contingencies	或有损失
related parties	关联方
CSRC(China Securities Regulatory Commission)	中国证监会

Notes

[1] Notes are an integral part of the financial statements and provide data on such subjects as

a profile of the company, basis of preparation, significant accounting policies and accounting estimates, lawsuits and other loss contingencies, and sales to related parties. 附注是用来披露含公司概况、编制基础、重要会计政策和会计估计、诉讼以及其他或有损失、关联方销售等方面内容，是财务报表必不可少的一部分。

Exercises

I. Discuss the following questions in English.

1. What are the three primary financial statements?

2. If you know the assets and the owners' equity of a business, how can you measure its liabilities?

3. Briefly describe the content and format of a balance sheet?

4. Identify the two basic categories of items on an income statement.

5. What is the main distinction between revenues and gains? And what is the main distinction between expenses and losses?

6. What is the purpose of a statement of cash flows? How does it differ from a balance sheet and an income statement?

7. Give two reasons why a business can have a steady stream of net income over a six-year period and still experience a cash shortage?

8. Differentiate among operating activities, investing activities, and financing activities.

9. If you could pick a single source of cash for your business, what would it be? Why?

10. Explain the link between the income statement and the statement of changes in owners' equity.

11. Explain the link between the balance sheet and the statement of changes in owners' equity.

12. What kinds of information are reflected in the notes to financial statements?

II. Choose the best word or phrase that fits the sentence.

1. Assets are, directly or indirectly, _____ by the creditors and shareholders of the firm.

　　A. funded　　　B. claimed　　　C. financed　　　　D. collected

2. Assets and liabilities are classified according to _____, that is, their expected use in operations or conversion to cash in the case of assets and time to maturity for liabilities.

　　A. currency　　　B. liquidity　　　C. flexibility　　　D. convenience

3. _____ assets are those assets that are in the form of cash or are expected to be turned into cash in the short run, usually within one year.

　　A. Current　　　B. Liquid　　　C. Short-term　　　D. Present

4. The _____ form of balance sheet lists the assets at the top, followed by liabilities and owners' equity below.

A. ledger   B. report   C. account   D. column

5.   The purpose of the income statement is to indicate how successful the business has been in meeting the objective of earning _____.

        A. revenues   B. incomes   C. gains   D. profits

6.   The portion of the income statement that deals with _____ items is interesting to investors and analysts alike, because this section discloses information about revenues and expenses that are a direct result of the regular business operations.

        A. non-operating   B. operating

        C. central   D. usual

7.   A firm may have income (loss) from other activities, such as _____ on sale or disposal of assets.

        A. gains or losses   B. revenues or expenses

        C. profits   D. incomes

8.   The statement shows how changes in balance sheet and income accounts affect _____.

        A. cash   B. cash on hand and cash in bank

        C. cash and marketable securities   D. cash and cash equivalents

9.   For a transportation company, investing cash flow should exclude _____.

        A. disposal of a track   B. making loans to others

        C. the effect of exchanging rate changes   D. purchase of a building

10.   The statement of changes in owner' equity details changes to the owners' equity portion of the _____ during a period of time.

        A. balance sheet   B. income statement

        C. Statement of retained earnings   D. cash flow statement

11.   Information provided in the financial statements is _____ by notes and other supplementary disclosures.

        A. augmented   B. increased

        C. enlarged   D. expended

III. Match each word on the left with its corresponding meaning on the right.

A	B
1. primary	(a) not having physical substance
2. supplementary	(b) the income arising from land or other property
3. estimate	(c) that part of the earnings of a corporation that is distributed to its shareholders
4. discharge	(d) grow or intensify
5. disposal	(e) added to complete or make up a deficiency
6. augment	(f) something left after other parts have been taken away
7. residual	(g) of first rank or importance or value
8. proceeds	(h) the act or means of getting rid of something

9. intangible　　　　　(i) free from obligations or duties

10. dividend　　　　　(j) an approximate calculation of quantity or degree or worth

IV. Fill in the blanks with words or phrases from the list below.

A.	depreciation	B.	function	C.	drawback	D.	facilitate
E.	cash-generating	F.	accrual-based	G.	gains	H.	recasts
I.	operations	J.	acquisition	K.	generated	L.	identically
M.	liabilities	N.	reconciliation	O.	convert	P.	possible

Cash flow statement report cash from __(1)__ either directly by reporting major categories of gross cash receipts and payments, or indirectly by reconciling __(2)__ net income to cash from operations. Both investing and financing cash flows are usually computed __(3)__ under the two methods: the direct method and indirect method. These statements are __(4)__ from the company's balance sheet and income statement. Enterprises using the direct method must also provide this __(5)__ from net income to operating cash flows.

Under the indirect method, cash from operation is computed by adjusting net income:

(1) Noncash revenues and expenses (e.g. __(6)__ expense);

(2) Non-operating items included in net income (e.g. __(7)__ from property sales); and

(3) Noncash changes in operating assets and __(8)__ (operating changes in receivables, payables, etc.).

Cash flow statement prepared using the indirect method has a significant __(9)__. Because the indirect format reports the net cash flow from operation, it does not __(10)__ the comparison and analysis of operating cash inflows and outflows by __(11)__ with the revenue and expense activities that generated them, as is __(12)__ from direct method cash flow statements. In the absence of __(13)__, divestitures, and significant foreign operations, the indirect method simply __(14)__ the income statement and the balance sheet, providing little new information on or insight into the specific components of a firm's __(15)__ ability. As a majority of firms prepare the cash flow statements using the indirect method, it is often necessary to __(16)__ an indirect statement into a direct one.

V. Translate the following sentences into Chinese.

1. The financial statements present an entity to the public in financial terms.

2. The purpose of a balance sheet is to show the financial position of a business on a given date, so it is often called the statement of financial position.

3. Current assets are assets that are expected to be converted to cash, sold, or consumed during the next 12 months or within the business' operating cycle.

4. Financial performance is assessed by giving a summary of how the business incurred its revenues and expenses—due to both operating and non-operating activities.

5. Selling, general and administrative expenses are the costs of everyday operations that are not directly related to merchandise purchases.

6. The most commonly used format for the cash flow statement is broken down into three sections: cash flows from operating activities, cash flows from investing activities, and cash flows

from financing activities.

7. The statement of changes in owners' equity presents a summary of the changes that occurred in the owners' equity of the entity during a specific period, such as a month or a year.

8. Note disclosure of loss contingencies is required when it is reasonably possible that a loss has been incurred or when it is probable that a loss had occurred but the amount cannot be reasonably estimated.

VI. Translate the following sentences into English.

1. 财务报表的基本目的是帮助决策者了解和评价企业的财务实力，盈利能力以及未来发展的前景。

2. 随着我国改革开放的深入和市场体制的完善，财务报告的作用日益突出。

3. 大多数企业也编制季度和月份财务报表，以便管理部门能随时掌握企业近期的盈利能力和财务状况。

4. 所谓账户式资产负债表就是将资产项目列在表的左边，将负债和所有者权益项目列在表的右边。

5. 利润表反映一段时期内企业的盈利活动所带来的收入、费用以及由此产生的净利润或净损失的变动情况。

6. 为了清楚地表明构成所有者权益的各组成部分当期的增减变动情况，所有者权益变动表应当以矩阵的形式列示。

7. 在具体编制现金流量表时，可以采用工作底稿法或 T 型账户法，也可以根据有关科目记录分析填列。

8. 附注是对在会计报表中列示项目所作的进一步说明，以及对未来能在这些报表中列示项目的说明等。

Reading Material 3

Delhaize Group

Financial Statements from Annual Report 2012

Delhaize Group is a limited liability company incorporated and domiciled in Belgium, with its shares listed on NYSE Euronext Brussels and on the New York Stock Exchange ("NYSE"), under the symbols "DELB" and "DEG", respectively.

The principal activity of Delhaize Group is the operation of food supermarkets. The Company is present in ten countries on three continents. The Group's sales network also includes other store formats such as convenience stores. In addition to food retailing, Delhaize Group engages in food wholesaling to affiliated stores in its sales network and independent wholesale customers and in retailing of non-food products such as pet products.

The contents contained in the financial statements of Delhaize Group are:

● Consolidated Balance Sheet
● Consolidated Income Statement

- Consolidated Statement of Comprehensive Income
- Consolidated Statement of Changes in Equity
- Consolidated Statement of Cash Flows
- Notes to the Financial Statements
- Supplementary Information
- Historical Financial Overview
- Certification of Responsible Persons
- Report of the Statutory Auditor
- Summary Statutory Accounts of Delhaize Group SA/NV

The following pages contain the five financial statements and an outline of notes to financial statement from the 2012 annual report of Delhaize Group.

You may spend 15 minutes having a glance at Delhaize Group's financial statements and the outline of notes, to use the consolidated financial statements and the data in Delhaize Group's annual report 2012 to get familiar with the English financial statements based on International Financial Reporting Standards.

Consolidated Balance Sheet

Consolidated Assets

(in millions of €)	Note	2012	2011[1]	2010
Goodwill	6	3,189	3,414	2,828
Intangible assets	7	848	878	634
Property, plant and equipment	8	4,331	4,550	4,075
Investment property	9	116	83	60
Investment in securities	11	11	13	125
Other financial assets	12	19	18	17
Deferred tax assets	22	89	97	95
Derivative instruments	19	61	57	61
Other non—current assets		53	48	19
Total non—current assets		**8,717**	**9,158**	**7,914**
Inventories	13	1,401	1,717	1,460
Receivables	14	634	697	637
Income tax receivable		21	10	1
Investment in securities	11	93	93	43
Other financial assets	12	—	22	3
Derivative instruments	19	—	1	5
Prepaid expenses		79	56	44
Other current assets		41	50	37
Cash and cash equivalents	15	932	432	758
		3,201	3,078	2,988
Assets classified as held for sale	5.2	18	56	—
Total current asset		**3,219**	**3,134**	**2,988**
Total assets		**11,936**	**12,292**	**10,902**

(1) 2011 was revised to reflect the effects of the completion in the second quarter of 2012 of the purchase price allocation of the Delta Maxi acquisition (see Note 4.1).

Consolidated Liabilities and Equity

(in millions of €)	Note	2012	2011[1]	2010
Share capital	16	51	51	51
Share premium	16	2,791	2,785	2,778
Treasury shares	16	(59)	(65)	(59)
Retained earnings	16	3,646	3,728	3,426
Other reserves	16	(60)	(47)	(34)
Cumulative translation adjustments	16	(1,178)	(1,038)	(1,094)
Shareholders' equity		**5,191**	**5,414**	**5,068**
Non-controlling interests	16	2	5	1
Total equity		**5,193**	**5,419**	**5,069**
Long-term debt	18.1	2,313	2,325	1,966
Obligations under finance leases	18.3	612	689	684
Deferred tax liabilities	22	570	624	543
Derivative instruments	19	10	20	16
Provisions	20, 21	369	289	233
Other non-current liabilities		70	98	68
Total non-current liabilities		**3,944**	**4,045**	**3,510**
Short-term borrowings	18.2	—	60	16
Long-term debt-current portion	18.1	156	88	40
Obligations under finance leases	18.3	62	61	57
Derivative instruments	19	4	—	—
Provisions	20,21	88	76	52
Income taxes payable		19	57	17
Accounts payable		1,884	1,845	1,574
Accrued expenses	23	437	442	393
Other current liabilities		145	199	174
		2,795	2,828	2,323
Liabilities associated with assets held for sale	5.2	4	—	—
Total current liabilities		2,799	2,828	2,323
Total liabilities		**6,743**	**6,873**	**5,833**
Total liabilities and equity		**11,936**	**12,292**	**10,902**

(1)2011 was revised to reflect the effects of the completion in the second quarter of 2012 of the purchase price allocation of the Delta Maxi acquisition (see Note 4.1).

Consolidated Income Statement

(in millions of €)	Note	2012	2011[(1)]	2010
Revenues		**22,737**	**21,110**	**20,850**
Cost of sales	24, 25	(17,170)	(15,749)	(15,497)
Gross profit		**5,567**	**5,361**	**5,353**
Gross margin		*24.5%*	*25.4%*	*25.7%*
Other operating income	27	122	118	85
Selling, general and administrative expenses	24	(4,871)	(4,497)	(4,394)
Other operating expenses	28	(428)	(169)	(20)
Operating profit		**390**	**813**	**1024**
Operating margin		*1.7%*	*3.9%*	*4.9%*
Finance costs	29.1	(258)	(203)	(215)
Income from investments	29.2	17	23	12
Profit before taxes and discontinued operations		**149**	**633**	**821**
Income tax expense	22	(24)	(156)	(245)
Net profit from continuing operations		**125**	**477**	**576**
Result from discontinued operations (net of tax)	5.3	(22)	(2)	(1)
Net profit		**103**	**475**	**575**
Net profit (loss) attributable to non-controlling interests		(2)	—	1
Net profit attributable to equity holders of the Group(Group share in net profit)		105	475	574

(in €)				
Earnings per share	31			
Basic		**1.27**	**4.74**	**5.74**
Net profit from continuing operations		1.05	4.71	5.73
Group share in net profit				
Diluted				
Net profit from continuing operations		1.26	4.70	5.69
Group share in net profit		1.04	4.68	5.68

(in thousands)			
Weighted average number of shares outstanding			
Basic	100,777	100,684	100,271
Diluted	101,134	101,426	101,160

---

(1) 2011 was adjusted for the reclassification of the Albanian operations to discontinued operations.

Consolidated Statement of Comprehensive Income

(in millions of €)	Note	2012	2011[1]	2010
Net profit		103	475	575
Deferred gain (loss) on discontinued cash flow hedge		—	—	—
Reclassification adjustment to net profit		—	—	1
Tax (expense) benefit		—	—	—
Deferred gain (loss) on discontinued cash flow hedge, net of tax	16,19	—	—	1
Gain (loss) on cash flow hedge		2	—	23
Reclassification adjustment to net profit		4	(5)	(15)
Tax (expense) benefit		(2)	2	(3)
Gain (loss) on cash flow hedge, net of tax	16, 19	4	(3)	5
Unrealized gain (loss) on financial assets available for sale		(1)	6	3
Reclassification adjustment to net profit		(6)	(4)	(1)
Tax (expense) benefit		1	—	—
Unrealized gain (loss) on financial assets available for sale, net of tax	16	(6)	2	2
Actuarial gain (loss) on defined benefit plans		(16)	(17)	1
Tax (expense) benefit		4	7	(1)
Actuarial gain (loss) on defined benefit plans net of tax	16, 21	(12)	(10)	—
Exchange gain (loss) on translation of foreign operations		(140)	53	263
Reclassification adjustment to net profit		—	—	—
Exchange gain (loss) on translation of foreign operations	16	(140)	53	263
Other comprehensive income		(154)	42	271
Attributable to non-controlling interests		(1)	(1)	—
Attributable to equity holders of the Group		(153)	43	271
Total comprehensive income for the period		(51)	517	846
Attributable to non-controlling interests	16	(3)	(1)	1
Attributable to equity holders of the Group		(48)	518	845

(1) 2011 was revised to reflect the effects of the completion in the second quarter of 2012 of the purchase price allocation of the Delta Maxi acquisition (see Note 4.1).

Consolidated Statement of Changes in Equity

(in millions of €, except number of shares)

Attributable to Equity Holders of the Group

	Issued Capital – Number of Shares	Issued Capital – Amount	Share premium	Treasury Shares – Number of Shares	Treasury Shares – Amount	Retained Earnings	Other Reserves – Discontinued Cash Flow Hedge Reserve	Other Reserves – Cash Flow Hedge Reserve	Other Reserves – Available-for-sale Reserve	Other Reserves – Actuarial Gains and Losses Reserve	Other Reserves – Cumulative Translation Adjustment	Share-holders' equity	Non-controlling interests	Total Equity
Balances at January 1, 2010	100,870,626	50	2,752	955,586	(54)	3,044	(9)	(6)	2	(27)	(1,360)	4,392	17	4,409
Other comprehensive income	—	—	—	—	(1)	—	—	5	2	(1)	266	271	—	271
Net profit	—	—	—	—	—	574	—	—	—	—	—	574	1	575
Total comprehensive income for the period	—	—	—	—	(1)	574	—	5	2	(1)	266	845	1	846
Capital increases	684,655	1	25	—	—	—	—	—	—	—	—	26	—	26
Treasury shares purchased	—	—	—	441,996	(26)	—	—	—	—	—	—	(26)	—	(26)
Treasury shares sold upon exercise of employee stock options	—	—	(11)	(408,722)	22	—	—	—	—	—	—	11	—	11
Excess tax benefit (deficiency) on employee stock options and restricted shares	—	—	1	—	—	—	—	—	—	—	—	1	—	1
Tax payment for restricted shares vest	—	—	(5)	—	—	—	—	—	—	—	—	(5)	—	(5)
Share-based compensation expense	—	—	16	—	—	—	—	—	—	—	—	16	—	16
Dividend declared	—	—	—	—	—	(161)	—	—	—	—	—	(161)	(1)	(162)
Purchase of non-controlling interests	—	—	—	—	—	(31)	—	—	—	—	—	(31)	(16)	(47)
Balances at December 31, 2010	101,555,281	51	2,778	988,860	(59)	3,426	(9)	(1)	4	(28)	(1,094)	5,068	1	5,069
Other comprehensive income	—	—	—	—	—	—	—	(3)	2	(12)	56	43	(1)	42
Net profit	—	—	—	—	—	475	—	—	—	—	—	475	—	475
Total comprehensive income for the period	—	—	—	—	—	475	—	(3)	2	(12)	56	518	(1)	517
Capital increases	336,909	—	13	—	—	—	—	—	—	—	—	13	—	13
Call option on own equity instruments	—	—	(6)	—	—	—	—	—	—	—	—	(6)	—	(6)

Treasury shares purchased	—	—	—	408,138	(20)	—	—	—	—	—	—	(20)	—	(20)
Treasury shares sold upon exercise of employee stock options	—	—	(10)	(213,050)	14	—	—	—	—	—	—	4	—	4
Excess tax benefit (deficiency) on employee stock options and restricted shares	—	—	1	—	—	—	—	—	—	—	—	1	—	1
Tax payment for restricted shares vested	—	—	(4)	—	—	—	—	—	—	—	—	(4)	—	(4)
Share-based compensation expense	—	—	13	—	—	—	—	—	—	—	—	13	—	13
Dividend declared	—	—	—	—	—	(174)	—	—	—	—	—	(174)	—	(174)
Non-controlling interests resulting from business combinations	—	—	—	—	—	—	—	—	—	—	—	—	15	15
Purchase of non-controlling interests	—	—	—	—	—	1	—	—	—	—	—	1	(10)	(9)
Balances at December 31，2011[1]	101,892,190	51	2,785	1,183,948	(65)	3,728	(9)	(4)	6	(40)	(1,038)	5,414	5	5,419
Other comprehensive income	—	—	—	—	—	—	—	4	(6)	(11)	(140)	(153)	(1)	(154)
Net profit	—	—	—	—	—	105	—	—	—	—	—	105	(2)	103
Total comprehensive income for the period	—	—	—	—	—	105	—	4	(6)	(11)	(140)	(48)	(3)	(51)
Capital increases	29,308	—	1	—	—	—	—	—	—	—	—	1	—	1
Treasury shares sold upon exercise of employee stock option	—	—	(6)	(139,813)	6	—	—	—	—	—	—	—	—	—
Tax payment for restricted shares vested	—	—	(2)	—	—	—	—	—	—	—	—	(2)	—	(2)
Share-based compensation expense	—	—	(13)	—	—	—	—	—	—	—	—	13	—	13
Dividend declared	—	—	—	—	—	(177)	—	—	—	—	—	(177)	—	(177)
Purchase of non-controlling interests	—	—	—	—	—	(10)	—	—	—	—	—	(10)	—	(10)
Balances at December 31, 2012	101,921,498	51	2,791	1,044,135	(59)	3,646	(9)	—	—	(51)	(1,178)	5,191	2	5,193

(1) 2011 was revised to reflect the effects of the completion in the second quarter of 2012 of the purchase price allocation of the Delta Maxi acquisition (see Note 4.1).

Consolidated Statement of Cash Flows

(in millions of €)	Note	2012	2011	2010
Operating activities				
Net profit attributable to equity holders of the Group (Group share in net profit)		105	475	574
Net profit attributable to non-controlling interests		(2)	—	1
Adjustments for:				
Depreciation and amortization		650	586	575
Impairment	28	288	135	14
Allowance for losses on accounts receivable		3	11	6
Income taxes	21.3	13	13	16
Share-based compensation	22	22	156	245
Finance costs		259	204	216
Income from investments		(17)	(23)	(12)
Other non-cash items		(16)	7	(2)
Changes in operating assets and liabilities:				
Inventories		291	(147)	(108)
Receivables		74	(10)	(39)
Prepaid expenses and other assets		(31)	(15)	(10)
Accounts payable		54	(24)	98
Accrued expenses and other liabilities		2	(4)	16
Provisions		38	4	(24)
Interest paid		(229)	(196)	(202)
Interest received		10	11	11
Income taxes paid		(106)	(77)	(58)
Net cash provided by operating activities		**1,408**	**1,106**	**1,317**
Investing activities				
Business acquisitions, net of cash and cash equivalents acquired	4.1	(12)	(591)	(19)
Business disposals. net of cash and cash equivalents disposed	5.1	3	—	—
Purchase of tangible assets (capital expenditures)	8.9	(596)	(675)	(568)
Purchase of intangible assets (capital expenditures)	7	(92)	(87)	(92)
Sale of tangible and intangible assets		39	11	14
Sale and maturity of (investment in) debt securities, net		(1)	72	(13)
Purchase of other financial assets		—	(21)	(2)
Sale and maturity of other financial assets		22	28	15
Settlement of derivatives instruments		—	(2)	—
Net cash used in investing activities		**(637)**	**(1,265)**	**665**
Cash flow before financing activities		**771**	**(159)**	**652**

Financing activities

Proceeds from the exercise of share warrants and stock options	16	(1)	13	32
Purchase of call option on own equity instruments	16	—	(6)	—
Treasury shares purchased	16	—	(20)	(26)
Purchase of non-controlling interests	4.2	(23)	(10)	(47)
Dividends paid	17	(180)	(173)	(161)
Dividends paid by subsidiaries to non-controlling interests		—	—	(1)
Escrow maturities		—	2	2
Borrowing under long-term loans, net of financing costs		621	408	(1)
Repayment of long-term loans		(564)	(224)	(42)
Repayment of lease obligations		(54)	(53)	(49)
Borrowings (repayments) of short-term loans, net		(60)	(85)	(49)
Settlement of derivative instruments		(1)	2	(1)
Net cash used in financing activities		**(262)**	**(146)**	**(343)**
Effect of foreign currency translation		(8)	(21)	10
Net (decrease) increase in cash and cash equivalents		**501**	**(326)**	**319**
Cash and cash equivalents at beginning of period	15	432	758	439
Cash and cash equivalents at end of period	15	933[1]	432	758

(1) Includes €1 million in assets classified as held for sale.

75 Notes to the Financial Statements

1. General Information
2. Significant Accounting Policies
3. Segment Information
4. Business Combinations and Acquisition of Non-controlling Interests
5. Divestitures, Disposal Group / Assets Held for Sale and Discontinued Operations
6. Goodwill
7. Intangible Assets
8. Property, Plant and Equipment
9. Investment Property
10. Financial Instruments by Category
11. Investments in Securities
12. Other Financial Assets
13. Inventories
14. Receivables
15. Cash and Cash Equivalents
16. Equity
17. Dividends
18. Financial Liabilities
19. Derivative Financial Instruments and Hedging
20. Provisions

21. Employee Benefits

22. Income Taxes

23. Accrued Expenses

24. Expenses from Continuing Operations by Nature

25. Cost of Sales

26. Employee Benefit Expenses

27. Other Operating Income

28. Other Operating Expenses

29. Financial Result

30. Net Foreign Exchange Losses (Gains)

31. Earnings Per Share ("EPS")

32. Related Party Transactions

33. Commitments

34. Contingencies

35. Subsequent Events

36. List of Consolidated and Associated Companies and Joint Ventures

Answers:

II.	1	C	2	B	3	A	4	B	5	D	6	B	7	A	8	D
	9	C	10	A	11	A										

III.	1	g	2	e	3	j	4	i	5	h	6	d	7	f	8	b
	9	a	10	c												

IV.	1	I	2	F	3	L	4	K	5	N	6	A	7	G	8	M
	9	C	10	D	11	B	12	P	13	J	14	H	15	E	16	O

 More Knowledge 知识扩展

IFRS——国际财务报告准则

国际财务报告准则(International Financial Reporting Standards, IFRS)是国际会计准则理事会(IASB)颁布的易于各国在跨国经济往来时执行的一项标准的会计制度。IFRS 是全球统一的财务规则,是按照国际标准规范运作的财务管理准则,用于规范全世界范围内的企业或其他经济组织的会计运作,使各国的经济利益可以在一个标准上得到保护,不至于因参差不一的准则导致不一样的计算方式,从而产生不必要的经济损失。

IFRS 的前身是 IAS(International Accounting Standards),由于社会的不断进步以及经济业务的日趋多样和复杂,老版本的 IAS 已逐渐不适用于当下,因此 IFRS 应运而生并逐步替代 IAS 的内容(例如,新出的 IFRS15 Revenue from contract with customers 将最早于 2017 年替代现有的 IAS18 Revenue 以及 IAS11 Construction Contract)。IFRS 的内容共分六部分。

IASB——国际会计准则理事会 IASB)的前身。国际会计准则理事会(International Accounting Standards Board,简称 IASB)。IASB 的前身是国际会计准则委员会(International Accounting Standards committee,简称 IASC),在 2000 年进行全面重组并于 2001 年年初改为国际会计准则理事会。

Chapter 4　Current Assets
流动资产

Learning Objectives

- Understand cash and internal control over cash　理解现金及其控制
- Understand petty cash fund　理解零用备用金
- Understand the bank reconciliation　理解银行往来备用表
- Understand and interpret marketable securities　理解并解释有价证券
- Understand accounts receivable and notes receivable　理解应收账款和应收票据
- Discuss credit sales and bad debts　讨论信用销售和坏账
- Understand discounting of notes receivable　理解应收票据的折扣率
- Understand inventory and inventory system　理解存货和存货制
- Discuss the various inventory costing methods　讨论各种存货成本计算方法
- Valuate inventory using lower of cost or market method　使用成本与市价孰低法评估存货

Listening Practice　听力练习

Chapter 4 English Listening.mp3

第 4 章答案和翻译的音频见右侧二维码。

Dictation: *Listen and complete the passage with the words or phrases according to what you've heard from the speaker.*

The growth of organizations, ____1____ in technology, government regulation, and the globalization of ____2____ during the twentieth century have spurred the development of accounting. As a result, a number of specialized fields of accounting have evolved in addition to ____3____ accounting and managerial accounting, which include auditing, cost accounting, tax accounting, budgetary accounting, ____4____ accounting and not-for-profit accounting, human resources accounting, environment accounting, social accounting, international accounting, etc. For example, tax accounting encompasses the preparation of tax ____5____ and the considerations of tax results of certain business transactions and their alternative actions for the company.

Wisdom　至理名言

Money begets (or breeds or gets) money. 金钱会产生(或繁殖或获得)金钱。
Boundless risk must pay for boundless gain. 无限的风险必须为无限的收益买单。

Mini Case 微型案例

Henson Company is a manufacturing business taking job orders. What's more, accounting for a manufacturing business is different from what we have been learning. The major difference is that a manufacturing business requires special accounting procedures and reports for costs. To be specific, cost accounting procedures are applied to compute the manufacturing costs and set the prices.

Then questions arise: What kinds of costs are there? How to account for costs? What is special for cost accounting in a manufacturing business? Why do we learn manufacturing cost accounting in particular?

4.1   Cash and Its Control
现金及其控制

A conversation between A—an accountant and S—a freshman majoring in accounting.

S: The business should establish one cash account, right?

A: Generally more than one. By its definition in the accounting, the cash not only includes paper money and coins the business holds, but also bank deposits and highly liquid instruments like checks. Therefore, the business at least has the cash on hand account and cash in bank account.

S: Accountants play a very important role in cash management, don't they?

A: Yes. Their responsibilities in cash management are really important.

S: I think accountants should provide accurate accounting for cash receipts, cash disbursements, and cash balances.

A: More than that. They should ensure that the business has sufficient cash for operations and meanwhile they should make good use of the cash and create some income.

S: By depositing the cash with the bank?

A: No. Generally, bank deposits don't generate income, so they should invest the idle cash, for example, by purchasing some marketable securities that may increase in value.

What is Cash

The measurement of cash classified as a current asset includes coins, currency, unrestricted funds on deposit with a bank (either checking accounts or savings accounts), **negotiable checks** and **bank drafts**. On the other hand, some items may be confused with cash but normally are categorized under other balance sheet captions. Among these items are **certificates of deposit, bank overdrafts, postdated checks, IOUs and travel advances.** [1] Most companies report cash and

cash equivalents together. Cash equivalents are short-term, highly liquid investments that are readily convertible into known amounts of cash and near their maturity. Examples of cash equivalent include **bearer bonds**, **money market funds**, and **commercial papers** which are short-term corporate debts. In summary, to be classified under the current assets-cash-caption on the balance sheet, amounts must be immediately available to pay current debts and may not be bound by any contractual or legal restrictions. [2] Items that do not meet these criteria must be reported elsewhere within the assets (liabilities) section on the balance sheet.

On a balance sheet, cash, the most liquid asset, is listed first in the current asset section. All unrestricted cash whether on hand or on deposit at banks is presented as a single item using the caption "cash and cash equivalent".

Cash and cash equivalents are completely liquid assets, and thus should get special respect from shareholders. This is the money that a company could immediately mail to you in the form of a fat dividend if it had nothing better to do with it.

 Internal Control Over Cash

Internal control is a plan of organization and a system of procedures implemented by company management and the board of directors, and designed to accomplish the following five objectives:

(1) **Safeguard** assets. A company must safeguard its assets against waste, inefficient, and fraud.

(2) Encourage employees to follow company policy. Everyone in an organization needs to work toward the same goals.

(3) Promote operational efficiency. Companies cannot afford to waste resources.

(4) Ensure accurate, reliable accounting records. Accurate records are essential.

(5) Comply with legal requirements. Companies, like people, are subject to laws, such as those of regulatory agencies like CSRC(China Securities Regulatory Commission), tax authorities and governing bodies.

Cash requires some specific internal controls because cash is relatively easy to steal and it is easy to convert to other forms of wealth. Moreover, all transactions ultimately affect cash.

Cash control systems, which are part of a firm's internal control systems, can be divided into two main functions: (1) control over **cash receipts** and (2) control over **cash disbursements**.

An adequate system of internal control over cash would include the following features:

(1) Responsibility for handling cash and checks should be separated from that for keeping records.

(2) All cash receipts are deposited intact in the bank each day.

(3) All major disbursements are made by checks, and an **imprest** (fixed amount) fund is used for **petty cash** disbursements. [3]

 Petty Cash Fund

Most business firms find it inconvenient and expensive to write checks for small expenditures. It would be wasteful to write separate checks for an executives' taxi fare, delivery of a package, or small purchases. Therefore, these expenditures are usually handled by establishing a **petty cash fund**. <u>Control can be maintained by handling the fund on an imprest basis and by following certain well-established procedures.</u> [4]

The petty cash fund is opened with a particular amount of cash. The size of the petty cash fund depends on the number and amount of minor expenditures. Many firms maintain funds that will last a month. A check is written for this amount, cashed, and the money turned over to the **custodian** in charge of the petty cash fund.

For each petty cash payment, the custodian keeps a record to list the items purchased. The sum of the cash in the petty cash fund plus the total of the paid records should be equal to the opening balance at all times.

The petty cash fund must be **reimbursed** at the end of an accounting period in order to journalize the petty cash disbursements. The expense accounts are debited each time when the fund is **replenished**. The petty cash account in the general ledger is affected only when the fund is established and when the estimated fund amount is increased or decreased. Otherwise, the petty cash account keeps the same balance at all time.

<u>Although expenditures from an imprest petty cash funds are made in currency and coin, the fund is established or increased by writing a check against the basic bank account.</u>[5] After reviewing expenditures, replenishment is also accomplished by issuing checks. Therefore, in the final analysis, all expenditures are actually controlled by checks.

 Bank Reconciliation

When a company opens a checking account at a bank, the bank will submit monthly statements to the company showing the beginning cash balance. This permits the company to have a double record of cash transactions, one being generated by the firms' recording procedures, and another being furnished by the bank. Control is provided by comparing the two records and accounting for any differences. <u>This important procedure is called reconciling the bank statement with the book record of cash transactions or, simply, making a **bank reconciliation**, which is a schedule explaining any of the differences between the bank statement balance and the book balance.</u> [6]

The books and the bank statement usually show different cash balances. Differences arise usually because of a time lag in recording transactions. Some reasons for the differences are:

(1) **Outstanding checks**. Checks issued by the company but not yet paid by the bank.

(2) Deposits not yet credited by the bank. Cash receipts recorded by the depositor but which reached the bank too late to be included in the bank statement for the current month.

(3) Charges made by the bank but not yet reflected on the depositor's books. Service charges and the cost of printed checks are usually deducted automatically by the bank. In addition, the

bank may pay cash by **electronic funds transfers (EFT)** on company's behalf.

(4) Credits made by the bank but not yet reflected on the depositor's books. For example, interest revenues on the company's checking account and an EFT receipt which the company has not yet recorded.

(5) Accounting errors made either by the depositor or by the bank.

Vocabulary

negotiable check	可转让支票
bank draft	银行汇票
certificates of deposit	存款证；存款单
bearer bond	不记名债券
money market fund	货币市场基金
commercial paper	商业汇票
internal control	内部控制；内控
safeguard	*n. & vt.* 保护，保卫
cash receipt	现金收入
cash disbursement	现金支出
imprest	*n.* 预付款 *& adj.* 预付的
petty cash	零用现金，小额现金
petty cash fund	零用备用金，零用金基金
custodian	*n.* 管理人；监护人；保管人
reimburse	*vt.* 偿还，付还，归还
replenish	*vt.* 补充；重新装满；把……装满
bank reconciliation	银行往来调节表；银行存款余额调节表
outstanding checks	未兑现支票
electronic funds transfers (EFT)	电子转账，电子汇款

Notes

[1] Among these items are certificates of deposit, bank overdrafts, postdated checks, IOUs and travel advances. 这些项目包括存款单、银行透支、远期支票、借据及差旅费预付款。

[2] In summary, to be classified under the current assets-cash-caption on the balance sheet, amounts must be immediately available to pay current debts and may not be bound by any contractual or legal restrictions. 总之，要在资产负债表上归入流动资产——现金项下的，其款额必须能立即用来偿付当前的债务，且不受任何契约的或法律的限制。

[3] All major disbursements are made by checks, and an imprest (fixed amount) fund is used for petty cash disbursements. 所有主要支出都使用支票，对零星的现金支出则另设(定额)预付资金。

[4] Control can be maintained by handling the fund on an imprest basis and by following

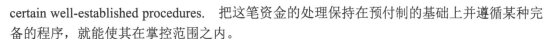

certain well-established procedures.　把这笔资金的处理保持在预付制的基础上并遵循某种完备的程序，就能使其在掌控范围之内。

[5] Although expenditures from an imprest petty cash funds are made in currency and coin, the fund is established or increased by writing a check against the basic bank account.　尽管从预付的零用备用金中支出的是纸币和硬币，但这笔资金的设置或增加，都是通过在基本银行账户中开出支票。

[6] This important procedure is called reconciling the bank statement with the book record of cash transactions or, simply, making a bank reconciliation, which is a schedule explaining any of the differences between the bank statement balance and the book balance.　这一重要程序称为将银行对账单与现金交易的账簿记录相调节，或简称为编制银行往来调节表，该表是用于说明银行对账单上的余额与企业账簿余额出现的不一致。

4.2　Marketable Securities
有价证券

A conversation between A—an accountant and S—a freshman majoring in accounting.

S: You said purchasing some marketable securities that might increase in value. What securities do you mean by marketable securities?

A: Stocks and bonds.

S: Aren't stocks somewhat risky?

A: In fact, bonds also have some risk. Without risk, there wouldn't be any gain. The purpose of investing in marketable securities is to gain profit from the cash lying idle by means of earning interest or dividends. Besides, these securities are likely to increase in value.

S: I wonder how the accounting entry should be made for the purpose of stocks.

A: The cost of the purchase includes the purchase price and incidental acquisition costs such as brokerage commissions and taxes. The accounting entry is to debit the marketable financial assets account and credit the cash in Bank account.

S: At the end of an accounting period when financial statements are to be prepared, is the amount of market securities recorded at cost?

A: No. A company should make subsequent measurement of its marketable securities according to their fair value, and not deduct the transaction expenses that may occur when it disposes of them in the future.

What are Marketable Securities

A corporation may have on hand a large amount of cash that is not needed immediately, but this cash may be needed later in operating the business. Rather than allow this excess cash to lie idle until it is actually needed, the corporation may invest all or a part of it in securities that can be quickly sold when cash is needed. Such securities are known as **marketable securities**, trading securities, short-term investment or <u>marketable financial assets</u> [1]. Marketable securities ordinarily consist of marketable debt securities (**government and corporate bonds**) and marketable equity securities (**preferred and common stock**) acquired with cash not immediately needed in operations.

<u>Although they may be retained as an investment for a number of years, they continue to be classified as temporary, if (1) they are marketable, and (2) management intents to sell them when cash needs developing or when good investment management indicates a change in the securities held.</u> [2] However, investments which are not readily marketable, or which management intends to hold on a long-term basis, are not classified as marketable financial assets.

Marketable securities can be easily purchased or sold at quoted market price on security exchanges. Investments in marketable securities are almost as liquid as cash itself. For this reason, marketable securities usually rank next to cash in liquidity and should be listed in the current asset section on the balance sheet immediately after cash and cash equivalent. Trading securities that are held for other than liquidity and temporary investment purposes should not be classified as current assets.

Accounting for Marketable Securities

Accounting for marketable securities is similar to that of other assets. <u>Investment in marketable equity securities is recorded, when acquired, at cost, which include the purchase price and incidental acquisition costs such as brokerage commissions and taxes.</u> [3]

Interest earned on debt obligations and dividends earned on equity securities are credited to revenue accounts such as interest earned and dividends earned or <u>income from investments</u> [4].

Sales of marketable securities may generate a gain or a loss representing the difference between cost and proceeds.

A year-end entry adjusts the carrying amount of the marketable securities to its current market value. The adjustment account either adds to the marketable securities carrying amount on the balance sheet or decreases it. Unrealized gain or loss is shown in the income statement. When a short-term investment is sold, the gain or loss is the difference between the sales proceeds and the last carrying amount on the balance sheet.

Vocabulary

marketable securities	可转售证券，有价证券
government bonds	政府债券
corporate bonds	公司债券
preferred stock	优先股
common stock	普通股

Notes

[1] marketable financial assets　对中文"交易性金融资产"会计科目的参考翻译，英文中的表述相类似的有"marketable securities, trading securities, temporary investments, short-term investments"

[2] Although they may be retained as an investment for a number of years, they continue to be classified as temporary, if (1) they are marketable, and (2) management intents to sell them when cash needs developing or when good investment management indicates a change in the securities held.　虽然这些证券作为投资也许会置留几年，但如果(1)他们可以随时出售，(2)当出现现金需求或是当合适的投资管理表明应该变换所持有的证券时，管理部门便会售出有价证券，他们仍被归类为临时性的。

[3] Investment in marketable equity securities is recorded, when acquired, at cost, which include the purchase price and incidental acquisition costs such as brokerage commissions and taxes.　有价证券投资在取得时按其成本入账，其中包括购价及各种附带的取得成本，例如经纪人佣金和税款。

[4] income from investments　对中文"投资收益"会计科目的参考翻译，英文中一般不设这样一个汇总的会计科目，而是分别计入利息或股利等，如"interest earned, dividends earned"。

4.3　Receivables
应收款项

A conversation between A—an accountant and S—a freshman majoring in accounting.

S: What's the difference between notes receivable and accounts receivable?

A: Notes receivable are a kind of promissory note the debtor issues to the creditor, promising to pay the creditor the principal and interest at a certain time. However, accounts receivable usually don't bear any interest.

S: What economic activities lead to accounts receivable?

A: The main activities are sales on credit. Credit sales are very popular in the modern business world. For many transactions, there is a time gap between the delivery and the payment.

S: What if accounts receivable prove to be uncollectible?

A: The chief problem in recording uncollectible accounts receivable is establishing the time at which to record the loss. Two general procedures are in use.

S: What are they?

A: Direct write-off method and allowance method. The former method requires that no entry should be made until a specific account has definitely been established as uncollectible. And the latter method suggests that companies estimate uncollectible accounts in advance rather than simply record them when accounts prove to be uncollectible.

What are receivables

Receivables are monetary claims against others. Receivables are acquired mainly by selling goods and services as well as by lending money. The two major types of receivables are **accounts receivable** and **notes receivable**.

A business' accounts receivables are the amount **collectible** from customers from the sale of goods and services. <u>Sales and profits can be increased by granting customers the privilege of making payment a month after the date of sale.</u> [1] Accounts receivable, which typically classified are current assets, are sometimes called trade receivables or receivables. The use of the word "trade" is usually to separate receivables arising from the selling of goods or provision of services to customers as opposed to non-trade receivables.

Notes receivables are more formal contracts than accounts receivable. Technically, a great distinction does not exist between trade accounts receivable and trade notes payable. A note receivable involves a formal **promissory note**, whereas an account receivable is only an informal promise to pay. <u>In addition, notes frequently carry a provision for interest on face amount of debt, and are **discounted** at the bank before their maturity date.</u> [2]

Other receivables are a miscellaneous category for all receivables other than accounts receivable and notes receivable. <u>Examples include advances to officers and employees, advances to subsidiaries, deposits as a guarantee of performance or payment, dividends and interest receivables, stock subscriptions receivable, and various other claims, such as claims against insurance companies for casualties sustained.</u> [3]

Internal Control for Receivables

Sales on any basis other than for cash make subsequent failure to collect the account a real possibility. <u>An **uncollectible** accounts receivable is a loss of revenue that requires, through proper entry in the accounts, a decrease in the assets accounts receivable and a related decrease in shareholders' equity.</u> [4] Internal control over collections on account is important. An essential step to ensure good control over accounts receivable is to have a separate account for each credit customer. Efficient business operations need information on how much each customer has purchased and paid, as well as how much remains to be collected.

When credit customers do not pay their debts, this **bad debt** becomes an expense for the business. According to the matching principle, expenses must be recorded in the period in which they are incurred and must be properly matched with the related revenues. Bad debt expenses are caused by selling goods on credit to customers who fail to pay bills. Therefore, the expenses should be recorded in the period during which the revenue is recorded.

Bad debt expense is an operating expense along with salaries, depreciation, rent and utilities. You may see companies label this as uncollectible—account expense, **impairment** of receivables expense or something similar. To measure bad debt expenses, accountants use the **allowance method** and the **direct write-off method**. Allowance method is a better alternative to the direct write-off method because it is in line with the matching principle of accounting.

## Allowance Method

In allowance method, the doubtful debts are estimated and bad debt expenses are recognized before the debts actually become uncollectible. An estimate is made of the expected uncollectible accounts from all sales made on account or the total of outstanding receivables. This estimate is entered as an expense and a reduction in accounts receivable in the period in which the sale is recorded. [5]

The best way to estimate uncollectibles uses the company's history of collections from customers and information on "loss events". The **percentage of sales method** matches costs with revenues because it relates the charge to the period in which the sale is recorded. Generally, the **percentage of outstanding receivables** is applied using an **aging schedule**, an approach that is more sensitive to the actual status of the accounts receivable. [6]

The first step in the allowance method is to pass an adjusting entry at the end of an accounting period to recognize the estimated bad debt expenses. Unlike direct write-off method, we do not credit accounts receivable at this stage because it is actually a **control account** of many individual debtor accounts and we do not yet know which particular debtor will make a **default**. We only know the estimated amount of receivables which are likely to end up uncollected. Therefore, a provision account called **allowance for doubtful accounts** is credited in the adjusting entry. Thus:

Bad Debt Expenses (**Asset impairment loss**)

    Allowance for Doubtful Accounts

The bad Debt expenses (asset impairment loss) account, just like any other expense account, is closed to the income summary (current year profit) account of the period. The allowance for doubtful debts is contra-asset account. It is presented on balance sheet by subtracting it from accounts receivable as shown below:

    Accounts Receivable

    Less: Allowance for Doubtful Accounts

    Accounts Receivable, net

In the next period, when a debt is actually determined as uncollectible, the following journal entry is passed to write it off.

    Allowance for Doubtful Debts

        Accounts Receivable

As more and more debts are written off, the balance in the allowance account decreases.

When any bad debt is recovered, two journal entries are passed. The first one reverses the write-off entry and the second one is a routine journal entry to record collection. Thus:

    Accounts Receivable

        Allowance for Doubtful Debts

    Cash in Bank

        Accounts Receivable

At the end of the next accounting period, bad debts are estimated again and the balance in the allowance account is adjusted.

Direct Write-off Method

Direct write-off method is one of the two most common accounting techniques of bad debts treatment. Instead of making end-of-period adjusting entries to record bad debt expenses on the basis of estimates, the companies recognize no expense until specific receivables are determined to be worthless. [7] In the direct write-off method, uncollectible accounts receivable are directly written off against income at the time when they are actually determined as bad debts. When debt is determined as uncollectible, a journal entry is passed in which bad debt expense account is debited and accounts receivable account is credited as shown below:

Bad Debts Expense(Asset impairment loss)

    Accounts Receivable

Direct write-off method does not use any allowance or reserve account.

Although the direct write-off method is simple, it has a major drawback. Often it violates the matching principle of accounting because it recognizes bad debt expense which is partly related to previous accounting period. For example if sales are made at the end of the accounting year 2013, bad debts will be realized in the beginning months of the accounting year 2014. Thus, the use of direct write-off method would cause deduction of expenses of the previous period against revenue of the current period which is contrary to the matching principle of accounting. [8]

Discounting Notes Receivables

The employment of receivables as an immediate source of cash is a common practice of many firms. Notes receivable can be converted into cash by selling them to a financial institution at a discount.

The following key terms are used in accounting for discounted notes:

(1) **Discount rate**: the annual percentage rate that the financial institution charges for buying a note and collecting the debt.

(2) **Discount period**: the length of time between a note's sale and its due date.

(3) **Bank discount**: the fee that the financial institution charges, is found by multiplying the note's **maturity value** by the discount rate and the discount period.

Notes are usually sold with recourse, which means the company discounting the note agrees to pay the financial institution if the maker **dishonors** the note.[9] Discounted note does not transfer the risk of bad debts to the financial institution. When notes receivable are sold with recourse, the company has a contingent liability that must be disclosed in the notes accompanying the financial statements.

 Vocabulary

accounts receivable	应收账款
notes receivable	应收票据
collectible	*adj*. 可收集的，可代收的； 适于收藏的
promissory note	本票，期票
discount	*vt*. 打折扣，减价出售；& *vi*. 折扣；贴现率；贴现
uncollectible	*adj*. 不可收回的；无法收集的
bad debt	坏账
impairment	*n*. 减值，损伤，损害
allowance method	备抵法
direct write-off method	直接注销法
Percentage of sales method	销售百分比法
percentage of outstanding receivables	账款余额百分比法
aging schedule	账龄表
control account	统制账户，控制账户：由明细账作为辅助的总分类账
default	*n*. 未履行，拖欠
allowance for doubtful accounts	坏账准备
asset impairment loss	资产减值损失
discount rate	贴现率，折现率
discount period	贴现期
bank discount	银行贴现费
maturity value	到期值，到期价值
dishonor	*n*. & *vt*. <商>(票据的)拒付

✏️ Notes

[1] Sales and profits can be increased by granting customers the privilege of making payment a month after the date of sale.　通过向客户提供可以在交易完成的一个月内再付款的优惠，来提高销售收入和盈利。

[2] In addition, notes frequently carry a provision for interest on face amount of debt, and are discounted at the bank before their maturity date.　此外，票据通常带有按债务面值计算利息的规定，并且可在到期日之前向银行贴现。

[3] Examples include advances to officers and employees, advances to subsidiaries, deposits as a guarantee of performance or payment, dividends and interest receivables, stock subscriptions receivables, and various other claims, such as claims against insurance companies for casualties sustained.　例子包括预付给高级职员和雇员的款项；预付给子公司的款项；履约或付款保证金存款；应收股利和利息；应收认购股款；以及其他各种要求权，例如因经确认的灾害

损失而向保险公司索赔的要求权。

[4] An uncollectible accounts receivable is a loss of revenue that requires, through proper entry in the accounts, a decrease in the assets accounts receivable and a related decrease in shareholders' equity. 一项无法收回的账款是收入的损失，它要求在账中作适当的记录来减少应收账款这一资产项目，同时相应地引起所有者权益的减少。

[5] This estimate is entered as an expense and a reduction in accounts receivable in the period in which the sale is recorded. 这一估计金额在记录销货的期间作为坏账费用及应收账款的减少入账。

[6] Generally, the percentage of outstanding receivables is applied using an aging schedule, an approach that is more sensitive to the actual status of the accounts receivable. 在应用账款余额百分比法时，通常可通过账龄表进行分析，这种方法能更为敏锐地反映应收账款的实际情况。

[7] Instead of making end-of-period adjusting entries to record bad debt expense on the basis of estimates, the companies recognize no expense until specific receivables are determined to be worthless. 公司不是在预估的基础上作期末调整会计分录来记录坏账损失，而是直至某一账款确定不再有价值时才确认损失。

[8] Thus, the use of direct write-off method would cause deduction of expenses of the previous period against revenue of the current period which is contrary to the matching principle of accounting. 因此，直接注销法的使用将使前期费用从当期收入中扣除，这与会计的配比原则相矛盾。

[9] Notes are usually sold with recourse, which means the company discounting the note agrees to pay the financial institution if the maker dishonors the note. 票据通常作为资源被出售，这就意味着如果出票人拒付票据，贴现的公司将承担向金融机构支付的义务。

4.4 Inventories
存货

A conversation between A—an accountant and S—a freshman majoring in accounting.

S: Does the inventory in the balance sheet refer to the goods the business has in stock?

A: Yes. For a manufacturing enterprise, inventory consists of raw materials, goods in the manufacturing process and finished goods.

S: For some businesses, their balance sheets don't carry the item "inventory".

A: Not all companies have inventories, particularly if they are involved in advertising, consulting, services or information industries. For those that do, however, inventories are extremely important.

S: Why?

A: The sale of inventory at a price greater than total cost is the primary source of income for manufacturing and retail business enterprises. Moreover, matching inventory cost against revenue is necessary for the proper determination of net income.

S: So, they need to take a physical count of the inventory as much as possible.

A: Not necessary. If the businesses keep a continuous record for each inventory item, they can determine the cost of ending inventory and the cost of goods sold from the accounts. Ordinarily, it is possible to take a complete physical inventory only at the end of a fiscal year.

 What is Inventory

Inventories are assets items held for sale in the ordinary course of business or goods that will be used or consumed in the production of goods to be sold.[1] In a **merchandising enterprise**, either wholesale or retail, inventory is composed of all goods owned and held for sale in the regular course of business. For a **manufacturing enterprise**, inventory consists of raw materials, goods in the manufacturing process and finished goods. The type of items included in the inventory is determined by the nature of the business, not the nature of the item. For example, a bus is a fixed asset for a public transport company but is inventory for a bus **dealership**.

There are four basic reasons for keeping an inventory:

(1) Time—the time lags present in the supply chain, from supplier to user at every stage, requires that you maintain certain amounts of inventory to use.

(2) Uncertainty—inventories are maintained as **buffers** to meet uncertainties in demand, supply and movements of goods.

(3) **Economies of scale**—ideal condition of "one unit at a time at a place where a user needs it, when he needs it" principle tends to incur lots of costs in terms of **logistics**. So bulk buying, movement and storing brings in economies of scale, thus inventory.[2]

(4) **Appreciation** in value—in some situations, some stock gains the required value when it is kept for some time to allow it to reach the desired standard for consumption, or for production. For instance, beer in the brewing industry.

Appropriate description and measurement of inventory demand careful attention because inventory is one of the most significant assets of many enterprises. Inventory is often the largest item in the current assets category, and must be accurately counted and valued at the end of each accounting period to determine a company's profit or loss. Inventories are particularly significant because they may materially affect both the income statement and balance sheet.

 Inventory System

There are two principal systems of inventory accounting — periodic and perpetual. Organizations with inventory items of small unit cost generally update their inventory records at the end of an accounting period or when financial statements are prepared, which is called **periodic inventory system**. When the periodic system is used, only the revenue from sales is recorded each time when a sale is made. No entry is made at the time of the sale to record the cost of the merchandise that has been sold. Consequently, a physical inventory must be taken in order to determine the cost of the inventory at the end of an accounting period.

Organizations whose inventory items have a large unit cost generally keep a day to day record of changes in the inventory, which is called **perpetual inventory system**, to ensure accurate and on-going control. A separate account of each type of merchandise is maintained in a subsidiary ledger. Increases in inventory items are recorded as debits to the proper accounts, and decreases are recorded as credits. The balances of the accounts are called the book inventories of the items on hand[3]. Regardless of the care with which the perpetual inventory records are maintained, their accuracy must be tested by **taking a physical inventory of** each type of commodity at least once a year. [4] The records are then compared with the actual quantities on hand and any differences are corrected.

The Various Inventory Costing Methods

Determining the cost of inventory is easy when the unit cost remains constant. But the unit cost usually changes. To compute cost of goods sold and the cost of ending inventory still on hand, we must assign unit cost to the items. The value of an inventory depends on the valuation method used, such as **specific identification** method, **first-in, first-out (FIFO)** method, **last-in, first-out (LIFO)** method and **weighted average** method.

(1) Specific identification

Some businesses deal in unique inventory items, such as automobiles, jewelry, and **real estate**. These businesses cost their inventories at the specific cost of the particular unit. The specific identification method determines the cost allocation according to the physical inventory flow. From a theoretical standpoint, the specific identification method is very attractive. However, this method is too expensive to use for inventory items that have common characteristics.

(2) First-in, first-out (FIFO)

The FIFO method is based on the assumption that costs should be charged against revenues in the order in which they were incurred. Under the FIFO method, the first costs into inventory are the first costs assigned to the cost of goods sold. Hence the inventory remaining is assumed to be made up of the most recent costs. Since most businesses tend to dispose of goods in the order of their acquisition, the FIFO method is generally in harmony with the physical movement of merchandise in an enterprise. [5]

During a period of **inflation** or rising prices, the use of the FIFO method will results in a greater amount of net income than the other methods. The reason is that the cost of the units sold is assumed to be in the order in which they were incurred, and earlier unit costs were lower than the more recent unit costs. Much of the benefit of larger amounts of gross profit is lost, however, as the inventory is continually replenished at ever higher prices.

(3) Last-in, first-out (LIFO)

The LIFO method is based on the assumption that the most recent costs incurred should be charged against revenues. LIFO costing is the opposite of the FIFO. Under the LIFO method, the last costs into inventory go immediately to the cost of goods sold. Hence the inventory remaining is assumed to be composed of the earlier costs. Although LIFO is frequently criticized from a theoretical standpoint that it does not match the usual flow of goods in a business, many firms would like to use it. There is the practical advantage of saving **income taxes** during a period of inflation.

From 2007, Chinese Accounting Standards **prohibits** the use of LIFO method.

(4) Weighted average

The weighted average method is based on the assumption that costs should be charged against revenues according to the weighted average unit costs of the goods sold.[6] The same weighted average unit costs are used in determining the cost of the merchandise remaining in the inventory. Unlike FIFO and LIFO, the individual inventory costs are no longer relevant once the inventory is purchased. The weighted average unit cost is determined by dividing the total cost of the identical units of each commodity available for sale during the period by the related number of units of that commodity.

 ## Lower of Cost or Market (LCM) Method

A frequently used alternative to valuing inventory at cost is to compare cost with market price and use the lower of the two. It should be noted that regardless of the method used, it is first necessary to determine the cost of the inventory. In China, "market", as used in the phrase, is interpreted to mean **net realizable value**, which may be defined as prospective selling price minus anticipated selling expenses. To the extent practicable, the market price should be based on quantities purchased from the usual source of supply.

The lower of cost or market method can be applied (1) to each item in the inventory, (2) to major classes or categories, or (3) to the inventory as a whole. The first procedure is the one usually followed in practice in China.

Two methods are used for recording inventory at market—direct method and allowance method. For companies reporting inventory under the lower of cost or market method, it is common to use the contra-asset inventory account—allowance to reduce inventory to LCM [7]. This balance sheet account is used to report the amount that the inventory's market amount is below the inventory's cost amount. The account of allowance to reduce inventory to LCM will have a credit balance for the amount that the market value of the inventory is less than the cost shown in the inventory account. [8] If the market value of the inventory is greater than cost, a zero balance appears in the account of allowance to reduce inventory to LCM.

 ## Vocabulary

inventory	*n.* 存货，存货清单；财产目录
merchandising enterprise	商业企业；商品流通企业

manufacturing enterprise	制造企业，生产企业
dealership	*n.* 代理权，经销权；代理商
buffer	*n.* 缓冲器；起缓冲作用的人(或物)
economies of scale	规模经济
logistics	*n.* 物流；后勤；逻辑学
appreciation	*n.* (尤指土地或财产的)增值
periodic inventory system	定期盘存制
perpetual inventory system	永续盘存制
take an (a physical) inventory of	对……进行(实物)盘点，对……进行盘存
specific identification	个别识别
first-in, first-out (FIFO)	先进先出
last-in, first-out (LIFO)	后进先出
weighted average	加权平均
real estate	*n.* 不动产，土地；房地产
inflation	*n.* 通货膨胀
income tax	所得税
prohibit	*vt.* 禁止，阻止，防止；不准许
Lower of Cost or Market (LCM) Method	成本与市价孰低法
net realizable value	可变现净值

Notes

[1] Inventories are assets items held for sale in the ordinary course of business or goods that will be used or consumed in the production of goods to be sold. 存货是正常营业过程中为了销售而持有的资产项目，或者是准备用来生产可供销售的商品或将在生产商品中消耗的资产。

[2] So bulk buying, movement and storing brings in economies of scale, thus inventory. 大宗购买、转移、储存带来规模经济，存货也适用。

[3] the book inventories of the items on hand 库存项目的账面盘存数

[4] Regardless of the care with which the perpetual inventory records are maintained, their accuracy must be tested by taking a physical inventory of each type of commodity at least once a year. 不管永续盘存的记录保持得多么仔细，它们的准确性必须通过至少每年一次对每类商品进行实物盘存来加以验证。

[5] Since most businesses tend to dispose of goods in the order of their acquisition, the FIFO method is generally in harmony with the physical movement of merchandise in an enterprise. 由于大多数企业倾向于按取得的顺序出售商品，一般地说，先进先出法是与企业商品实物流动相一致的。

[6] The weighted average method is based on the assumption that costs should be charged against revenues according to the weighted average unit costs of the goods sold. 加权平均法所依据的假设是按已售商品的加权平均单价从收入中抵减。

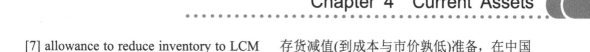

[7] allowance to reduce inventory to LCM 存货减值(到成本与市价孰低)准备，在中国计入"存货跌价准备"科目，参考翻译为"provision for decline in value of inventory"。

[8] The account of allowance to reduce inventory to LCM will have a credit balance for the amount that the market value of the inventory is less than the cost shown in the inventory account. 存货减值准备账户有贷方余额，金额为存货账户成本与存货市场价值的差额。

Exercises

I. Discuss the following questions in English.

1.   What are cash equivalents? Provide two examples. Why these items are often combined with cash for the purpose of balance sheet presentation?

2.   Mention some principles to be observed by a business in establishing internal control over cash.

3.   Why are some cash payments made from a petty cash fund but not by check?

4.   Why should a petty cash fund be reimbursed at the end of an accounting period?

5.   What is the amount to be reported on the balance sheet for a marketable security?

6.   Why are marketable securities always current assets?

7.   What are the differences between accounts receivable and notes receivable?

8.   Why must bad debt expense be estimated if such an estimate is possible?

9.   Why is estimated bad debt expense credited to the allowance for doubtful account rather than to the accounts receivable account?

10.   What are the period inventory system and the perpetual inventory system? Describe the major differences between them.

11.   In what types of situations is the specific identification method applied to inventory valuation?

12.   When costs are rising, which method reports higher net income?

13.   What is the meaning of market as it is used in determining the lower of cost or market for inventory?

II. Choose the best word or phrase that fits the sentence.

1.   The measurement of cash classified as a current asset includes coins, currency, unrestricted funds on deposit with a bank, negotiable checks and _____.

  A. bank overdrafts   B. postdated checks

  C. bank drafts   D. travel advances

2.   _____ is a plan of organization and related measures adopted by an entity to safeguard assets, encourage adherence to company policies, promote operational efficiency, and ensure accurate and reliable accounting records.

  A. Internal rule   B. Internal control

C. Regulation   D. Internal system

3. The petty cash fund must be _____ at the end of an accounting period in order to journalize the petty cash disbursements.

    A. returned   B. repaid

    C. reimbursed   D. reinvested

4. _____ is a document explaining the reasons for the differences between a depositor's records and the bank's records about the depositor's cash in bank.

    A. Bank reconciliation   B. Bank statement

    C. Checking account   D. Certificate of deposit

5. Marketable securities can be easily purchased or sold at _____ market price on securities exchanges.

    A. fixed   B. stated

    C. announced   D. quoted

6. Other receivables are a _____ category for all receivables other than accounts receivable and notes receivable.

    A. various   B. miscellaneous

    C. combined   D. mixed

7. In _____ method, the doubtful debts are estimated and bad debt expense is recognized before the debts actually become uncollectible.

    A. allowance   B. provision

    C. direct write-off   D. reverse

8. Direct write-off method _____ the matching principle of accounting because it recognizes bad debt expense which is partly related to the previous accounting period.

    A. breaks   B. violates

    C. trespasses   D. destroys

9. When notes receivable are sold with recourses, the company has _____ liability that must be disclosed in the notes accompanying the financial statements.

    A. a probable   B. a possible

    C. an uncertain   D. a contingent

10. When the _____ is used, only the revenue from sales is recorded each time when a sale is made.

    A. periodic inventory system   B. perpetual inventory system

    C. physical inventory system   D. continuous inventory system

11. The _____ method is based on the assumption that costs should be charged against revenues in the order in which they were incurred.

    A. specific identification   B. FIFO

    C. LIFO   D. weighted average

III. Match each word on the left with its corresponding meaning on the right.

A	B
1. negotiable	(a) the occurrence of a change for the worse
2. custodian	(b) fill something that had previously been emptied
3. impairment	(c) a reserve of money set aside for some purpose
4. petty	(d) a general and progressive increase in prices
5. perpetual	(e) continuing forever or indefinitely
6. bond	(f) legally transferable to the ownership of another
7. fund	(g) one having charge of buildings or a collection of valuable objects
8. inflation	(h) refuse to accept
9. replenish	(i) small and of little importance
10. dishonor	(j) a certificate of debt that is issued by a government or corporation in order to raise money

IV. Fill in the blanks with words or phrases from the list below.

A.	division	B.	relatively	C.	transactions	D.	merchandise
E.	group	F.	posting	G.	credit	H.	warrant
I.	added	J.	sales	K.	advantage	L.	least
M.	occurring	N.	separately	O.	purchase	P.	tabular

An accounting journal may be one of a (1)＿＿ of special journals or it may be a general journal. The general journal is a (2)＿＿ simple record in which any type of business transactions can be recorded. In contrast to the general journal, a special journal is designed to record a specific type of frequently (3)＿＿ business transactions. Most firms use, in addition to a general journal, at (4)＿＿ the following special journals:

Special Journal	Specific Transaction to be Recorded
Sales journal	Sales on (5)＿＿ terms
Cash receipts journal	Receipts of cash (including cash (6)＿＿)
Invoice register (purchase journal)	Purchases of (7)＿＿ and other items (supplies, fixed assets, etc.) on credit terms
Cash disbursements	Payment of cash (including cash (8)＿＿)

When special journals are used, only those transactions that do not occur often enough to (9)＿＿entry in a special journal are recorded in the general journal.

A major (10)＿＿of special journals is that their use permits a (11)＿＿ of labor. Nevertheless, the most significant advantage of using special journal is the time saved in (12)＿＿ from the journals to the ledger. When a general journal is used, each entry must be posted (13)＿＿ to the general ledger. The (14)＿＿ arrangement of special journals, however, often permits all entries to a given account to be (15)＿＿ and posted as a single aggregate posting. The more the (16)＿＿ that are involved, the greater the savings in posting time.

V. Translate the following sentences into Chinese.

1.　Current assets are defined as cash and other assets that are reasonably expected to be realized in cash or to be sold or consumed within one year or within the normal operating cycle of the business, whichever is longer.

2.　A petty cash fund is usually established for an amount sufficient to handle the payment of small expenditures for a period of month or a reasonable length of time.

3.　The bank statement will show the beginning and ending cash balance deposits, collections made by the bank for the company, checks paid, deductions from service fees and other charges.

4.　Marketable securities are investments that are highly liquid, meaning that they can be quickly sold in the secondary financial markets in large amounts for cash.

5.　Accounts receivable are a legally enforceable claim for payment to a business by its customer for goods supplied and/or services rendered in execution of the customer's order.

6.　The allowance for bad debt is the money set aside to cover the potential for bad customers, based on the kind of receivables problems the company may or may not have had in the past.

7.　Inventories are the components and finished products that a company has currently stockpiled to sell to customers.

8.　First-in, first-out (FIFO) is one of the methods commonly used to calculate the value of inventory on hand at the end of an accounting period and the cost of goods sold during the period.

VI. Translate the following sentences into English.

1.　现金对任何一家企业来说都是一项必不可少的资产。

2.　良好的内部控制意味着将各工作任务的职责划分清楚并指派给适当的员工，否则在发生差错时将很难确定是谁的责任。

3.　银行存款余额调节表是用来解释企业记录的支票账户余额与银行对账单上所列明的余额之间存在差额的一种报表。

4.　交易性金融资产主要是指企业为了近期内出售而持有的金融资产，例如企业以赚取差价为目的从二级市场购入的股票、债券、基金等。

5.　应收账款和应收票据是两种最常见的应收款项。

6.　备抵法要求企业估计其坏账费用以便在期末时编制调整分录。

7.　在永续盘存制下，每完成一笔购货或销货业务，我们都会更新一次存货账户的余额，但是由于某些事件的发生，有可能会导致存货的账面余额与实际余额不符。

8.　企业应当根据各类存货的实物流转方式、企业管理的要求、存货的性质等实际情况，合理地选择发出存货成本的计算方式，以合理确定当期发出存货的实际成本。

9.　在确定发出存货的成本时，企业可以采用先进先出法、移动加权平均法、月末一次加权平均法和个别计价法四种方法。

Reading Material 4

Retail Inventory Method

Accounting for inventory in a retail operation presents several challenges. Retailers with certain types of inventory may use the specific identification method to value their inventories. Such an approach makes sense when individual inventory units are significant, such as automobiles, pianos, or fur coats. However, imagine attempting to use such an approach at Wal-Mart, True-Value Hardware, Sears, or Bloomingdale's—high-volume retailers that have many different types of merchandise. It would be extremely difficult to determine the cost of each sale, to enter the cost codes on the tickets, to change the codes to reflect declines in value of the merchandise, to allocate costs such as transportation, and so on.

An alternative is to compile the inventories at retail prices. In most retail concerns, an observable pattern between cost and price exists. Retail prices can therefore be converted to cost through use of a formula. This method, called the retail inventory method, requires that a record be kept of (1) the total cost and retail value of goods purchased, (2) the total cost and retail value of the goods available for sale, and (3) the sales for the period. Here is how it works: The sales for the period are deducted from the retail value of the goods available for sale, to produce an estimated inventory (goods on hand) at retail. The ratio of cost to retail for all goods passing through a department or firm is then determined by dividing the total goods available for sale at cost by the total goods available at retail.

The inventory valued at retail is converted to the ending inventory at cost by applying the cost to retail ratio. Use of the retail inventory method is very common. The retail inventory method is illustrated in Table 4-1 with assumed data for Star Supermarket.

Table 4-1　An Illustration of Retail Inventory Method

Star Supermarket (current period)	Cost	Retail
Beginning inventory	$14,000	$ 20,000
Purchases	63,000	90,000
Goods available for sale	$77,000	110,000
Deduct: Sales		85,000
Ending inventory, at retail		$ 25,000
Ratio of cost to retail ($77,000/$110,000)		70%
Ending inventory at cost (70% of $25,000)		$17,500

To avoid a potential overstatement of the inventory, the retailer makes periodic inventory counts, especially in operations where loss due to shoplifting and breakage is common. There are different versions of the retail inventory method—the conventional (lower of average cost or market) method, the cost method, the LIFO retail method, and the dollar value LIFO retail method. Regardless of which version is used, the retail inventory method is sanctioned by the International Revenue Service(IRS), various retail associations, and the accounting profession. One of its advantages is that the inventory balance can be approximated without a physical count.

The retail inventory method is particularly useful for any type of interim report, because a fairly quick and reliable measure of the inventory value is usually needed. Insurance adjusters often use this approach to estimate losses from fire, flood, or other types of casualty. This method also acts as a control device because any deviations from a physical count at the end of the year have to be explained. In addition, the retail method expedites the physical inventory count at the end of the year. The crew taking the physical inventory need record only the retail price of each item; there is no need to look up each item's invoice cost, thereby saving time and expense.

The retail inventory method of computing inventory is used widely (1) to permit the computation of net income without a physical inventory count, (2) as a control measure in determining inventory shortages, (3) in regulating quantities of merchandise on hand, and (4) for insurance information.

One characteristic of the retail inventory method is that it has an averaging effect on varying rates of gross profit. When applied to an entire business where rates of gross profit vary among departments, no allowance is made for possible distortion of results because of such differences. Some companies refine the retail method under such conditions of computing inventory separately by departments or by classes of merchandise with similar gross profit. In addition, the reliability of this method assumes that the distribution of items in inventory is similar to the "mix" in the total goods available for sale.

Answers:

II.	1	C	2	B	3	C	4	A	5	D	6	B	7	A	8	B
	9	D	10	A	11	B										
III.	1	f	2	g	3	a	4	i	5	e	6	j	7	c	8	d
	9	b	10	h												
IV.	1	E	2	B	3	M	4	L	5	G	6	J	7	D	8	O
	9	H	10	K	11	A	12	F	13	N	14	P	15	I	16	C

 More Knowledge　知识扩展

应收账款控制与融资

应收账款控制与融资在为新客户或现有客户制定信用额度前应对企业客户进行评价，通常可以利用"5C"系统进行。"5C"即评估客户信用特征的5个方面，包括品质(character)、能力(capacity)、资本(capital)、抵押(collateral)和条件(conditions)。品质：客户的信誉，即履

行偿债义务的可能性，企业必须设法了解客户的历史付款记录，了解是否有拖欠的不良记录。能力：客户的偿债能力，包括流动资产的数量和质量以及与流动负债的比例。观察客户的经济状况，尤其关注客户的现金流状况，看其是否有足够的现金支付能力。资本：客户的财务状况和支付能力。通过客户的审计报告、会议纪要等，洞察报表数字后面的隐含因素，调查是否有被抵押和冻结的资产。抵押：客户拒付欠款或无力偿债时能被用作抵押的资产的数量和质量。条件：可能影响客户付款能力的经济环境。了解社会中介机构对客户的评价，调查客户所在行业的发展趋势和变化政策。根据以上 5 项特性，给客户划定不同的等级，不同的等级给予不同的授信额度。

应收账款保理业务(factoring)是一种金融业务或产品：企业把由于赊销而形成的应收账款有条件地转让给保理商(如银行)，保理商为企业提供资金，并负责管理、催收应收账款和坏账担保等业务，企业可借此收回账款，加快资金周转。

Chapter 5 Non-Current Assets
非流动资产

Learning Objectives

- Understand fixed assets and their acquisition 理解固定资产和资产购置
- Explain depreciation and compare the alternative deprecation methods 解释折旧和可替代折旧法
- Understand disposal of fixed assets 理解固定资产的清理
- Understand impairment of fixed assets 理解固定资产的减值
- Understand the definition of intangible assets and issues in accounting for them 理解无形资产的定义和解释无形资产的事项
- Understand some types of intangible assets 理解无形资产的几个类型
- Understand long-term investments 理解长期投资
- Describe how to account for equity securities 描述如何解释股权
- Describe how to account for debt securities 描述如何解释债券
- Identify the different classes of investments in securities 辨别证券投资的不同级别

Chapter 5 English Listening.mp3

Listening Practice 听力练习

第 5 章原文翻译和答案的音频见右侧二维码。

Dictation: *Listen and complete the passage with the words or phrases according to what you've heard from the speaker.*

Financial statements are necessary ____1____ of information about companies for a wide variety of users. Those who use financial statement information include company management ____2____, investors, creditors, governmental oversight agencies and the Internal Revenue Service. Users of financial statement information do not ____3____ need to know everything about accounting to use the information in basic statements. However, to ____4____ use financial statement information, it is helpful to know a few simple concepts and to be ____5____ with some of the fundamental characteristics of basic financial statements.

Wisdom 至理名言

A cow for her milk, a hen for her eggs, and a stock, for her dividends. 养奶牛是为了牛奶，养母鸡是为了鸡蛋，买股票是为了股息。

An orchard for fruit, bees for their honey, and stocks, besides, for their dividends. 种植果园是为了水果，养蜜蜂是为了蜂蜜，炒股票是为了股息。

 **Mini Case** 微型案例

Apple's stock buyback

Since Apple said in January that it would bring back most of the $252 billion it held abroad under the new tax law, investors have wondered what the company would do with the enormous cash pile.

Apple said it would buy back an additional $100 billion in stock, by far the largest increase in its already historic record of returning capital to investors. The company didn't provide a timeline for the repurchases. Apple also increased its dividend by 16 percent to 73 cents a share, pushing past Exxon Mobil to become the largest dividend payer, according to S&P Dow Jones Indices.

Apple's stock buyback fits into a broader trend of companies using the financial windfall from President Trump's tax cut to reward shareholders. Share buybacks, which are reaching record levels, are great for investors, including executives and employees, because they reliably lift stock prices by limiting the supply of shares for sale.

But critics say the actions can take money away from potential investments in hiring or research and development, and can increase economic inequality because they typically benefit wealthier people.

5.1　Fixed Assets
固定资产

A conversation between A—an accountant and S—a freshman majoring in accounting.

S: What do non-current assets mean?

A: They mean those lasting assets the business purchases for use in business operations rather than for resale to customers.

S: What specific assets do they include?

A: They consist of three major categories, namely, fixed assets, intangible assets and long-term investment. Fixed assets, which are usually referred to as property, plant and equipment, mainly include buildings, land, furniture and fixtures, machines and vehicles.

S: Some balance sheets list land, buildings, and office equipment separately. Do these items fall into the category of fixed assets you mentioned?

A: Yes. If all these are grouped into one single category, the category is called fixed assets or property, plant and equipment.

S: We dealt with the depreciation of fixed assets when we were discussing the accounting cycle, right?

A: Right. In accounting, depreciation is the allocation of the cost of a tangible asset to expense in the periods in which services are received from the assets.

What are Fixed Assets

Fixed assets, also known as property, plant and pquipment, are long-lived tangible assets acquired for continued use in carrying on the normal operations of the business and not intended for resale. [1]

These assets are expected to be used for more than one accounting period. Fixed assets are generally not considered to be a liquid form of assets unlike current assets. Examples of common types of fixed assets include buildings, land, furniture and **fixtures**, machines and vehicles.

The term "fixed asset" is generally used to describe tangible fixed assets. This means that they have a physical substance unlike intangible assets which have no physical existence such as **copyright** and **trademarks**.

Fixed assets are not held for resale but for the production, supply, rental or administrative purposes. Assets that held for resale must be accounted for as inventory rather than fixed asset. For example, if a company is in the business of selling cars, it must not account for cars held for resale as fixed assets but instead as inventory assets. However, any vehicles other than those held for the purpose of resale may be classified as fixed assets such as delivery trucks and employee cars.

Fixed assets are normally expected to be used for more than one accounting period which is why they are part of non-current assets of the entity. Economic benefits from fixed assets are therefore derived in the long term.

The primary phases of accounting for operational assets are:

(1) Measuring and recording the cost of the asset at the acquisition date.

(2) After acquisition, measuring the expense of using the asset during its useful life.

(3) Recording disposal of operational assets.

Acquisition of Fixed Assets

At the date of acquisition, a fixed asset is measured and recorded **in conformity with** the cost principle. In other words, historical cost is the usual basis for valuating fixed assets. Historical cost is measured by the cash equivalent price of obtaining the asset and getting it ready for its intended use. The cost of a fixed asset is its purchase price, including **import duties** and other deductible trade discounts and **rebates**. In addition, it should also include any cost directly **attributable** to bringing the asset to the location and condition necessary for it to be capable of operating in the manner intended by management. [2]

Some examples of "directly **attributable cost**" are costs of employee benefits arising directly from the construction or acquisition of the items, cost of **site preparation**, initial delivery and **handling costs**, **installation** and **assembly** costs.

To be recorded as part of the cost of a fixed asset, expenditure must be normal, reasonable and necessary in preparing it for its intended use. If an asset is damaged during **unpacking**, the repairs are not added to its cost. Instead, they are charged to an expense account. Nor is a paid traffic fine for moving heavy machinery on city streets without a proper permit part of the machinery's cost; but payment for a proper permit, like charges incurred to modify or **customize** a new fixed asset, is included in the cost.[3]

Depreciation of Fixed Assets

After acquisition, fixed assets (expect land) decrease in economic utility to the user because of a number of causative factors, such as wear and tear, the passage of time, obsolescence, technological changes.[4] These causative factors always impact on such assets during the periods in which the assets are being used to generate revenues.

Depreciation is the systematic allocation of the cost of an asset over its useful life. The depreciation process matches the asset's expense against revenue to measure income, as the matching principle directs. We should notice that depreciation is not a process of valuation, and depreciation does not mean **setting aside** cash to replace assets as they wear out.

For financial reporting purposes, companies may choose from several different depreciation methods. Before studying some of the methods that companies use to depreciate assets, we should understand the following definitions.

(1) **Acquisition cost**, which we have discussed, is the overall cost of purchasing a fixed asset.

(2) Estimated **useful life** is an estimate of the productive life of an asset. Although usually expressed in years, an asset's useful life may also be based on units of activity, such as items produced, hours used, or miles driven.

(3) Estimated **residual value** equals the value, if any, that a company expects to receive by selling or exchanging an asset at the end of its useful life.

There are four depreciation methods: **straight-line method**, **unit-of-production method**, **double-declining-balance method** and **sum-of-the-years-digits method**.

Straight-line depreciation method is the method that companies most frequently use for financial reporting purposes. If straight-line depreciation method is used, an asset's annual depreciation expense is calculated by dividing the asset's depreciable cost by the number of years in the asset's useful life. The formula for straight-line depreciation method is shown below:

$$\text{Annual depreciation expense} = \frac{\text{Cost} - \text{Residual valuel}}{\text{Useful life (years)}}$$

Unit-of-production method is based on the assumption that the revenue-generating benefits derived each period from a depreciable asset are related directly to the periodic output of the asset.[5] It relates acquisition cost less estimated residual value to the estimated productive output;

therefore, a depreciation rate per unit of output and depreciation expense is computed as follows:

$$\text{Annual depreciation expense} = \frac{\text{Cost} - \text{Residual valuel}}{\text{Total units of production}} \times \text{Units of actual production}$$

Unlike the two depreciation methods discussed above, double-declining-balance method and sum-of-the-years-digits method are two **accelerated depreciation methods**. An accelerated depreciation method yields larger depreciation expenses in the early years of an asset's life and less depreciation in later years.

The most common accelerated method is the double-declining-balance method, which uses a depreciation rate that is twice of the straight-line rate and applies it to the asset's beginning-of-period book value. [6] The amount of depreciation declines each period because book value declines each period. The formula is shown below:

$$\text{Annual depreciation expense} = \frac{2 \times \text{Beginning period book value}}{\text{Useful life (years)}}$$

Estimated residual value is not taken into account in figuring depreciation except in the last two years of an asset's useful life, when depreciation method is changed to the straight-line method and the amount of the carrying value down to the estimated residual value in the last year.[7] Allocating the remaining book value over the remaining life by the straight-line method does not represent a change in depreciation methods. Rather, a switch to the straight-line method is part of the double-declining-balance method. This is the way in which we arrive at the residual value.

Sum-of-years-digits method is a depreciation method that results in a more accelerated write-off than the straight-line method, and less accelerated than the double-declining-balance method. Under this method the annual depreciation is determined by multiplying the depreciable cost by a schedule of fractions that is successively smaller each year. The formula is shown below:

$$\text{Annual depreciation expense} = (\text{Cost} - \text{Residual valuel}) \times \frac{\text{Remaining useful life}}{\text{Sum of digits}}$$

Assume that, a machine is purchased by Store Corporation on December 31, 2008. The data and estimates needed for computation of annual depreciation expense are:

Acquisition cost	$120,000
Useful life: years	5
Useful life: units of production	20,000
Number of units per year respectively	3,000; 6,000; 4,000; 5,000; 2,000
Residual value	$20,000

Compute the depreciation expense for this machine over its useful life using all the four methods. The results are as follows:

(in thousands of $)

Annual period	Straight-Line		Units-of-Production		Double-Declining-Balance		Sum-of-the-Years-Digits	
	Depreciation expense	Book value	Depreciation expense	Book value	Depreciation expense	Book value	Depreciation expense	Book value
2008		120		120		120		120
2009	20	100	15	105	48	72	33.33	86.67
2010	20	80	30	75	28.8	43.2	26.67	60
2011	20	60	20	55	17.28	25.92	20	40
2012	20	40	25	30	2.96	22.96	13.33	26.67
2013	20	20	10	20	2.96	20	6.67	20
Total	100		100		100		100	

It shows depreciation expense for each year of the machine's useful life under each of the four methods. These methods allocate different amounts of depreciation to each period. However, they all result in the same total amount of depreciation, which is the asset's depreciable amount, over the life of the assets.

Disposals of Fixed Assets

Eventually, fixed assets will cease to serve a company's needs. The assets may wear out or become obsolete. A disposal involves removing all traces of the fixed asset from the balance sheet, so that the related fixed asset account and accumulated depreciation account are reduced. Meanwhile, a gain or loss is recognized for the difference between the amounts recovered on the assets and its book value. In Chinese practice, the gain or loss would be reported as "**non-operating revenue**" or "**non-operating expense**" in the year of asset disposal.

The general steps in accounting for a disposal of fixed assets are described as:

(1) Record depreciation up to the date of disposal—this also updates accumulated depreciation;

(2) Record the removal of the disposed asset's account balances—including its accumulated depreciation;

(3) Record any cash (and/or other assets) received or paid in the disposal;

(4) Record any gain or loss.

In Chinese practice, all entries of disposal of fixed assets transactions should use "**fixed assets pending disposal**" for the steps of disposal fixed assets. The entry should be done in China as follows:

(1) Update the depreciation.

　　Depreciation expense [8]

　　　　Accumulated depreciation

(2) Remove the disposed asset's account balances.

　　Fixed assets pending disposal

        Accumulated depreciation

        <u>Provision for fixed assets impairment</u>[9]

            Fixed assets

(3) Receive cash in the disposal.

        Cash in bank

            Fixed assets pending disposal

Pay cash in the disposal

        Fixed assets pending disposal

            Cash in bank

(4) If an asset is sold and received cash, a gain would be recognized when the amount of cash received is more than that of the asset book value. The entry would be:

        Fixed assets pending disposal

            Non-operating revenue

If an asset is **scrapped** or abandoned without cash recovery or with little cash recovery, a loss would be recognized. The entry would be:

        Non-operating expense

            Fixed assets pending disposal

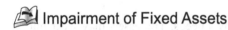 Impairment of Fixed Assets

An asset is **impaired** when its carrying value is higher than its **recoverable amount**. Recovery amount is the higher or fair value less cost to sell and value in use. The determination of recoverable amount, and many other aspects of impairment of assets, is quite complicated. However, it is important to know the basic concepts of impairment. Many companies in the financial crisis have reported billions of impairment losses.

An enterprise should examine its fixed assets at the end of each period. When a provision for impairment loss has been made for a fixed asset, the depreciation rate and depreciation charge for the fixed asset should be recalculated based on the asset's carrying amount and its remaining useful life.

<u>If there are indications that the factors based on which an impairment loss for a fixed asset was recognized in prior periods have been changed, resulting in the recoverable amount of the fixed asset becoming higher than its carrying amount, the impairment loss recognized in prior periods can not be reversed.</u>[10]

 Vocabulary

fixture	*n.* (房屋等的)固定装置
copyright	*n.* 版权，著作权
trademark	*n.* (注册)商标
in conformity with	和……相适应，和……一致

import duty	进口税
rebate	*n.* 折扣；回扣
attributable	*adj.* 可归因于……的；由……引起的
attributable cost	可归属成本
site preparation	整地；现场准备；场地整理
handling cost	装卸费；手续费；处理费
installation	*n.* 安装；装置
assembly	*n.* 装配；组配
unpacking	*n.* 取出货物，拆包[箱]
customize	*vt.* 定制，定做
set aside	把……放置一旁；不理会；取消；留出
acquisition cost	置业费，购置成本
useful life	有用年限；使用寿命
residual value	残值，剩余价值
straight-line method	直线法，年限平均法
unit-of-production method	工作量法，产量法
double-declining-balance method	双倍余额递减法
sum-of-the-years-digits method	年数总和法
accelerated depreciation method	加速折旧法
non-operating revenue	营业外收入
non-operating expense	营业外支出
fixed assets pending disposal	固定资产清理
scrap	*vt.* 废弃；取消；抛弃；报废
impair	*vt.* 减值，损害，削弱
recoverable amount	可收回金额

✎ Notes

[1] Fixed assets, also known as property, plant and equipment, are the long-lived tangible assets acquired for continued use in carrying on the normal operations of the business and not intended for resale. 固定资产是企业购置并持续用于正常经营活动而不是准备出售的长期有形资产。

[2] In addition, it should also include any cost directly attributable to bringing the asset to the location and condition necessary for it to be capable of operating in the manner intended by management. 此外，它(固定资产成本)还应该包括为了使资产到达管理者所要求的指定位置和预定可使用状态所发生的任何可直接归属成本。

[3] Nor is a paid traffic fine for moving heavy machinery on city streets without a proper permit part of the machinery's cost; but payment for a proper permit, like charges incurred to

modify or customize a new fixed asset, is included in the cost. 在运送重型机器途中所发生的交通罚款也不能算作机器的成本，但如果是合理的支出，如改装或定制新固定资产的支出便属于该固定资产成本。

[4] After acquisition, fixed assets (expect land) decrease in economic utility to the user because of a number of causative factors, such as wear and tear, the passage of time, obsolescence, technological changes. 购置之后，由于诸多因素如磨损、时间流逝、陈旧及技术变革等的影响，使固定资产(除土地外)为使用者带来的经济效用不断下降。

[5] Unit-of-production method is based on the assumption that the revenue-generating benefits derived each period from a depreciable asset are related directly to the periodic output of the asset. 工作量法基于这样的假设：应折旧资产在获取收入的每期受益与期间资产产出直接相关。

[6] The most common accelerated method is the double-declining-balance method, which uses a depreciation rate that is twice of the straight-line rate and applies it to the asset's beginning-of-period book value. 其中最常用的是双倍余额递减法，使用直线折旧率的二倍乘以期初账面价值计算折旧费用。

[7] Estimated residual value is not taken into account in figuring depreciation except in the last two years of an asset's useful life, when depreciation method is changed to the straight-line method and the amount of the carrying value down to the estimated residual value in the last year. 在计算资产折旧时不考虑预计残值，除非在某项资产折旧年限到期前两年内，改用直线法计提折旧，使账面金额在最后一年减至预计残值。

[8] Depreciation expense 折旧费用，在中国"累计折旧"直接计入"制造费用""管理费用""销售费用"，而不是"折旧费用"。

[9] Provision for fixed assets impairment 固定资产减值准备：是指由于固定资产市价持续下跌，或技术陈旧、损坏、长期闲置等原因导致其可收回金额低于账面价值的，应当将可收回金额低于其账面价值的差额作为固定资产减值准备。

[10] If there are indications that the factors based on which an impairment loss for a fixed asset was recognized in prior periods have been changed, resulting in the recoverable amount of the fixed asset becoming higher than its carrying amount, the impairment loss recognized in prior periods can not be reversed. 如果有迹象表明，在前期导致固定资产减值损失确认的因素已经改变，使该固定资产的可回收金额已高于账面金额，在前期已确认的减值损失不得转回。

5.2 Intangible Assets
无形资产

A conversation between A—an accountant and S—a freshman majoring in accounting.

S: What's the definition of intangible assets?

A: Intangible assets are assets which are used in the operation of the business but have no physical substance and are non-current. Examples are patents, copyrights, franchises, licenses and trademarks.

S: Neither do accounts receivable have physical substance. Why aren't they included in the category of intangible assets?

A: By intangible assets, here we mean that first they are long-lived assets and they can contribute to the production, operation, and development of the business. In other words, they should bring about the increased value. However, accounts receivable are not long-lived assets, and nor can they increase the value of the business.

S: Are intangible assets subject to depreciation?

A: Subject to depreciation are fixed assets, while intangible assets are subject to amortization. Nonetheless, both depreciation and amortization are based on the same principle. They are both designed to offset the revenue of an accounting period with the cost incurred in the effort to generate that revenue.

What are Intangible Assets

Intangible assets are non-monetary assets which are without physical substance and **identifiable**. [1] The three critical attributes of an intangible asset are identifiably, control and future economic benefits.

An intangible asset is identifiable when it: (1) is separable (capable of being separated and sold, transferred, licensed, rented, or exchanged, either individually or together with a related contract) (2) or arises from contractual or other legal rights, regardless of whether those rights are transferable or separable from the entity or from other rights and obligations. [2]

Examples of possible intangible assets include computer software, **patents**, copyrights, **motion picture films**, customer lists, **licenses**, **import quotas**, **franchises**, and customer and supplier relationships.

Intangibles can be acquired by separate purchase, as part of a **business combination**, by a government **grant**, by exchange of assets or by self-creation.

Recognition **criteria** require an entity to recognize an intangible asset, whether purchased or self-created (at cost) if, and only if it is probable that the future economic benefits that are attributable to the asset will flow to the entity, and the cost of the asset can be measured reliably.[3]

Intangible assets normally have limited lives; however, they seldom, if ever, have a residual value. Intangible assets have a limited life because the rights or privileges that give them value terminate or simply disappear. Therefore, the acquisition cost of an intangible asset must be written off over its estimated economic life. This systematic write-off is usually called **amortization**. Intangible assets are generally **amortized** on straight-line basis over their useful lives, unless the asset has an indefinite useful life, in which case it is not amortized.

In that event of periodic amortization of the cost, it would be charged as expense for each of the useful life. The debit is to an expense account, and the credit is to an account entitled **accumulated amortization**, which is identical in nature to an accumulated depreciation account.

Main Types of Intangible Assets

A patent is a set of exclusive rights granted by a **sovereign state** to an inventor or **assignee** for a limited period of time in exchange for detailed public disclosure of an invention. An invention is a solution to a specific technological problem and is a product or a process. Patents are a form of **intellectual property**. The initial cost of a patent is the cash or cash equivalent price paid when the patent is acquired. A patent is amortized, in accordance with the matching principle, over the shorter of its economic life or its remaining legal life.

A trademark is a recognizable sign, design or expression which identifies products or services of a particular source. [4] A permanent exclusive right to the use of a trademark, brand name, or commercial symbol may be obtained by registering it with the government. The cost of developing a trademark or brand name often consists of **advertising campaigns** which should be treated as expense when incurred. If a trademark is purchased, however, the cost may be **substantial**. Since a trademark or a brand name does not expire as long as it is used, the question arises as to whether any of the cost of such an asset should be amortized and, if so, over what period of time. Conservatism suggests that any cost incurred in purchasing a trademark should be written off within a few years of its incurrence. If the use of the trademark is discontinued or its contribution to earnings becomes doubtful, any unamortized cost should be written off immediately.

A copyright is an exclusive right of protection given to a creator of a published work, such as a song, film, painting, photograph, or book. Copyrights are protected by law and give the creator the exclusive right to reproduce and sell the artistic or published work for the life of creator plus 50 years. [5] The cost of obtaining a copyright in some cases is minor and therefore is chargeable to expense when paid. Only when a copyright is purchased will the expenditure be material enough to warrant its being **capitalized** and spread over the useful life. The revenue from copyrights is usually limited to only a few years, and the purchase cost should be amortized over the years in which the revenue is expected.

A franchise is a right granted by a company or government unit to conduct a certain type of business in a specific geographical area. [6] Examples of governmental franchise include the right to operate buses or other public vehicles on city streets and the **monopoly** right to operate a power company. An example of a franchise for business organizations is the right to operate a McDonald's restaurant in a specific neighborhood. The cost of franchises varies greatly and often may be quite substantial. When the cost of a franchise is small, it may be charged immediately to expense or amortized over a few years. When the cost is material, amortization should be based on the life of the franchise if limited.

 Vocabulary

identifiable	*adj*. 可辨认的，可识别的
patent	*n*. 专利；专利品；专利权；专利证
motion picture film	电影(胶)片
license	*n*. 许可证，执照；特许
import quota	进口配额
franchise	*n*. 特许权；经销权
business combination	企业合并
grant	*n*. 授给物(如财产、授地、专有权等)
criterion(复数 criteria)	*n*. (批评、判断等的)标准，准则；规范
amortization	*n*. 摊销；分期偿还
amortize	*vt*. 摊销；分期偿还(债务)
accumulated amortization	累计摊销
sovereign state	主权国，独立国
assignee	*n*. 受托人，代理人；受让人；被指定人
intellectual property	知识产权
advertising campaign	广告运动，广告战
substantial	*adj*. 大量的；结实的，牢固的；重大的
capitalize	*vt*. 使……资本化
monopoly	*n*. 垄断；专卖

Notes

[1] Intangible assets are non-monetary assets which are without physical substance and identifiable.　无形资产是没有实物形态的可辨认非货币性资产。

[2] An intangible asset is identifiable when it: (1) is separable (capable of being separated and sold, transferred, licensed, rented, or exchanged, either individually or together with a related contract) (2) or arises from contractual or other legal rights, regardless of whether those rights are transferable or separable from the entity or from other rights and obligations.　无形资产具有"可辨认性"是指：(1)可分离的(能够从企业中分离出来，单独或与有关合同一起用于出售、转让、授权、出租、交换)，(2)源自于合同性权利或其他法定权利，无论这些权利是否可以从企业或其他权利和义务中转移或者分离。符合其中之一即可。

[3] Recognition criteria require an entity to recognize an intangible asset, whether purchased or self-created (at cost) if, and only if it is probable that the future economic benefits that are attributable to the asset will flow to the entity, and the cost of the asset can be measured reliably. 无论是外购还是内部研发，只有同时满足以下两个确认标准企业才可(按成本)确认该项为无形资产：与该资产有关的未来经济利益很可能流入企业；该资产的成本能够可靠地计量。

[4] A trademark is a recognizable sign, design or expression which identifies products or services of a particular source.　商标是用来辨认特定产品或劳务的可识别的符号、设计或表述。

[5] Copyrights are protected by law and give the creator the exclusive right to reproduce and sell the artistic or published work for the life of creator plus 50 years. 著作权指作者在有生之年及去世后 50 年内对其艺术品、出版物依法享有的再版和出售的专属权利。

[6] A franchise is a right granted by a company or government unit to conduct a certain type of business in a specific geographical area. 特许权是公司或政府单位授予的可以在某一特定区域内从事某一特定业务的权利。

5.3　Long-Term Investments
长期投资

A conversation between A—an accountant and S—a freshman majoring in accounting.

S: What's the difference between short-term investments and long-term investments?

A: It lies in the company's motive for owning them. Short-term investments consist of stocks, bonds, etc. which a company has bought and will sell shortly when the business is in an urgent need of cash. The investments made under long-term investments may never be sold.

S: Please give an example of assets classified as long-term investments.

A: Debt and equity securities that do not meet current asset requirements.

S: They are bonds and stocks, aren't they?

A: Yes. Debt securities reflect a creditor relationship and include investment in bonds. Equity securities reflect an owner relationship and include shares of stock issued by other companies.

S: But how to distinguish them between short-term and long-term investments.

A: Short-term investments are defined as those that meet two tests: (1) ready marketability and (2) management intention to convert them to cash in the short run. Those not meeting these two tests are classified as long-term investments.

What are Long-Term Investments

Long-term investments and funds are investments a company intends to hold for more than one year. They can consist of stocks and bonds of other companies, real estate, and cash that have been set aside for a specific purpose or project. In addition to investments a company plans to hold for an extended period of time, long-term Investments also consist of the stock in a company's affiliates and subsidiaries.

Long-term investments are investments made by a company in order to secure an additional income stream or a **strategic** goal. For example, a long-term stock investor may outline investment goals for any time longer than one year, while a long-term bond investor may hold a bond until it matures 10 or more years later. Long-term investing involves more uncertainty than short-term investing because, in general, market trends are more easily predictable in the short-term.

In China, the long-term investments can be divided into three sections: (1) equity securities, (2) debt securities, and (3) other long-term investments.

In this part, we will discuss measuring and reporting of long-term investments in both equity securities and debt securities.

 Accounting for Long-Term Equity Investments

Equity investments are described as securities representing ownership such as common stock. Accounting for **long-term equity investments** involves measuring the investment amount that should be reported on the balance sheet and the periodic investment revenue that should be reported on the income statement. In accordance with the cost principle, long-term investments in equity securities of another company are measured and recorded, at the dates of acquisition of the shares, as the total consideration given to acquire them.

Subsequent to acquisition, measurement of the investment amount and the investment revenue depends upon the relationship between the investor and the investee company. The relevant characteristic of the relationship is the extent to which the investing company can exercise significant influence or control over the operating and financial policies of the other company. [1] Two methods are available to account for different levels of ownership of another company's shares, which are **cost method** and **equity method**.

The following long-term equity investments should be measured by employing the cost method:

(1) A long-term equity investment of an investing enterprise that is able to control the invested enterprise.

(2) A long-term equity investment of the investing enterprise that does not joint control or does not have significant influences on the invested entity, and has no offer in the active market and its **fair value** cannot be reliably measured. [2]

The price of a long-term equity investment measures by employing the cost method should be included at its initial investment cost. If there are additional investments or disinvestments, the cost of the long-term equity investment should be adjusted. The dividends or profits declared to distribute by the invested entity should be recognized as the current investment income.

A long-term equity investment of the investing enterprise that does **joint control** or significant influences over the invested entity should be measured by employing the equity method. Under the equity method, each year the investor company recognizes its proportionate part of the net income (or net loss) of the investee corporation as investment revenue rather than awaiting the declaration of dividends. [3] No cash dividend is received at the time when investment revenue is recorded under the equity method; the **offsetting** debit is to the investment account. Thus, both the investment account and income from investment account of the investor company reflect the investor's proportionate share of the income (and losses) of the investee corporation. When dividends are received, cash in bank is debited, and the investment account is credited.

 Accounting for Debt Securities

Investors may buy bonds at their dates of issuance or at subsequent dates during the life of the bonds. Regardless of the timing of the bonds' acquisition, at the end of each accounting period the investor must measure the (1) cost, adjusted for the cumulative amount of discount or **premium** that has been amortized, and (2) interest revenue earned.

At the date of acquisition, a bond investment is measured, recorded, and reported in accordance with the cost principle. The purchase cost, including all incidental acquisition costs (such as transfer fees and **broker commissions**), is debited to an investment account such as "held-to-maturity investments" or "available-for-sale financial assets" [4] in China. The amount recorded under the cost principle is the current cash equivalent amount; and it may be the same as the maturity amount (if acquired **at par**), less than the maturity amount (if acquired at discount), or more than the maturity amount (if acquired at a premium). The premium or discount on a bond investment usually is not recorded in a separate account as is done for bonds payable; rather, the investment account reflects the current book or carrying amount.

If the bond investment was acquired at par，the carrying value amount remains constant over the life of the investment. In this situation, revenue earned from the investment each period is measured as the amount of cash interest collected (or accrued).

When a bond investment is purchased at a discount or premium, measurement of the carrying value of the investment after the date of acquisition necessitates adjustment for the investment account balance from acquisition cost to maturity amount at each period over the life of the investment. [5] This adjustment is the periodic amortization is made as a debit or credit to the investment account, depending on whether there was a discount or premium at acquisition, so that the investment account at the end of each period reflects related current carrying amount.

When a bond investment is acquired at a discount or premium, the revenue from interest each period is measured as the cash interest collected (or accrued) plus or minus the periodic amortization of discount or premium. [6] Bond discount or premium may be amortized by using **effective-interest method,** which will be explained in Chapter 6.

 Classification and Reporting of Investments

Accounting for investments in securities depends on three factors: (1) security type, either debt or equity, (2) the company's intent to hold the security either short-term or long-term, and (3) the company's (investor's) percent ownership in the other company's (**investee**'s) equity securities. Table 5-1 indentifies four classes of securities using three factors.

Table 5-1　Investments in Securities

Classification	Security Type	Reporting
Marketable financial assets	Debt and equity securities[a] that are actively traded	• Current assets • Market value • Unrealized gains and losses reported on the income statement

Table 5-1(Continued)

Classification	Security Type	Reporting
Held-to-maturity investments	Debt securities intended to be held until maturity	● Non-current assets ● Amortized cost
Available-for-sale financial assets	Debt and equity securities[a]	● Non-current assets ● Market value ● Unrealized gains and losses reported in the equity section of the balance sheet
Neither significant influence nor control[b]	Equity securities	● Non-current assets ● Cost method
Significant influence[b]	Equity securities	● Non-current ● Equity method
Controlling influence[b]	Equity securities	● Non-current assets ● Consolidation

[a] Holding less than 20% of voting stock (equity securities only)

[b] Recording in long-term equity investments account

 Vocabulary

strategic	*adj.* 战略(上)的；战略性的
long-term equity investments	长期股权投资
cost method	成本法
equity method	权益法
fair value	公允价值
joint control	共同控制
offset	*vt.* 抵消；补偿
premium	*n.* 溢价；费用；保险费；奖赏，奖励
broker commission	经纪人佣金
at par	与票面价值相等；按票面价格
effective-interest method	实际利息法
investee	*n.* 接受投资者

Notes

[1] The relevant characteristic of the relationship is the extent to which the investing company can exercise significant influence or control over the operating and financial policies of the other company. 这种关系的相关特征表现为投资公司对另一家公司的经营与财务政策施加重大影响和控制的程度。

[2] A long-term equity investment of the investing enterprise that does not joint control or does not have significant influences on the invested entity, and has no offer in the active market

and its fair value cannot be reliably measured. 投资企业对被投资单位不具有共同控制或重大影响，在活跃市场中没有报价，公允价值不能可靠计量长期股权投资。

[3] Under the equity method, each year the investor company recognizes its proportionate part of the net income (or net loss) of the investee corporation as investment revenue rather than awaiting the declaration of dividends. 在权益法下，投资公司每年按所占比例将被投资公司的一部分净利润(或净亏损)确认为投资收益，而不是等待股利发放。

[4] "held-to-maturity investments" or "available-for-sale financial assets" 持有至到期投资或可供出售金融资产。持有至到期投资主要是债券性投资，通常具有长期性质，但期限较短(1 年以内)的债券投资，符合持有至到期投资条件的，也可将其划分为持有至到期投资。可供出售金融资产可以是企业购入的在活跃市上有报价的股票、债券和基金等，没有划分为以公允价值计量且其变动计入当期损益的金融资产或持有至到期投资等金融资产的，可归为此类。

[5] When a bond investment is purchased at a discount or premium, measurement of the carrying value of the investment after the date of acquisition necessitates adjustment for the investment account balance from acquisition cost to maturity amount at each period over the life of the investment. 当债券投资以折价或溢价购入时，在取得日后对这项投资的账面价值进行计量时，有必要在投资期内每期都对投资账户的余额进行调整，使之由取得成本调整到到期值。

[6] When a bond investment is acquired at a discount or premium, the revenue from interest each period is measured as the cash interest collected (or accrued) plus or minus the periodic amortization of discount or premium. 以折价或溢价购入债券投资时，每期的利息收益可计量为收到(或应计)的现金利息加上或减去折价或溢价的每期摊销额。

Exercises

I. Discuss the following questions in English.

1. What characteristics of a fixed asset make it different from other assets?

2. What is the general rule for cost's inclusion for fixed assets?

3. What does the term depreciation mean in accounting?

4. Does the balance in the accumulated depreciation account represent funds to replace the fixed asset when it wears out? If not, what does it represent?

5. Identify events that might lead to disposal of a fixed asset.

6. What are the characteristics of an intangible asset?

7. Give some examples of intangible assets.

8. Under what conditions investments should be classified as non-current assets?

9. In accounting for investments in equity securities, when should the cost method be used?

10. On a balance sheet, what valuation must be reported for debt securities classified as

held-to-maturity investments?

11.   For investments in available-for-sale financial assets, how are the unrealized gains and losses reported?

II. Choose the best word or phrase that fits the sentence.

1.   _____ are long-lived tangible assets acquired for continued use in carrying on the normal operations of the business and not intended for resale.

    A. Long-term assets   B. Fixed assets

    C. Non-current assets   D. Permanent assets

2.   Depreciation is the systematic allocation of the cost of an asset over its _____ life.

    A. estimated   B. economic

    C. useful   D. mature

3.   A(n) _____ depreciation method yields larger depreciation expenses in the early years of an asset's life and less depreciation in later years.

    A. accelerative   B. accelerated

    C. stepped-up   D. speeded

4.   An asset is impaired when its carrying value is higher than its _____.

    A. fair value   B. market value

    C. replacement cost   D. recoverable amount

5.   Intangible assets are non-monetary assets which are without physical substance and _____.

    A. identifiable   B. unidentifiable

    C. recognizable   D. unrecognizable

6.   _____ is not classified as an intangible asset.

    A. Goodwill   B. Trademark

    C. Copyright   D. Franchise

7.   The acquisition cost of an intangible asset must be _____ over its estimated economic life.

    A. depreciated   B. amortized

    C. depleted   D. reversed

8.   Long-term investments are investments made by a company in order to secure an additional income stream or a _____ goal.

    A. specific   B. subject

    C. sound   D. strategic

9.   Subsequent to acquisition, measurement of the investment amount and the investment revenue depends upon the _____ between the investor and the investee companies.

    A. brotherhood   B. connection

    C. relationship   D. kinship

10.   Under the cost method, the dividends or profits declared to distribute by the invested

entity should be recognized as _____.

    A. the prior investment income   B. the investment cost

    C. unrealized gain   D. the current investment income

11. When a bond investment is acquired _____, the revenue from interest each period is measured as the cash interest collected plus the periodic amortization of the difference.

    A. at a discount   B. at par

    C. at premium   D. on credit

III. Match each word on the left with its corresponding meaning on the right.

A	B
1. decline	(a) the act or means of getting rid of something
2. rebate	(b) a document granting an inventor sole rights to an invention
3. goodwill	(c) make worse or less effective
4. equity	(d) following in time or order
5. subsequent	(e) the ownership interest of shareholders in a corporation
6. accelerate	(f) an asset valued according to the reputation a business has acquired
7. disposal	(g) the act of constructing something
8. patent	(h) move faster
9. assembly	(i) a reduction in the price during a sale
10. impair	(j) go down in value

IV. Fill in the blanks with words or phrases from the list below.

A.	bargain	B.	formula	C.	overvalue	D.	historical
E.	impairment	F.	fair	G.	target	H.	drop
I.	scandal	J.	regional	K.	flavors	L.	gains
M.	accounted for	N.	amortized	O.	decades	P.	subjective

Goodwill arises when one company acquires another, but pays more than the (1)___ market value of the net assets (total assets-total liabilities). According to International Financial Reporting Standards (IFRS), goodwill is never (2)___. Instead, management is responsible to value goodwill every year and to determine if (3)___ is required. If the fair market value goes below (4)___ cost (what goodwill was purchased for), impairment must be recorded to bring it down to its fair market value. However, an increase in the fair market value would not be (5)___ in the financial statements.

The amount the acquiring company pays for the (6)___ company over the target's book value usually accounts for the value of the target's goodwill. If the acquiring company pays less than the target's book value, it (7)___ "negative goodwill", meaning that it purchased the company at a (8)___ in a distress sale.

Goodwill is difficult to price, but it does make a company more valuable. For example, a company like Coca-Cola (who has been around for (9)___, makes a wildly popular product based on a secret __(10)__ and is generally positively perceived by the public), would have a lot of goodwill. A competitor, which is a small, __(11)__ soda company that has only been in business for five years, has a small customer base, specializes in unusual soda __(12)__ and recently faced a __(13)__ over a contaminated batch of soda, would have far less goodwill, or even negative goodwill.

Because the components that make up goodwill have __(14)__ values, there is a substantial risk that a company could __(15)__ goodwill in an acquisition. This overvaluation would be bad news for shareholders of the acquiring company, since they would likely see their share values __(16)__ when the company later has to write down goodwill.

V. Translate the following sentences into Chinese.

1. Fixed assets are tangible assets used in a company's operations that have a useful life of more than one accounting period.

2. Acquisition cost of a fixed asset includes all normal and reasonable expenditures necessary to get the asset in place and ready for its intended use.

3. If fixed assets are used up in about equal amounts each accounting period, straight-line method produces a reasonable matching of expense with revenues.

4. Disposal of a fixed asset is the withdrawal of a fixed asset from use upon the completion of its useful life or due to lower productivity in its later life.

5. An intangible asset, like any other asset, has value because of certain rights and privileges conferred by law upon the owner of the asset.

6. Intangible assets normally have limited lives; however, they seldom, if ever, have a residual value.

7. The long-term investment account differs largely from the short-term investment account in that the short-term investments will most likely be sold, whereas the long-term investments may never be sold.

8. Cost method is a method of accounting whereby the investment is carried at its cost.

9. Some companies have the ability to significantly influence the operating decisions and management policies of the other companies.

VI. Translate the following sentences into English.

1. 固定资产是指企业为生产商品、提供劳务、出租或经营管理而持有的、使用寿命超过一个会计年度的有形资产。

2. 固定资产的成本，是指企业构建某项固定资产达到预定可使用状态前所发生的一切合理、必要的支出。

3. 折旧的基本目的是实现配比原则，即从一个会计年度的收益中扣减掉为实现收益而付出的商品或服务成本。

4. 可选用的折旧方法包括年限平均法、工作量法、双倍余额递减法和年数总和法等。

5. 固定资产减值准备是指由于固定资产市价持续下跌，或技术陈旧、损坏、长期闲置等原因导致其可收回金额低于账面价值的，应当将可收回金额低于其账面价值的差额作为固定资产减值准备。

6. 无形资产主要包括专利权、非专利技术、商标权、著作权、土地使用权、特许权等。

7. 商誉的存在无法与企业自身分离，不具有可辨认性，不属于无形资产。

8. 长期投资是指不满足短期投资条件的投资，即不准备在一年或长于一年的经营周期之内转变为现金的投资。

9. 长期股权投资是指企业持有的对其子公司、合营企业及联营企业的权益性投资以及企业持有的对被投资单位不具有控制、共同控制或重大影响，且在活跃市场中没有报价、公允价值不能可靠计量的权益性投资。

Reading Material 5

Natural Resources and Their Depletion

Natural resources, often called wasting assets, include petroleum, minerals, and timber. Natural resources are characterized by two main features: (1) the complete removal (consumption) of the asset, and (2) replacement of the asset only by an act of nature. Unlike plant and equipment, natural resources are consumed physically over the period of use and do not maintain their physical characteristics. For the most part, the accounting problems associated with natural resources are similar to those encountered in the plant asset area. The questions to be answered are:

(1) How is the cost basis for write-off (depletion) established?

(2) What pattern of allocation should be employed?

Establishment of Depletion Base

The costs of natural resources can be divided into three categories: (1) acquisition cost of deposit, (2) exploration costs, and (3) development costs. The acquisition cost of the deposit is the price paid to obtain the property right to search and find an undiscovered natural resource or the price paid for an already discovered resource. In some cases, property is leased and special royalty payments are paid to the lesser if a productive natural resource is found and is commercially profitable. Generally, the acquisition cost is placed in an account titled "undevelopment property" and assigned to the natural resource if exploration efforts are successful. If they are unsuccessful, the cost is written off as a loss.

As soon as the enterprise has the right to use the property, considerable exploration costs are entailed in finding the resource. The accounting treatment for these costs varies: some firms expend all exploration costs; Some capitalize only those costs that are directly related to successful projects (successful efforts approach); and others adopt full-cost approach (capitalization of all costs whether related to successful or unsuccessful projects).

The final costs that are incurred in finding natural resources are development costs, which are classified in two ways: (1) tangible equipment costs, and (2) intangible development costs. Tangible equipment costs include all of the transportation and other heavy equipment necessary to extract the resources and get it ready for production or shipment. Tangible equipment costs are normally not considered in the depletion base; instead, separate depreciation charges are employed because the asset can be moved from one drilling or mining site to another. Depreciation expense is, therefore, based on a service life relevant to its total usefulness. Intangible development costs, on the other hand, are considered part of the depletion base. These costs are for such items as the drilling costs, tunnels, shafts, and wells, which have no tangible characteristics, but are needed for the production of the natural resources.

Write-off of Resource Cost

As soon as the depletion base is established, the next problem is determining how the natural resource cost should be allocated to accounting periods. Normally, depletion is computed on the unit of production method, which means that depletion is a function of the number of units withdrawn during the period.

For example, Baker Oil Co. has acquired the right to use 500 acres of land to explore for oil. The lease cost is $50,000; the related exploration costs for a discovered oil deposit on the property are $100,000; and intangible development costs incurred in erecting and drilling the well are $850,000. Total costs related to the oil deposit before the first gallon is extracted are, therefore, $1,000,000. It is estimated that the well will provide approximately 500,000 barrels of oil. The depletion rate established is computed in the following manner:

Total cost / Total estimated units available = Depletion charge per unit

$1,000,000 / 500,000 = $2.00 per barrel

If 100,000 barrels are withdrawn in the first year, then the depletion charge for the year is $200,000. The entry to record the depletion is:

Depletion expense   200,000

    Accumulated depletion   250,000

In some instances an accumulated depletion account is not used, and the credit goes directly to the natural resources asset account. In the income statement the depletion cost is part of the cost of producing the product. The balance sheet presents the cost of the property and the amount of depletion entered to date as follows:

Oil deposit (at cost) $1,000,000

Less: accumulated depletion   200,000

Balance $800,000

Answers:

II.	1	B	2	C	3	B	4	D	5	A	6	A	7	B	8	D
	9	C	10	D	11	A										
III.	1	j	2	i	3	f	4	e	5	d	6	h	7	a	8	b
	9	g	10	c												
IV.	1	F	2	N	3	E	4	D	5	M	6	G	7	L	8	A
	9	O	10	B	11	J	12	K	13	I	14	P	15	C	16	H

知识扩展

1. 金融工具

金融工具是指形成一个企业金融资产并形成另一个企业金融负债或权益性工具的合同。

2. 金融资产

金融资产是指下列资产：①现金；②从另一个企业收取现金或其他金融资产的合同权利；③在潜在有利的条件下，与另一个企业交换金融工具的合同权利；④另一个企业的权益性工具。国际会计准则理事会于 2014 年 7 月发布的 IFRS 9 采用业务模式和合同现金流量特征标准，将金融资产予以分类。为切实解决我国企业金融工具相关会计实务问题、实现我国企业会计准则与国际财务报告准则的持续全面趋同，2017 年 3 月 31 日，财政部修订发布了《企业会计准则第 22 号——金融工具确认和计量》《企业会计准则第 23 号——金融资产转移》和《企业会计准则第 24 号——套期保值》3 项金融工具会计准则，随后，于 2017 年 5 月 2 日，修订发布了《企业会计准则第 37 号——金融工具列报》。修订后的金融工具确认和计量准则规定以企业持有金融资产的"业务模式"和"金融资产合同现金流量特征"作为金融资产分类的判断依据，将金融资产分类为：①以摊余成本计量的金融资产；②以公允价值计量且其变动计入其他综合收益的金融资产；③以公允价值计量且其变动计入当期损益的金融资产，取消了贷款和应收款项、持有至到期投资和可供出售金融资产的 3 个原有分类，提高了分类的客观性和会计处理的一致性。

3. 投资性房地产

IAS 40(International Accounting Standard 40)—Investment property，国际会计准则第 40 号——投资性房地产)指出，投资性房地产是指为赚取租金或为资本增值，或两者兼有而由业主或融资租赁的承租人持有的房地产(土地或建筑物，或建筑物的一部分，或两者兼有)，但不包括：①用于商品或劳务的生产或供应，或用于管理目的的房地产；或②在正常经营过程中销售的房地产。企业可以选择公允价值模式或成本模式计量。在对投资性房地产重估价变动或公允价值变动的处理上，IAS 40 规定采用公允价值模式的房地产的公允价值变动产生的利得和损失需记录在利润表中。

Chapter 6 Liabilities
负债

Learning Objectives

- Understand accounts payable and advance from customers 理解应付账款和预收账款
- Understand notes payable and short-term loans 理解应付票据和短期借贷
- Understand current maturities of non-current debt 理解非流动债务的当前到期日
- Understand payables as payroll and taxes 理解工资和税收形式的应付款
- Understand bonds payable and account for bonds payable 了解应付债券并说明原因
- Understand liabilities arisen from capital leases 理解融资租赁产生的负债
- Understand long-term loans 理解长期借贷

 Listening Practice 听力练习

第 6 章听写原文翻译和答案的音频见右侧二维码。

Chapter 6 English
Listening.mp3

Dictation: *Listen and complete the passage with the words or phrases according to what you've heard from the speaker.*

Intellectual property _____1_____ are the rights given to persons over the creations of their minds. They usually give the creator an _____2_____ right over the use of his / her creation for a certain _____3_____ of time. Intellectual property rights are customarily divided into two main areas: copyright and rights _____4_____ to copyright and industrial property.

Copyright and rights related to copyright. The rights of authors of literary and artistic works (such as books and other writings, musical compositions, paintings, sculptures, computer programs and films) are protected by _____5_____, for a minimum period of 50 years after the death of the author.

 Wisdom 至理名言

You can't fool all of the people all of the time. 你不可能一直愚弄所有的人。

Mini Case 微型案例

Soto Company is seeking a large bank loan for plant expansion. The bank looks very closely

at the current ratio. The auditor proposes reclassifications of some items. Among these a note payable issued 4 years ago matures in 6 months from the reporting date. The auditor wants to reclassify it as a current liability. The controller says "No" because "we are probably going to refinance this note with other long-term debts". If you were the auditor, how would you respond to the controller?

6.1 Current Liabilities
流动负债

A conversation between A—an accountant and S—a freshman majoring in accounting.

S: I think accounts receivable and accounts payable are two aspects of a transaction. They may have arisen from the credit sale, right?

A: Right. The company is the crediter of accounts receivable, and the debtor of accounts payable. Generally, you don't have to pay any interest for accounts payable.

S: So accounts payable represent interest-free loans from suppliers. If a credit purchase is done, the entry is to debit inventory and credit accounts payable, right?

A: Right. Under periodic inventory system, many companies have no inventory subsidiary system, so the newly-purchased goods are usually recorded in purchases first, and are transferred to inventory at the end of an accounting period.

S: Is it possible that a current liability is converted into another current liability?

A: Just the same as the existence of the possibility of accounts receivable being converted into notes receivable, accounts payable can also be converted into notes payable. For example, the obligation arising from a credit purchase is recorded in accounts payable before a note payable like a promissory note is issued. The debt in notes payable usually involves a certain amount of interest.

Accounts Payable and Advance from Customers

Accounts payable are the most commonly seen current liabilities. They represent balances owed by a business to its suppliers and are shown as a liability on a company's balance sheet. These extensions of credit are the practical result of a time lag between the receipt of a good, supply, or service and the corresponding payment. Accounts payable usually do not require the payment of interest. Accounts payable have no associated fee or interest, so they represent **interest-free** loans from suppliers.

A liability for unearned revenue arises when a customer pay in advance. Upon the receipt of an advance payment from a customer, the company debits cash on hand or cash in bank account and credits a liability account as "unearned revenue". This liability is then converted to revenue as the related services are performed or the relevant goods are delivered. In China, we use "**advance from customers**" account title instead of "unearned revenue".

Notes Payable

In western countries, **notes payable** represent obligations to banks or other creditors based on formal written agreements. In China, notes payable, in contrast to notes receivable, are just trade notes payable. Business firms borrow funds from banks or other lenders frequently by signing an agreement and that is called loans rather than notes payable in Chinese practice.

Notes payable usually require the borrower to pay an interest charge. Normally, the interest rate is stated separately from the **principal** amount of the note.

In theory, notes payable should be measured by the **present value** of the future outlay of cash required to liquidate them. But, in practice, notes payable, like all the other current liabilities, are usually recorded in accounting records and reported in financial statements at their **face amount**. Because of the short time periods involved, frequently less than one year, the difference between the present value of a current liability and the maturity value is usually not large. The slight overstatement of liabilities that results from carrying current liabilities at maturity value is justified on the grounds of **expediency**, conservatism, and immateriality. [1]

When the note is issued, the generally accepted practice is to report note payable at its face amount, and no liability is recorded for the interest charge. At the maturity date or the end of the period, the interest charge should be recorded as an expense.

 Short-Term Loans

Short-term loan[2] is an account shown in the current liabilities portion of a company's balance sheet. This account is comprised of short-term bank loans taken out by a company that is due within one year.

Companies can obtain trade credit from suppliers in the form of accounts payable to obtain production materials or various accrued expenses such as unpaid salaries as a result of employee services.[3] But to obtain short-term cash proceeds that can be used at their own **discretion**, companies may have to borrow short-term loans from banks or other creditors.

If a company has more short-term loan than available cash or investments to cover the debt's payments, the company could be forced to take on additional debt and could be in poor financial health.

 Current Maturities of Non-Current Debt

Current maturities of non-current debt [4] are a portion of the balance sheet that represents the total amount of long-term debt that must be paid within the next year. The balance sheet has a liability section, which is broken down into long-term and current debts. When a debt payment is set to be made in longer than a year's time, it is recorded in the long-term debt section, and when that payment becomes due within a year, it moves to the current maturities of non-current debt section.

Payroll Liabilities [5]

Payroll, also called employee **compensation**, is a substantial expense for many companies, particularly if they are involved in advertising, consulting, services or information industries.

Employee compensation takes many different forms. A salary is employee pay stated at a monthly or yearly rate. A wage is employee pay stated at an hourly rate. Sales employees earn a **commission**, which is percentage of the sales the employee has made. A **bonus** is an amount over and above regular compensation. There may be some kinds of deductions, such as employees' income taxes and employees' contribution to **provident funds**. Payroll expense represents employee pay before **subtractions** for taxes and other deductions.

Taxes Payable

Taxes payable fall into a liability account that reports the amount of taxes that a company owes as of the end of the reporting period. When taxes need to be paid out by the company, the company will record the amount of taxes in the taxes payable account.

Most countries have some forms of **turnover tax**. A turnover tax is an indirect tax, applicable to a production process or stage. This tax is usually called **goods and service tax**, **value-added tax** or simply **sales tax**. In China, there are several turnover taxes, such as value-added tax, **consumption tax** and **business tax**. Taxes payable account is debited and cash credited when it **remits** these collections to the government. This kind of taxes payable is not an expense. It arises because laws require sellers to collect this cash from customers for the government.

In addition, at the end of each accounting period, the amount of accrued income taxes is estimated and recorded in an adjusting entry. Income tax payable is common current liabilities of corporations. It conforms to the matching principle, that is, income tax payable should be matched with the income that caused the income tax effect. On the other hand, income tax payable should follow **taxes law**. Numerous items create differences between taxable income and pretax accounting income. For purposes of accounting recognition, these differences are of two types: (1) **timing differences** and (2) **permanent differences**. We will discuss this issue in the reading material of this chapter.

Vocabulary

accounts payable	应付账款
interest-free	*adj.* (贷款等)无息的
advance from customers	预收账款
notes payable	应付票据
principal	*adj.* 本金的；最重要的；主要的；资本的 & *n.* 本金
present value	现值
face amount	面值

expediency	*n.* 适宜；方便；合算；利己
discretion	*n.* 自行决定的自由
payroll	*n.* 职工薪酬，工资名单；工资总支出，工薪总额
compensation	*n.* 补偿，赔偿，报酬，薪酬
commission	*n.* 佣金，手续费
bonus	*n.* 奖金，额外津贴；红利，额外股息
provident fund	公积金；福利基金；准备基金
subtraction	*n.* 减，减法；减除法；减去
taxes payable	应交税费
turnover tax	流转税
goods and service tax	商品及服务税
value-added tax	增值税
sales tax	销售税
consumption tax	消费税
business tax	营业税
remit	*vt.* 汇款；宽恕；免除；缓和，恢复
taxes law	税法
timing difference	暂时性差异
permanent difference	永久性差异

Notes

[1] The slight overstatement of liabilities that results from carrying current liabilities at maturity value is justified on the grounds of expediency, conservatism, and immateriality. 按到期值反映流动负债而导致的对负债的略微高估，可以用便利、谨慎和非重大性等理由，来说明这样做是恰当的。

[2] Short-term loan 短期借款的参考翻译，英文比较常见的表述为 "short-term notes payable"。

[3] Companies can obtain trade credit from suppliers in the form of accounts payable to obtain production materials or various accrued expenses such as unpaid salaries as a result of employee services. 公司可以利用商业信用在供应商那里以应付账款形式获得生产材料或各种各样的应计费用，如员工劳务而产生的未付工资。

[4] Current maturities of non-current debt 一年内到期的非流动负债，英文中比较常见的表述有 "Current portion of long-term debt"。

[5] Payroll Liabilities 参考翻译 "工资负债"。对应的中文说法为 "应付职工薪酬"，参考翻译为 "Payroll Payable"。

6.2 Non-Current Liabilities
非流动负债

A conversation between A—an accountant and S—a freshman majoring in accounting.

A: A bond is a certificate promising to pay its holder a specified sum of money plus interest at a stated rate. Most of such bonds are traded on the securities exchange. Generally, they mature in 5 to 30 years after their date of issuance.

S: Stock issuance and bond issuance are both common ways of financing. Then compared with the stock issuance, what's the major advantage of financing by issuing bonds.

A: The greatest advantage of financing by issuing bonds is that interest payments are deductible in determining income subject to corporate income taxes. Dividends paid to shareholders are not tax deductible.

S: Does the bond issuance involve complicated formalities?

A: Somewhat complicated. First, the bond issuance should be approved by the board of directors, and then approval must be obtained from China Securities Regulatory Commission. Only after that can the bonds be sold to an investment banking firm called Underwriter. And the underwriter sells the bonds to the public.

S: The underwriter can profit from it, right?

A: Right. The price at which the underwriter sells the bonds to the public is higher than that at which the bonds were bought from the issuing company.

Bonds Payable

A bond is its issuer's written promise to pay an amount identified as the par value of the bond with interest. Bonds are the most important instrument by which corporations finance their long-term investment projects. Bonds are a means of dividing long-term debt into a number of small units. In this way, a sum of money larger than that which could be obtained from a single credit source may be borrowed from a large number of investors.[1] The terms of the borrowing are contained in a contract between the corporation and the bondholders, which is known as the **bond indenture**. This contract is usually held by a trustee who acts as an independent third party to protect the interests of both the borrower and the bondholders.

These are the broad classifications of bonds:

(1) **Registered and Unregistered Bonds**

Registered bonds are payable only to the registered holder whose name appears on the **debenture**. Only on executing a **transfer deed** and filing a copy of it with the company, they can be transferred.[2]

Unregistered bonds are also called as **bearer debentures** and are payable to the **bearer**. They are negotiable and can be transferred by simple **endorsement**.

(2) Convertible and Non-Convertible Bonds

A convertible bond is a type of bond that the holder can convert it into a specified number of shares of common stock in the issuing company or cash of equal value.

Non-convertible debentures are duly paid back when they are mature.

(3) Callable and Non-Callable Bonds

A callable bond is a type of bond that allows the issuer of the bond to retain the privilege of redeeming the bond at some point before the bond reaches its date of maturity.

Non-callable bonds cannot be **redeemed** early by the issuer.

Bonds may be issued to the general public through the intermediary of an investment banker, or they may be privately placed with a single institution or sold to investment dealers, who in turn retail the bonds in smaller lots to individual investors. Investment dealers may **underwrite** the bond issue, in which case they guarantee a certain price to the issuer and take the risk in selling the issue to the public.[3]

The market price of bonds is determined by the difference between the **effective interest rate** (also referred to as **yield rate**) and the **coupon rate**. If the effective interest rate is identical to the coupon rate, the bonds will sell at face amount. If the effective interest rate is higher than the coupon rate, the bonds will sell at a discount. Conversely, if the effective interest rate is less than the coupon rate, the bonds will sell at a premium.[4]

To illustrate this point, assume that $1,000,000 of five-year life, 7% bonds are offered for sale. The bond contract, which promises $1,000,000 at the end of the fifth year and $70,000 annual interest, then is offered to investment dealers. Under two different assumptions as to the effective annual interest rate, the prices are determined as follows, using the appropriate present values:

Assumption 1: an effective interest rate of 8%:

Present value of $1,000,000 due in 5 years, interest paid annually:

$$\$1,000,000 \times 0.680583^{[5]} = \$680,583$$

Present value of $7,000 every year for 5 years:

$$\$7,000 \times 3.992710^{[5]} = 279,490$$
$$\$960,073$$

The journal entry necessary to record the issuance of the bonds are:

Cash in bank	960,073	
Discount on bonds payable [6]	39,927	
Bonds payable—face amount	1,000,000	

Assumption 2: an effective interest rate of 6%:

Present value of $100,000 due in 5 years, interest paid annually:

$$\$1,000,000 \times 0.747258^{[5]} = \$747,258$$

Present value of $7,000 every year for 5 years:

$$\$70,000 \times 4.212364^{[5]} = 294,866$$
$$\$1,042,124$$

The journal entry necessary to record the issuance of the bonds are:

Cash in bank	1,042,124	
Bonds payable—face amount		1,000,000
Premium on bonds payable[6]		42,124

At the date of interest payment, interest expense must be measured and recorded. <u>Because differences between the effective rate and the coupon rate of interest are reflected in bond prices, the amount of premium or discount affects the periodic interest expense to the issuer.</u> [7] It is clear that correct measurement of interest expense calls for amortization of premium or discount.

Discount and premium can be amortized through effective interest methods. Using the case that bonds are issued at discount (Assumption 1), the effective interest method of amortization can be illustrated by the schedule of Table 6-1.

Table 6-1　The Schedule of Interest Expense and the Amortization

Period	Year Interest Paid	Effective Interest	Discount Amortization	Bond Discount Balance	Carrying Amount
At time of issuance				39,927	960,073
1	70,000	76,806	6,806	33,121	966,879
2	70,000	77,350	7,350	25,771	974,229
3	70,000	77,938	7,938	17,833	982,167
4	70,000	78,573	8,573	9,259	990,741
5	70,000	79,259	9,259	0	1,000,000

The journal entry for Year 1 would be:

(Financial) Expense	76,806	
Cash in bank		70,000
Discount on bonds payable[6]		6,806

The journal entry for Year 5 would be:

(Financial) Expense	79,259	
Bonds payable—face amount	1,000,000	
Cash in bank		1,079,259
Discount on bonds payable[6]		9,259

Capital Lease

A **lease** is a rental agreement in which the **lessee** agrees to make rent payments to the property owner (**lessor**) in exchange for the use of the asset. Leasing allows the lessee to acquire the use of a needed asset without having to make the large **up-front** payment that purchase agreements require.

There are two main types of lease: **operating lease** and **capital lease**. An operating lease is a lease whose term is short compared to the useful life of the asset or piece of equipment being leased. An operating lease is not capitalized; it is accounted for as an expense.

If the terms of the lease meet any of the following conditions, it will be recognized as a capital lease or **finance lease**:

(1) Lease transfers substantially all risks and **rewards** of the asset to lease.

(2) Lease transfers ownership of assets to lessee at the end of the lease.

(3) Lease term represents substantial part of the asset's useful life.

(4) Present value of lease payments represents substantial part of fair value of the asset.

A capital lease would be considered as a purchased asset for accounting purposes. Since a finance lease is capitalized, both assets and liabilities in the balance sheet increase. When a capital lease is signed, the lessee will record the present value of his/her lease payments on his/her books.[8]

As the asset is being used, it is depreciated in accordance with the entity's usual depreciation policy. The lease liability is amortized by dividing each payment into an interest expense component and a lease liability component.

Assume that on Jan. 1, 2014, Meihua Company signed a capital lease that requires a payment of $20,000 per year for the next five years. The present value of the lease payment is determined to be $75,816 (using a 10% interest rate). On signing this lease agreement, Meihua Company would record the following entry:

Lease asset   75,816

　　Lease liability [9]   75,816

When the first payment is made on Dec. 31, 2014, the $20,000 payment is first applied to the interest for the lease liabilities for the period, which is $7,581.6 ($75,816×10%), and the balance of $12,418.4 ($20,000~$7,581.6) reduces the lease liability.

The entry would be:

Lease liability   12,418.4

(Financial) Expense   7,581.6

　　Cash in bank   20,000

In the subsequent period, less and less interest will be charged, and higher portions of the lease payments will go towards reducing the lease liability. This schedule is shown in Table 6-2.

Table 6-2　The Lease Amortization Schedule

Period	Begin Balance	Payment	Interest	Principle	End Balance
1	75,816	20,000	7,582	12,418	63,398
2	63,398	20,000	6,340	13,660	49,737
3	49,737	20,000	4,974	15,026	34,711
4	34,711	20,000	3,471	16,529	18,182
5	18,182	20,000	1,818	18,182	0

📖 Long-Term Loans

Unlike bonds, <u>long-term loans</u>[10] are typically transacted with a single lender such as a bank. Bank loans usually carry fixed maturities and interest rates as well as a monthly or quarterly repayment schedule. The long-term loan usually has a maturity of 3~10 years although long-term bank loans can stretch out as far as 20 years depending on its purpose.

Long-term bank loans are always supported by a company's **collateral**, usually in the form of the company's assets. The loan contracts usually contain **restrictive covenants** detailing what the company can and cannot do financially during the term of the loan. For example, the bank may specify that the company cannot take on more debts during the life of the long-term loan. Long-term loans are usually repaid by the company's cash flow over the life of the loan or by a certain percentage of profits that are set aside for this purpose.

📖 Vocabulary

bond indenture	债券契约，债券发行契约，债券信托契约
registered bonds	记名债券
unregistered bonds	不记名债券；无记名债券
debenture	*n.* 公司债券
transfer deed	(产权等)过户文契，转让契约
bearer debentures	不记名债券
bearer	*n.* 持票人
endorsement	*n.* 认可，支持；背书；签注(文件)
convertible bonds	可转换债券
non-convertible bonds	不可转换债券
callable bonds	可赎回债券
non-callable bonds	不可赎回债券
redeem	*vt.* 赎回；挽回；兑换；履行；补偿；恢复
underwrite	*vt.* 承购包销；签名承认(担保)，签名接受(保险)
effective interest rate	实际利率；有效利率
yield rate	投资实得率，收益率，报酬率
coupon rate	息票利率，票面利率
lease	*n.* 租约；租契；租赁物；租赁权 & *vt.* 出租；租借
lessee	*n.* 承租人，租户
lessor	*n.* 债主
up-front	*adj.* 在前面的；坦率的；预付的
operating lease	经营租赁
capital lease	融资租赁
rewards	*n. & vt.* 报酬；报答；赏金；酬金

finance lease	融资租赁
collateral	*n.* 担保物
restrictive covenant	限制性条款，限制性契约

Notes

[1] In this way, a sum of money larger than that which could be obtained from a single credit source may be borrowed from a large number of investors.   通过这种方式，就可以向众多的投资者借得高于从单一信用渠道所能借得的一大笔资金。

[2] Only on executing a transfer deed and filing a copy of it with the company, they can be transferred.   他们(记名债券)转让时，必须背书(签署转让契约)并到债券发行公司登记。

[3] Investment dealers may underwrite the bond issue, in which case they guarantee a certain price to the issuer and take the risk in selling the issue to the public.   投资经纪商可以对发行的债券进行包销，在这种情况下，他们保证付给发行者一定的价格并承担向公众售出这些债券的风险。

[4] If the effective interest rate is higher than the coupon rate, the bonds will sell at a discount. Conversely, if the effective interest rate is less than the coupon rate, the bonds will sell at a premium.   如果实际利率高于票面利率，债券将折价出售。相反的，如果实际利率低于票面利率，债券将溢价出售。

[5] 0.680583 和 3.992710，0.747258 和 4.212364 是现值系数和年金现值系数，可以查表获得，也可以通过公式计算求得，公式分别为 $P=F/(1+i)n$，$P=A[(1+i)n-1]/i(1+i)n$。其中 P 为现值(present value)，F 为终值(future value)，A 为年金(annuity)，i 为利率(interest rate)，n 为期数。

[6] Discount on bonds payable 和 Premium on bonds payable   参考翻译为"应付债券折价"和"应付债券溢价"。根据中国企业会计准则，无论是按面值发行，还是折价或溢价发行，均按债券面值记入"应付债券"科目的"面值"明细科目，实际收到的款项面值的差额记入"利息调整"明细科目，参考翻译为"bonds payable—interest adjustments"。

[7] Because differences between the effective rate and the coupon rate of interest are reflected in bond prices, the amount of premium or discount affects the periodic interest expense to the issuer.   由于实际利率和票面利率之间的差异已反映在债券的价格上，所以溢价或折价金额会影响发行者的利息费用。

[8] When a capital lease is signed, the lessee will record the present value of its lease payments on its books.   当签订融资租赁协议时，承租人在账簿中记录租赁付款额的现值。中国会计实务中，在租赁期开始日，将租赁开始日租赁资产公允价值与最低租赁付款额现值两者中较低者，加上初始直接费用，作为租入资产的入账价值，借记"固定资产"等科目，按最低租赁付款额，贷记"长期应付款"科目，按其差额，借记"未确认融资费用"科目。"长期应付款"的参考翻译为"long-term payables"，"未确认融资费用"属于负债类科目，其参考翻译为"unrecognized financing charges"。

[9] Lease liability   租赁负债，在中国记入"长期应付款"科目，除了应付融资租赁款外，分期付款方式购入固定资产和无形资产等发生的应付款项也记入"长期应付款"科目。

[10] long-term loans　长期借款的参考翻译。英文中的"long-term notes payable"(长期应付票据)与长期借款的含义比较接近。长期借款涉及的会计科目有"长期借款——本金""长期借款——利息调整""应付利息"等，参考翻译为"long-term loan—principal""long-term loan—interest adjustments""interest payable"。

Exercises

I. Discuss the following questions in English.

1.　What is the difference between a current liability and a non-current liability?

2.　Why does a creditor prefer a note payable to an account payable?

3.　Are current maturities of non-current debt are shown in the current liabilities section? Why?

4.　What determines the amount deducted from an employee's pay for income taxes?

5.　Define turnover taxes and provide some examples.

6.　What is the main difference between a bond and a share of stock?

7.　Under what condition of bond issuance does a discount on bonds payable arise?

8.　How do you compute the amount of interest a bond issuer pays in cash each year?

9.　How should unamortized discount on bonds payable be reported on the financial statements? How about unamortized premium on bonds payable?

10.　What's the difference between capital lease and operating lease?

II. Choose the best word or phrase that fits the sentence.

1.　A liability for _____ arises when a customer pay in advance.

　　A. deferred expense　　　　　　B. deferred revenue

　　C. accrued expense　　　　　　D. accrued revenue

2.　The slight overstatement of liabilities that results from carrying current liabilities at maturity value is justified on the grounds of _____, conservatism, and immateriality.

　　A. expediency　　　　　　B. expedient

　　C. facilitate　　　　　　D. facility

3.　The balance sheet has a liability section, which is _____ into long-term debt and current debt.

　　A. broken in　　　　　　B. broken into

　　C. broken down　　　　　　D. broken off

4.　Sales employees earn a _____, which is the percentage of the sales the employee has made.

　　A. salary　　　　　　B.wage

　　C. commission　　　　　　D. bonus

5.　Taxes Payable account is debited and cash credited when it _____ these collections to the government.

    A. liquidates   B. pays

    C. sends   D. remits

6.   A _____ bond is a type of bond that allows the issuer of the bond to retain the privilege of redeeming the bond at some point before the bond reaches its date of maturity.

    A. callable   B. non-callable

    C. convertible   D. non-convertible

7.   If the effective interest rate is higher than the coupon rate, the bonds will sell at _____.

    A. a discount   B. par

    C. a premium   D. face amount

8.   Discount and premium of a bond issuance can be amortized through _____ methods.

    A. accurate interest   B. actual interest

    C. effective interest   D. coupon interest rate

9.   A lease is a rental agreement in which the _____ agree to make rent payments to the property owner (lessor) in exchange for the use of the asset.

    A. charger   B. trustee

    C. lessor   D. lessee

10. When a capital lease is signed, the lessee will record the _____ on his/her books.

    A. fair value of the lease asset

    B. present value of his/her lease payments

    C. future value of his/her lease payments

    D. total amount of his/her lease payments

III. Match each word on the left with its corresponding meaning on the right.

A	B
1. advance	(a) send (money) in payment
2. indenture	(b) freedom to act or judge on one's own
3. principal	(c) something (such as money) given or received as payment
4. debenture	(d) a certificate or voucher acknowledging a debt
5. discretion	(e) exchange or buy back for money
6. contribution	(f) a tenant who holds a lease
7. compensation	(g) an amount paid before it is earned
8. redeem	(h) a voluntary gift (as of money or service or ideas) made to some worthwhile cause
9. lessee	(i) formal agreement between the issuer of bonds and the bondholders as to terms of the debt
10. remit	(j) the original amount of a debt on which interest is calculated

IV. Fill in the blanks with words or phrases from the list below.

A.	discounted	B.	interest	C.	calculations	D.	obligations
E.	notion	F.	worth	G.	stream	H.	specified
I.	ordinary	J.	inflation	K.	future	L.	finance
M.	power	N.	terminology	O.	invested	P.	annuity

The time value of money is the principle that a certain currency amount of money today has a different buying (1)____ from that of the same currency amount of money in the future. The value of money at a future point of time would take account of interest earned or (2)____ accrued over a given period of time. This (3)____ exists both because there is an opportunity to earn interest on the money and because inflation will drive prices up, thus changing the "value" of the money. The time value of money is the central concept in (4)____ theory. However, the explanation of the concept typically looks at the impact of (5)____ and assumes, for simplicity, that inflation is neutral.

For example, $100 of today's money (6)____ for one year and earning 5% interest will be worth $105 after one year. Therefore, $100 paid now or $105 paid exactly one year from now both have the same value to the recipient who assumes 5% interest; using time value of money (7)____, $100 invested for one year at 5% interest has a future value of $105.

The method also allows the valuation of a likely (8)____ of income in the future, in such a way that the annual incomes are discounted and then added together, thus providing a lump-sum "present value" of the entire income stream.

All of the standard (9)____ for time value of money derive from the most basic algebraic expression for the present value of a future sum, "discounted" to the present by an amount equal to the time value of money. For example, a sum of FV to be received in one year is (10)____ (at the rate of interest r) to give a sum of PV at present: $PV = FV - r \cdot PV = FV/(1+r)$.

Some standard calculations based on the time value of money are:

Present value is the current (11)____ of a future sum of money or stream of cash flows given a specified rate of return. Future cash flows are discounted at the discount rate, and the higher the discount rate is, the lower the present value of the (12)____ cash flows. Determining the appropriate discount rate is the key to properly valuing future cash flows, whether they be earnings or (13)____.

An (14)____ is a series of equal payments or receipts that occur at evenly spaced intervals. Leases and rental payments are examples.

Present value of an annuity is the payments or receipts occurred at the end of each period for an (15)____ annuity while they occur at the beginning of each period for an annuity due.

Present value of a perpetuity is an infinite and constant stream of identical cash flows.

Future value is the value of an asset or cash at a (16)____ date in the future that is equivalent in value to a specified sum today.

Future value of an annuity is the future value of a stream of payments (annuity), assuming the payments are invested at a given rate of interest.

V. Translate the following sentences into Chinese.

1. A single liability can be divided between the current and non-current sections if a company expects to make payments toward it in both the short and long terms.

2. Accounts payable are amounts owed to suppliers for products or services purchased on credit.

3. Under a note payable agreement, a borrower obtains a specific amount of money from a lender and promises to pay it back with interest over a predetermined time period.

4. Payroll liabilities are often large and arise from salaries and wages earned, from employee benefits, and from payroll taxes levied on the employer.

5. Income tax payable is calculated according to the prevailing tax law in the company's home country.

6. Bond payments can be especially burdensome when income and cash flow are low.

7. Many bond issuers try to set a contact rate of interest equal to the market rate they expect as of bond issuance date.

8. Firms often choose to lease long-term assets rather than buy them for a variety of reasons—the tax benefits are greater to the lessor than the lessees, leases offer more flexibility in terms of adjusting to changes in technology and capacity needs.

VI. Translate the following sentences into English.

1. 应付账款是指企业因购买材料、物资和接受劳务供应等而付给供货单位的账款。

2. 在我国应收票据、应付票据仅指"商业汇票"，包括"银行承兑汇票"和"商业承兑汇票"两种，属于远期票据，付款期一般在 1 个月以上，6 个月以内。其他的银行票据(支票、本票、汇票)等，都是作为货币资金来核算的，而不作为应收应付票据。

3. 短期借款是指企业用来维持正常的生产经营所需的资金或为抵偿某项债务而向银行或其他金融机构等外单位借入的、还款期限在一年以下或者一年的一个经营周期内的各种借款。

4. 一年内到期的非流动负债是反映企业各种非流动负债在一年之内到期的金额，包括一年内到期的长期借款、长期应付款和应付债券。

5. 应付职工薪酬是指企业为获得职工提供的服务而给予各种形式的报酬以及其他相关支出。

6. 应交税费是指企业根据在一定时期内取得的营业收入、实现的利润等，按照现行税法规定，采用一定的计税方法计提的应交纳的各种税费。

7. 公司债券是指公司依照法定程序发行、约定在一定期限还本付息的有价证券。

8. 长期应付款是指企业除了长期借款和应付债券以外的长期负债，包括应付融资租入固定资产的租赁费、以分期付款方式购入固定资产发生的应付款项等。

Reading Material 6

Accounting for Income Taxes

Business income is generally subject to federal, state, and local income taxes. In computing income taxes payable to governmental units, business must complete tax returns including a statement showing the amount of net income subject to tax. In general, the form and content of the tax return income statement are similar to the form and content of the accounting income statement. Taxable income in the tax return, however, is computed in accordance with prescribed tax regulations and rules, while accounting income in the income statement is measured in accordance with generally accepted accounting principles and standards. And, because the basic objectives of measuring taxable income are different from the objectives of measuring accounting income, tax rules are frequently different from accounting principles. Therefore, differences between taxable income and accounting income exist.

Numerous items create differences between taxable income and pretax accounting income. For the purpose of accounting recognition, these differences are of two types: (1) timing differences and (2) permanent differences.

Timing differences arise when items of revenue and expense are included in the computation of accounting income in one period and in the computation of taxable income in a different period. Timing differences originate in one period and reverse or "turn around" in one or more subsequent periods. When they originate, some timing differences result in reporting less tax expense than the amount of taxes currently payable; when these timing differences reverse, the accounting tax expense is greater than the taxes paid. For other timing differences, accounting tax expense exceeds taxes payable in the period the timing differences originate, and is less than taxes payable in the period of reversal. Inter-period tax allocation was required to account for the tax effects of transactions which involve timing differences in China.

Some differences between taxable income and accounting income are permanent. Permanent differences are items that (1) enter into accounting income but never into taxable income or (2) enter into taxable income but never into accounting income. Congress has enacted a variety of tax law provisions in an effort to attain certain political, economic, and social objectives. Some of these provisions exclude certain revenues from taxation, limit the deductibility of certain expenses, and permit the deduction of certain other expenses in excess of costs incurred. A corporation that has tax-free income, nondeductible expenses, or allowable deductions in excess of cost has an effective tax rate that is different from the statutory tax rate. The apparent discrepancy between the reported tax and the "normal" tax is not allocated between accounting periods. Since permanent differences affect only the period in which they occur, they are not reversed or offset by corresponding differences in subsequent periods. The Chinese Accounting Standards stated that the inter-period tax allocation was not appropriate for permanent differences.

Two different methods of inter-period tax allocation for timing differences have been used: (1) the deferred method, and (2) the liability method.

Under the deferred method the amount of differed income tax based on tax rates comes into effect when timing differences originate. The balance in deferred taxes is not adjusted to reflect subsequent changes in tax rates or the imposition of new taxes. Consequently, the balance in deferred taxes may not be representative of the actual amount of additional taxes payable or receivable in the periods that timing differences reverse. The deferred method had been used in the USA for many years till it was replaced by the liability method in 1987. From 2007, Chinese Accounting Standards prohibits the use of differed method.

Under the liability method the amount of deferred income tax based on the tax rates is expected to be in effect during the periods in which the timing differences reverse. Advocates of this method believe that the initial computation of deferred taxes is a tentative estimate which is subject to future adjustment if the tax rate changes or new taxes are imposed. Ordinarily, the most reasonable assumption about the future tax rates is that the current tax rate will continue. However, if a rate change is known or reasonably certain at the time of the initial computation, the anticipated rate would be used under the liability method. Under this method deferred taxes are viewed as economic liabilities for taxes payable or assets for prepaid tax. Therefore, it would be appropriate to discount them to the present value of the amounts which is ultimately expected to be paid or received. In China, present accounting standards require that the liability method be used for inter-period tax allocation.

Answers:

II.	1	B	2	A	3	C	4	C	5	D	6	A	7	A	8	C
	9	D	10	B												
III.	1	g	2	i	3	j	4	d	5	b	6	h	7	c	8	e
	9	f	10	a												
IV.	1	M	2	J	3	E	4	L	5	B	6	O	7	N	8	G
	9	C	10	A	11	F	12	K	13	D	14	P	15	I	16	H

 More Knowledge　知识扩展

1. 金融负债

金融负债是指属于下列合同义务的负债：①向另一个企业交付现金或其他金融资产的合同义务；②在潜在不利的条件下，与另一个企业交换金融工具的合同义务。金融负债应当在初始确认时划分为下列两类：①以公允价值计量且其变动计入当期损益的金融负债，包括交易性金融负债和指定为以公允价值计量且其变动计入当期损益的金融负债；②摊余成本计量的金融负债。

2. 金融资产减值

基于减值客观证据的金融资产减值处理会导致信用损失的延迟确认，且不同类别的金融资产减值模型不同，增大人为操纵空间，在 2008 年国际金融危机中被视为重大缺陷，IFRS 9 提供了一种全新的减值模式——预期信用损失模式，考虑包括前瞻性信息在内的各种可获得信息，不再采用"已发生损失法"。对于购入或源生的未发生信用减值的金融资产，企业应当判断金融工具的违约风险自初始确认以来是否显著增加：①如果已显著增加，企业应当采用概率加权法计算确定该金融工具在整个存续期的预期信用损失，以此确认和计提减值准备；②如果未显著增加，企业应当按照相当于该金融工具未来 12 个月内预期信用损失的金额确认和计提减值准备。我国修订后的金融工具确认和计量准则也对金融工具减值确认方法提出了上述要求。

Chapter 7　Owners' Equity
所有者权益

Learning Objectives

- Know different forms of business organization: sole proprietorships, partnerships and corporations 了解不同形式的商业组织：独资企业、合伙企业和股份有限公司
- Understand types of corporate capital 了解公司资本的类型
- Know the meaning of authorized stock 了解授权股票的含义
- Understand the issuance of common stock 了解普通股的发行
- Understand retained earnings 了解留存收益
- Understand the restriction and appropriation of retained earnings 了解留存收益的限制用途和盈余公积
- Understand cash dividends and stock dividends 了解现金股利和股票股利

Chapter 7 English
Listening.mp3

Listening Practice　听力练习

第 7 章原文翻译和答案的音频见右侧二维码。

Dictation: *Listen and complete the passage with the words or phrases according to what you've heard from the speaker.*

Intangible assets are long-term assets that are without physical _____1_____ and not held for sale but are useful in the _____2_____ of a business. Such assets include patents, copyright and trademarks. Their value to an _____3_____ is generally derived from the rights or privileges granted by governmental authority.

The basic_____4_____of accounting for intangible assets are (1) determining the initial cost, (2) recognizing the periodic cost expiration. This is called amortization. Amortization results from the passage of time or a _____5_____ in the usefulness of the intangible asset.

Wisdom　至理名言

Why do corporations pay dividends? Why do investors pay attention to dividends? Perhaps the answers to these questions are obvious. Perhaps the answers are not so obvious. I claim the answers to these questions are not obvious at all. The harder we look at the dividend picture, the more it seems like a puzzle, with pieces that just don't fit together. What should the individual investor do about dividends in his portfolio? We don't know. What should the corporation do about dividend policy? We don't know. 为什么公司要支付股息？投资者为什么关注股息？也许这些问题的答案是显而易见的。也许答案并不那么明显。我认为这些问题的答案一点也不明显。我们越看股息走势图，就越觉得它像一幅拼图，一块块的碎片无论怎么拼接都不合适。个人投资者应该如何处理投资组合中的股息？我们不知道。公司应该如何对待股利政策？我们不知道。

The prime purpose of a business corporation is to pay dividends to its owners. 商业公司的主要目的是向其所有者支付股息。

 **Mini Case** 微型案例

Esther is considering investing $2,000 and wishes to know which of the following two companies offers the better alternative. The Mark Company earned net income of $45,000 last year on average total assets of $200,000 and average shareholders' equity of $150,000. The company's shares are selling for $10 per share; 45,000 shares of common stock are outstanding. The Luke Company earned net income of $23,500 last year on average total assets of $100,000 and average shareholders' equity of $75,000. The company's shares are selling for $8 per share; 25,000 shares of common stock are outstanding. Which stock should Esther purchase?

Owner's equity is defined as the excess of total assets over total liabilities. It is a residual amount that represents the book value of the owners' interest in the business enterprise. Because of the reporting principles and certain legal differences, owners' equity appears somewhat differently on the balance sheet of sole proprietorships, partnerships, and corporations.

In this chapter, we will focus on owners' equity of corporations. We will learn more about equity and equity transactions, and discuss some of the decisions a company faces when issuing shares and paying dividends.

7.1 Forms of Business Organization
企业组织形式

A conversation between A—an accountant and S—a freshman majoring in accounting.

S: I think there are more sole proprietorships and partnerships than corporations, aren't there?

A: Yes. The reason is that sole proprietorships and partnerships are easy to form. When one or more people agree to start a business, and go through a simple registration formality, a sole proprietorship or a partnership is formed.

S: When one or more people retire, the partnership is likely to become a proprietorship or cease its existence.

A: Yes. The life of the sole proprietorship and partnership is limited, but the liability is unlimited. They are all personally responsible for all the debts of the firm. Besides, the property is owned by all the partners. When a partner invests a building, inventory, or other properties in a partnership, he doesn't retain any personal right to the assets contributed. The property becomes jointly owned by the partners.

S: I think the income of the partnership is also owned by all partners.

A: The income of the partnership is distributed according to the partnership agreement. Some partnerships distribute the income in proportion to the partners' investment, and some distribute the income equally to the partners.

A business can be organized in one of several ways, and the form its owners choose will affect the company's and owners' legal liability and income tax treatment. There are three types of business structures: sole proprietorships, partnerships, and corporations.

 Sole Proprietorship

The vast majority of small businesses start out as sole proprietorships. These firms are owned by one person, usually the individual who has day-to-day responsibility for running the business. Sole proprietorships own all the assets of the business and the profits generated by it. They also assume complete responsibility for any of its liabilities or debts.

Advantages of a sole proprietorship are:

(1) Easiest and least expensive form of ownership to organize.

(2) Lowest amount of regulatory burden.

(3) Direct control of decision making.

(4) Minimal **working capital** required to start up.

(5) Profits from the business flow directly to the owner's **personal tax return**.

(6) The business is easy to **dissolve**, if desired.

Disadvantages of a sole proprietorship are:

(1) Sole proprietors have unlimited liability and are legally responsible for all debts against the business.[1]

(2) May be at a disadvantage in raising funds and are often limited to using funds from personal savings or consumer loans.

(3) May have a hard time attracting **high-caliber** employees, or those that are motivated by the opportunity to own a part of the business.

(4) Some employee benefits such as owner's **medical insurance premiums** are not directly deductible from business income (only partially as an adjustment to income).

Partnership

In a partnership, two or more people share ownership of a single business. Like proprietorships, the law does not distinguish between the business and its owners. The partners

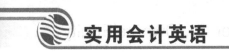
should have a legal agreement that sets forth how decisions will be made, profits will be shared, **disputes** will be resolved, how future partners will be admitted to the partnership, how partners can be bought out, what steps will be taken to dissolve the partnership, and so on.[2]

Advantages of a partnership are:

(1) Partnerships are relatively easy to establish; however, time should be invested in developing the partnership agreement.

(2) With more than one owner, the ability to raise funds may be increased.

(3) The profits from the business flow directly to the partners' personal tax return.

(4) Prospective employees may be attracted to the business if given the **incentive** to become a partner.

(5) The business usually wins benefit from partners who have **complementary** skills.

Disadvantages of a partnership are:

(1) Partners are jointly and individually liable for the actions of the other partners.

(2) Profits must be shared with others.

(3) Since decisions are shared, disagreements can occur.

(4) Some employee benefits are not deductible from business income on tax returns.

(5) The partnership may have a limited life; it may end upon the withdrawal or death of a partner.

The term "partnership" has changed over the years, as business people have come to add new features to the old business form. These new partnership types are intended to help mitigate the liability issues with partnerships. The three most used partnership types are **general partnership**, **limited partnership** and **limited liability partnership (LLP)**.

A general partnership is a partnership with only general partners. It is like a proprietorship in most ways except that it has more than one owner. Each general partner takes part in the management of the business, and also takes responsibility for the liabilities of the business. If one partner is sued, all partners are held liable. General partnerships are the least desirable for this reason.

A limited partnership includes both general partners and limited partners. A limited partner does not participate in the day-to-day management of the partnership and his/her liability is limited. In many cases, the limited partners are merely investors who do not with to participate in the partnership other than to provide an investment and to receive a share of the profits. [3]

An LLP is a partnership in which some or all partners (depending on the jurisdiction) have limited liabilities. Therefore, it exhibits elements of partnerships and corporations. In the LLP, all partners have limited liability, and one partner is not responsible or liable for another partner's misconduct or **negligence**. LLPs are most commonly used by professionals such as accountants, doctors and lawyers.

 Corporation

A corporation is considered by law to be a unique entity, separate and apart from those who own it. A corporation can be taxed; it can be sued; it can enter into contractual agreements. The owners of a corporation are its shareholders. The shareholders **elect** a board of directors to oversee the major policies and decisions. The corporation has a life of its own and does not dissolve when ownership changes.

Advantages of a corporation are:

(1) Shareholders have limited liability for the corporation's debts or judgments against the corporation.

(2) Generally, shareholders can only be held accountable for their investment in stock of the company.

(3) A corporation may deduct the cost of benefits it provides to officers and employees.

(4) Stocks which represent the ownership to the corporation are highly liquid and can be transferred any time the owner wishes.

Disadvantages of a corporation are:

(1) The process of incorporation requires more time and money than other forms of organization.

(2) Corporations must meet requirements of national corporation law, which subject the corporation to regulation and control.[4]

(3) Incorporating may result in higher overall taxes, as dividends paid to shareholders are not deductible from business income; thus this income can be taxed twice.

It is required by the law that the owners' equity of a corporation be divided into two parts: capital stock, which is the amount, invested in the company, and retained earnings, which represent the cumulative earnings of the company less any distribution of these earning called dividends. Single proprietorships or partnerships, however, do not have to distinguish between amounts invested by the owners and any undistributed earnings. In the next, we will discuss corporation accounting.

📖 Vocabulary

working capital	营运资本，营运资金
personal tax return	个人纳税申报单
dissolve	*vt.* 使消失，使消逝，消除；使终止
high-caliber	*adj.* 高质量的
medical insurance premiums	医疗保险费
dispute	*n.* 辩论；争端
incentive	*n.* 动机；刺激 & *adj.* 刺激性的；鼓励性质的
complementary	*adj.* 互补的；补充的，补足的
general partnership	普通合伙公司
limited partnership	有限合伙公司
limited liability partnership	*n.* 有限责任合伙

negligence	*n.* 疏忽；过失；粗心大意
elect	*vt.* 选举；挑出，挑选；决定

Notes

[1] Sole proprietors have unlimited liability and are legally responsible for all debts against the business.　独资企业主对企业欠下的所有债务依法承担无限责任。

[2] The partners should have a legal agreement that sets forth how decisions will be made, profits will be shared, disputes will be resolved, how future partners will be admitted to the partnership, how partners can be bought out, what steps will be taken to dissolve the partnership, and so on.　应该有一份关于合伙人的法定协议，可以详细地解释如何制定决策、分配利润、解决争议、新合伙人如何入伙，合伙人如何退伙，以及合伙企业的解散程序等。

[3] In many cases, the limited partners are merely investors who do not with to participate in the partnership other than to provide an investment and to receive a share of the profits.　在许多情况下，有限责任合伙人只是投资者，他们只参与合伙企业的投资以及分红，而绝不参与经营。

[4] Corporations must meet requirements of national corporation law, which subject the corporation to regulation and control.　股份公司必须遵守国家的公司法，受其监管和控制。

7.2　Corporate Capital
公司资本

A conversation between A—an accountant and S—a freshman majoring in accounting.

S: Owners' equity represents the net assets of the corporation, doesn't it?

A: Yes, it does. The amount of owners' equity is the total amount of the corporation's assets minus the total amount of the corporation's liabilities. There are two sources of owners' equity. One is the investment of the shareholders, and the other is the earnings from the operations of the business. So it can also be called shareholders' equity.

S: The two sources are capital stock and retained earnings respectively in the balance sheet. I'm not very clear about the sources of capital stock?

A: Simply put, capital stock is the recording of the cash or other assets invested by shareholders. The corporation issues the shareholders with shares of capital as evidence of their ownership when the corporation receives their invested capital.

S: For the section of capital stock, some balance sheets carry detailed items.

A: That's true. Detailed items of various preferred and common stocks can be included in the capital stock.

S: Is the amount of owners' equity equal to the amount of the corporation's cash?

A: Generally no. Owners' equity can be represented in any form of the assets.

Types of Capital Stock

Ownership in a corporation is evidenced by a **stock certificate**. This capital stock may be either common stock or preferred stock.

Common stock is a form of corporate equity ownership. Common stock being primarily used in the United States, and the terms "voting share" and "ordinary share" are also used frequently in other parts of the world. <u>If a corporation issues common stock, its shareholders usually have certain basic rights to be exercised in proportion or the number of common stock they own.</u>[1] These rights include: (1) right to vote for directors; (2) right to receive dividends declared by the board of directors; (3) right to share in the distribution of cash or other assets if the corporation is liquidated; and (4) **preemptive** <u>right to purchase additional shares of capital stock in proportion to present holdings in the event that the corporation increase the amount of stock outstanding</u>[2].

Common stock may be either **par value** or **no-par value**. Par value stock appears in the accounts as a fixed amount per share that is specified in the corporation's **charter** or **bylaws**. No-par value stock has a stated value, which is fixed by the board of directors. <u>The stated value governs the amounts to be entered in the capital stock account just as if it were a par value.</u> [3] In Chinese practice, par value is 1 *yuan* for all the <u>listed corporations</u> [4].

Another type of capital stock is called preferred stock, which normally possesses four major features: (1) preference as to dividends at a stated rate or amount; (2) preference as to assets in event of liquidation of the corporation; (3) redeemable (callable) at the option of the corporation; and (4) absence of voting rights. <u>Preferred stock can be either cumulative or non-cumulative, participating or non-participating, depending on the agreement reached between the corporation and the preferred shareholders.</u> [5]

At present, there is just one kind of stock—common stock in China. Since the current Corporation Law has no comment on the preferred stock, the issuance of preferred stock is forbidden in China.

 Authorized Stock

In issuing stock, the stock must be **authorized** by the government, generally in the **certificate of incorporation** or charter. Next, shares are offered for sale and contracts to sell stock. The number of shares the corporation can issue is called **authorized stock**, which represents the maximum number of common shares that can be issued legally by the company as stated in the company's charter. **Outstanding stock** is the stock that is in the hands of a stockholder.

In Chinese practice, we use **legal capital system** [6]. Legal capital is specified in China as the par value of the authorized shares. In China, the number of outstanding stock should be equal to the authorized stock.

Accounting for Issuance of Stock

When shares are issued the person **subscribing** must pay cash or equivalent value of at least the par amount. [7] Shares may be issued by the company to shareholders in return for cash or other value equal to or greater than its par value.

Paid-in capital (paid in capital or contributed capital)[8] refers to capital contributed to a corporation by investors through purchase of stock from the corporation (**primary market**) (not through purchase of stock in the open market from other stockholders (**secondary market**)). Paid-in capital represents the funds raised by the business from equity, but not from ongoing operations. It includes capital stock as well as additional paid-in capital[9].

Paid-in capital (contributed capital) = A + B:

A = Capital stock (share capital, common stock or preferred stock)

B = Additional paid-in capital (paid-in capital in excess of par)

The user should be aware of the use of the term, otherwise it may be misleading.

According to the convention, the capital stock account reflects the par or stated value, and the premium (i.e. issuing price less par or stated value) is shown separately, in additional paid-in capital account.[10]

To illustrate, assume that Crown Corporation received a charter from the government authorizing the issuance of 200,000 shares of $1 par value common stock. If 200,000 shares of stock were issued at $3, and the proceeds were received by Crown Corporation, the following entry would be made:

Cash in bank	600,000	
Capital stock		100,000
Additional paid-in capital		500,000

Capital stock is a company balance sheet entry listed under stockholder's equity, often shown **alongside** the balance sheet entry for additional paid-in capital.

Treasury Stock

A company may purchase its stock that was previously issued. Such stock is called **treasury stock**. More specifically, treasury stock is a corporation's own stock that was sold, issued, reacquired subsequently and still held by the corporation, without voting, dividend, or other shareholder rights.

It is usual in USA for corporations to reacquire shares of their own stock by purchase in the open market. Many public companies spend millions of dollars each year to purchase back their own shares. Corporations purchase their own shares for several reasons:

(1) It offers employee **share option** compensation or an **employee share ownership plan** but it does not wish to issue new shares, so it purchases the shares from the market and then passes them to employees upon exercise of the share options or purchase of the shares.

(2) The management wants to avoid a **takeover** by an outside party.

(3) The management wants to increase its reported earnings per share.

When a corporation purchases its own capital stock, the assets (usually cash) of the corporation and the stockholders' equity are reduced by equal amounts. When treasury stock is sold, the opposite effects occur. Usually the purchase and sale prices of treasury stock are different, necessitating recognition of the difference in an appropriately designated paid-in capital account in the entry to record the sale.

In China, the current Corporation Law restricts the purchase of treasury stock.

 Vocabulary

stock certificate	股票，股票证书
preemptive	*adj.* 先买的，有先买权的
par value	票面价值，面值，平价
no-par value	无面值
charter	*n.* 许可证；纲领；宪章
bylaw	*n.* 次要法规，(社、团制定的)规章制度
authorize	*vt.* 授权，批准，委托
certificate of incorporation	公司注册证；登记执照
authorized stock	法定股本，核定股本，额定股本
outstanding stock	外发股本
legal capital system	法定资本制
subscribe	*vt. & vi.* 认购；订阅，订购；捐赠；署名
primary market	一级市场；初次市场(即证券发行机构)
secondary market	二(中，次)级市场
alongside	*prep. & adv.* 在……旁边；横靠；傍着
treasury stock	库存股
share option	股票认购权
employee share ownership plan	职工持股计划
takeover	*n.* 收购；接管；验收

Notes

[1] If a corporation issues common stock, its shareholders usually have certain basic rights to be exercised in proportion or the number of common stock they own.　如果公司发行普通股，其股东通常可根据所拥有的普通股比例或份数行使一些基本权利。

[2] preemptive right to purchase additional shares of capital stock in proportion to present holdings in the event that the corporation increase the amount of stock outstanding　在公司增加外发股票时，可按现在的持股比例享有优先购买额外股份的权利。

[3] The stated value governs the amounts to be entered in the capital stock account just as if it were a par value.　设定价值决定着股本账户所记录的金额，就如同它有面值一样。

[4] listed corporations　上市公司。英文中比较常见的"上市公司"的说法还有"listed

company" "public company (corporation)" "quoted company"。

[5] Preferred stock can be either cumulative or non-cumulative, participating or non-participating, depending on the agreement reached between the corporation and the preferred shareholders. 根据公司与优先股股东所达成的协议，优先股可分为累积的或非累积的，参与分配或不参与分配的。

[6] legal capital system 法定资本制。法定资本制是指公司在设立时，必须在章程中对公司的资本总额作出明确规定，并需由股东全部认足，否则公司不能成立。

[7] When shares are issued, the person subscribing must pay cash or equivalent value of at least the par amount. 发行股票时，认购者必须支付不少于票面等价的现金或资本值。

[8] paid-in capital (paid in capital or contributed capital) 参考翻译为"实缴资本"，也可翻译成"实收资本"，但二者的含义是不同的，简单来说，实缴资本=实收资本+资本公积。

[9] capital stock as well as additional paid-in capital 股本和资本公积。英文中股本的说法可以是"capital stock" "share capital" "common stock"或"preferred stock"，资本公积的说法可以是"additional paid-in capital" "paid-in capital in excess of par"。"股本"和"资本公积"的英文参考翻译为"capital stock (share capital)"和"capital surplus"。

[10] According to the convention, the capital stock account reflects the par or stated value, and the premium (i.e. issuing price less par or stated value) is shown separately, in additional paid-in capital account. 根据惯例，"股本"账户反映的是面值或设定价值，溢价(即发行价格减面值或设定价值)应单独列示于称作"资本公积"的账户。

7.3 Retained Earnings
留存收益

A conversation between A—an accountant and S—a freshman majoring in accounting.

A: Could you tell me what is the main difference between retained earnings and net income?

S: Retained earnings are the result of business accumulation for a long time, while the net income is only the operating result for an accounting period, right?

A: Right. But retained earnings are not a simple addition of net incomes of all the past periods. The company may have distributed some dividends to the shareholders. Would you please guess how the amount of retained earnings is calculated at the end of a period?

S: I think we should add the net income of this period to retained earnings at the beginning of this period and then subtract the dividends to the share holders or withdrawals by the shareholders over the period.

A: Absolutely right. Retained earnings may carry either a debit balance or a credit balance.

S: What does it mean if it carries a debit balance?

A: This happens when a company's losses or distribution to shareholders are greater than its profits from operations. In such a case, the firm is said to have a deficit in retained earnings.

What are Retained Earnings

Retained earnings generally consist of a company's cumulative net income less any net losses and dividends declared since its **inception**. It is important to note that retained earnings are not the assets themselves, but the existence of retained earnings means that net assets generated by profitable operations have been kept in the company to help it **boost** or to meet other business needs. [1] Retained earnings are part of stockholders' claims on the company's net assets, but this does not imply that a certain amount of cash or other assets is available to pay shareholders.

Factors that may cause the retained earnings account to increase or decrease include certain transactions or events related to the income or loss from operations, the declaration of shareholder dividends and **prior period adjustments**.

(1) Income or loss from operations

Whether a company reports net income or suffers a net loss, the operating results from a company's fiscal year is recorded to retained earnings, resulting in a increase or decrease in the account.

(2) Declaration of **cash dividends**

When a corporation announces a dividend to its shareholders, the retained earnings account is decreased. Since dividends are distributed on a per share basis, retained earnings are decreased by the total of outstanding shares multiplied by the **dividend rate** on each share of stock. [2]

(3) Prior period adjustments

If an error is made on a previously issued income statement (as opposed to a change in estimate), a corporation must restate its beginning retained earnings balance. If the error understated the corporation's net income, the beginning retained earnings balance must be increased (a credit to retained earnings). If the error had overstated the corporation's net income, the beginning retained earnings balance must be decreased (a debit to retained earnings).

Retained earnings are an equity account that represents the accumulated portions of net income that a business reinvests into its operations. In most cases, retained earnings have a credit balance, receiving a credit when it increases and a debit when it decreases. However, it is possible that a business distributes more to its owners than it earns and ends up with negative retained earnings with a debit balance.

Restrictions and Appropriations

After companies deduct the costs of business from sales revenue, retained earnings represent the remaining funds on financial statements. However, those earnings do not necessarily go straight to shareholders. This is because earnings themselves are sometimes **slated** for specific purposes, such as reinvestment into business projects. In such cases these earnings are designated as **appropriated** or **restricted retained earnings**; in other instances, earnings are considered **unappropriated**.

The term "restricted retained earnings" refers to both **statutory** and contractual restrictions.

In China, a certain percentage of income should be restricted if the corporation has profit until the company's legal accumulation fund exceeds 50% of registered capital.[3] The main purpose of legal accumulation funds is to protect creditors from overpayment of dividends and it is good for the growth of the corporation. The term "appropriated retained earnings" refers to a voluntary transfer of amounts from the retained earnings account to the appropriated retained account to inform users of special activities that require funds.[4] An appropriation might occur when a corporation is expanding its factory and its cash must be preserved.

A board of directors can vote to appropriate, or restrict, some of the corporation's retained earnings. An appropriation (or restriction) will result in two retained earning accounts instead of one: unappropriated retained earnings, and Appropriated (restricted) retained earnings [5].

The subdividing of retained earnings is a way of disclosing the appropriation on the balance sheet directly. By displaying the appropriated retained earning account on the balance sheet, the corporation is communicating a certain situation and is potentially limiting itself from declaring dividends by having reduced the balance in its regular (the unappropriated) retained earnings. Legally, dividends can be declared only if there is a credit balance in retained earnings.

To record an appropriation of retained earnings, the retained earning account is debited, and appropriated retained earning account is credited. [6]

Vocabulary

inception	*n.* 开始，开端，初期
boost	*vt.* 促进，提高；增加
prior period adjustments	前期调整项目
cash dividend	现金股利
dividend rate	股利率，股息率
slate	*vt.* 安排或指定
appropriate	*vt.* 占用，拨出
restricted retained earnings	限定用途留存收益
unappropriated	*adj.* 未被占用的，未被指定的；未分配

Notes

[1] It is important to note that retained earnings are not the assets themselves, but the existence of retained earnings means that net assets generated by profitable operations have been kept in the company to help it boost or to meet other business needs. 需要注意的是，留存收益本身不是资产，但留存收益的存在意味着盈利运作所产生的净资产被企业留存下来，用于促进企业发展或满足企业的其他需要。

[2] Since dividends are distributed on a per share basis, retained earnings are decreased by the total of outstanding shares multiplied by the dividend rate on each share of stock. 由于股利是以每股为基础分配的，留存收益减少的金额应该是外发股本与每股股利的乘积。

[3] In China, a certain percentage of profit should be restricted if the corporation has net

income until the company's legal accumulation fund exceeds 50% of registered capital. 在中国，在法定公积金累计额为公司注册资本的50%以上时，不可再提取，否则如果公司有净利润就应该按利润的确定比例提取法定公积金。"legal accumulation fund"为中文"法定公积金"的参考翻译。

[4] The term "appropriated retained earnings" refers to a voluntary transfer of amounts from the retained earnings account to the appropriated retained account to inform users of special activities that require funds. 已拨定留存收益是指公司自愿将留存收益账户中的部分金额转至已拨定留存收益账户，来告知报表使用者公司的某些特定活动需要使用资金。

[5] Unappropriated retained earnings, and appropriated (restricted) retained Earnings 未指定用途留存收益和已拨定(限定用途)留存收益。前者与我国会计中的"未分配利润"比较类似，后者与"盈余公积"类似。"未分配利润"的参考翻译为"undistributed profits"，"盈余公积"的参考翻译为"earnings surplus"，"法定公积金"的参考翻译为"legal accumulation fund"，"任意公积金"的参考翻译为"optional accumulation fund"。

[6] To record an appropriation of retained earnings, the retained earning account is debited, and appropriated retained earning account is credited. 记录已拨定留存收益时，借记"留存收益"账户，贷记"已拨定留存收益"账户。会计实务中，企业提取盈余公积时，借记"利润分配"科目，贷记"盈余公积"科目。利润分配的参考翻译为"profit distribution"。

7.4 Dividends
股利

A conversation between A—an accountant and S—a freshman majoring in accounting.

S: Dividends refer to the cash that a corporation distributes to its shareholders, don't they?

A: Yes. But besides cash, dividends can be stock, which we call stock dividends. Of course, the dividends in cash form are called cash dividends.

S: Is the distribution of dividends decided by the top management of the corporation?

A: No. Only the board of directors has the right to decide whether or not to distribute dividends, the amount of dividends, and the dividend form.

S: How is the entry for the cash dividends distribution to be made?

A: Because a dividend is decided on one date and paid at a later date, two separate entries are necessary. On the declaration day the entry is to debit profit distribution and credit dividends payable. Then on the payment day, the entry is to debit dividends payable and credit cash in bank.

S: What about stock dividends?

A: Stock dividends will not lead to a change of assets and owners' equity. The distribution of stock dividends only transfers part of retained earnings into the invested capital of the shareholders.

A dividend is a distribution of cash (or other assets) or capital stock to shareholders by a corporation. Dividends must be approved by the board of directors of the corporation (i.e. a dividend declaration) before they can be paid. The term "dividend", without any qualifier, usually is understood to mean a cash dividend, which is the most common type. A dividend distribution of the corporation's own share is called a **stock dividend**.

Cash Dividends

A cash dividend is money paid to stockholders, normally out of the corporation's current earnings or accumulated profits. Dividends are **analogous** to withdrawals by the owner of a sole proprietorship. As such, dividends are not expenses and do not appear on the corporation's income statement.

Corporations routinely need cash in order to replace inventory and other assets whose replacement costs have increased or to expand capacity. As a result, corporations rarely distribute all of their net income to shareholders. Young, growing corporations may pay no dividends at all, while more mature corporations may distribute a significant percentage of their profits to shareholders as dividends.

Before dividends can be distributed, the corporation's board of directors must declare a dividend. The date the board of directors declares the dividend is known as the **declaration date** and it is on this date that the liability for the dividend is created. Legally, corporations must have a credit balance in retained earnings in order to declare a dividend. Practically, a corporation must also have a cash balance large enough to pay the dividend and still meet upcoming needs, such as asset growth and payments on existing liabilities.[1]

A cash dividend to shareholders involves two entries. The first entry occurs on the date that the board of directors declares the dividend. In this entry, the account retained earnings is debited and **dividends payable** is credited for the amount of the dividend that will be paid. In China, corporations debit an account profit distribution [2] instead of debiting retained earnings. Until such time as the company actually pays the shareholders, the cash amount of the dividend is recorded within a dividends payable account as a current liability. The second entry occurs on the date of the payment to the shareholders. On that date the current liability account dividends payable is debited and the asset account cash in bank is credited.

Stock Dividends

A stock dividend is a proportional distribution by a corporation of its own shares to its shareholders. A corporation may choose to distribute share dividends for these reasons:

(1) To continue dividends but **conserve** cash

A company may need to conserve cash and yet wish to continue dividends in some form. So the corporation may distribute shares as dividends instead.

(2) To reduce the market price of its share

Distribution of a stock dividend usually causes the share's market price to fall because of the increased number of outstanding shares that result from it. The objective is to make the shares less expensive and therefore attractive to more investors.

(3) To provide evidence of management's confidence

Distribution of a stock dividend is to provide evidence of management's confidence that the company is doing well and will continue to do well. [3]

To record a stock dividend, retained earnings are debited with the par value of the dividend shares with the credit being to the capital stock account. [4] Total equity is unchanged, and no asset or liability is affected.

In Chinese practice, the entry of stock dividends is only recorded at the date of payment, and stock dividends should be disclosed in financial statement.

📖 Vocabulary

stock dividend	股票股利
analogous	*adj.* 相似的，可比拟的
declaration date	股息宣告日
dividends payable	应付股利
conserve	*vt.* 保护，保藏，保存

🖋 Notes

[1] Practically, a corporation must also have a cash balance large enough to pay the dividend and still meet upcoming needs, such as asset growth and payments on existing liabilities.   实务中，公司必须有足够多的现金余额，支付股利的同时又能够满足即将到来的需要，如资产增长、支付即期债务。

[2] profit distribution   利润分配的参考翻译。在会计处理上，未分配利润是通过"利润分配"科目进行核算的，"利润分配"科目应当分别以"提取法定盈余公积""提取任意盈余公积""应付现金股利或利润""转作股本的股利""盈余公积补亏"和"未分配利润"等进行明细核算。

[3] Distribution of a stock dividend is to provide evidence of management's confidence that the company is doing well and will continue to do well.   发放股票股利说明公司管理层对公司目前的良好业绩和未来保持良好业绩的信心。

[4] To record a stock dividend, retained earnings are debited with the par value of the dividend shares with the credit being to the capital stock account.   记录股票股利，按股利股票面值借记"留存收益"，贷记"股本"科目。会计实务中，应借记"利润分配——转作股本的股利"，贷记"股本"科目。

Exercises

I. Discuss the following questions in English.

1.   What are the advantages and disadvantages of the sole proprietorship form of business?

2.   What are the different types of partnerships?

3.   Why is a corporation's income said to be taxed twice?

4.   What is the preemptive right of common shareholders?

5.   What is the difference between authorized shares and outstanding shares?

6.   What things can debit or credit retained earnings? Specifically what types of transactions or accounts?

7.   What do negative retained earnings mean?

8.   What is the difference in unappropriated retained earnings and appropriated (restricted) retained earnings?

9.   When and how should you record a dividend payment?

10.   What type of an account is the dividends payable account?

11.   How does declaring a stock dividend affect the corporation's assets, liabilities and shareholders' equity? What are the effects of the eventual distribution of that stock?

II. Choose the best word or phrase that fits the sentence.

1.   The vast majority of small businesses start out as _____.

    A. sole proprietorships   B. partnerships

    C. limited partnerships   D. corporations

2.   _____ are most commonly used by professionals such as accountants, doctors and lawyers.

    A. General partnerships   B. Limited partnerships

    C. Limited liability partnerships   D. Corporations

3.   The shareholders elect _____ to oversee the major policies and decisions.

    A. chief executive officer (CEO)   B. a board of directors

    C. general manager   D. chief accountant

4.   If a corporation issues common stock, its shareholders usually have _____ right to purchase additional shares of capital stock in proportion to present holdings in the event that the corporation increases the amount of stock outstanding.

    A. anticipated   B. advanced

    C. preemptive   D. previous

5.   In China, the number of outstanding stock should be _____ the authorized stock.

    A. less than   B. more than

    C. close to   D. equal to

6.   According to the convention, the capital stock account reflects the par or stated value, and the premium is shown separately, in _____ account.

    A. paid-in capital   B. capital surplus

    C. retained earnings   D. appropriated retained earnings

7.   Treasury stock is a corporation's own stock that was sold, issued, reacquired subsequently and still held by the corporation, has _____ voting, dividend, or other shareholder rights.

    A. entire   B. restricted

    C. limited   D. no

8.   It is important to note that retained earnings are not the assets themselves, but the existence of retained earnings means that net assets generated by _____ operations have been kept in the company to help it grow or to meet other business needs.

    A. profitable   B. continuos

    C. effective   D. normal

9.   The term "appropriated retained earnings" refers to a(n) _____ transfer of amounts from the retained earnings account to the appropriated retained account to inform users of special activities that require funds.

    A. arbitrary   B. compulsive

    C. voluntary   D. reasonable

10.   Dividends payable are dividends that a company's _____ has declared to be payable to its shareholders.

    A.chief executive officer (CEO)   B. board of directors

    C. chief financial officer (CFO)   D. publicity department

11.   A stock dividend is a(n) _____ distribution by a corporation of its own shares to its shareholders.

    A. additional   B. complementary

    C. attached   D. proportional

III. Match each word on the left with its corresponding meaning on the right.

A	B
1. elect	(a) similar or correspondent in some respects though otherwise dissimilar
2. dispute	(b) an event that is a beginning
3. analogous	(c) come to an end
4. option	(d) failure to act with the prudence that a reasonable person would exercise under the same circumstances
5. takeover	(e) keep in safety and protect from harm, decay, loss, or destruction
6. inception	(f) have a disagreement over something
7. incentive	(g) the right to buy or sell property at an agreed price

8. dissolve   (h) select by a vote for an office or membership

9. negligence   (i) a change by sale or merger in the controlling interest of a corporation

10. conserve   (j) a positive motivational influence

IV. Fill in the blanks with words or phrases from the list below.

A.	rises	B.	option	C.	dividends	D.	control
E.	flexibility	F.	unique	G.	break	H.	attend
I.	approximately	J.	deregulated	K.	insight	L.	interest
M.	portion	N.	enhancing	O.	expand	P.	supporting

Stock market investment gives you the (1)_____ opportunity to take a direct part in the growth and success of companies. When you buy shares in a company, it means that you actually own a (2)_____ of that company. As part owner, you benefit by receiving part of the profits or (3)_____ and sharing in the growth of the value of the company.

The company benefits by raising funds or capital when your shares and other shares are first sold. These funds are used to operate and (4)_____ the business.

In general, share investments produce better returns than fixed (5)_____ investments, particularly when money is invested long term.

Although there are rises and falls in the stock market, history shows that over the long term, the value of the stock market (6)_____. In the US, which has a long history of (7)_____ stock market, the average real return per year after inflation is (8)_____ 10%.

Direct investment in the stock market also gives you (9)_____ over where you put your money. You decide which companies you want to invest in and when the time is right for you to sell your shares. If you want to be in control, stock market investment is a good (10)_____.

Another attractive feature of stock market investment is the (11)_____ to change your investments when your personal circumstances change. For example, if you need money for a well-earned (12)_____, an extension on our house or your children's education, all you need to do is sell your shares.

Stock market investment allows you to follow your investment. You'll receive regular information from companies you invest in and can (13)_____ meetings. This enables you to gain a unique (14)_____ into the results and strategies of the organization and learn a lot in the process.

Market investment also allows you to follow a particular interest you have. For example, you may have lived all you life in a forestry area and are interested in (15)_____ this industry and benefiting from its success, by investing in listed forestry stocks.

V. Translate the following sentences into Chinese.

1. The only owner's equity accounts of a sole proprietorship needed are a capital account for the proprietor and a drawing account for the proprietor.

2. A partnership is formed by two or more persons reaching mutual agreement as to the

terms of the partnership.

3.   The transfer of shares from one stockholder to another usually has no effect on the corporation or its operations except when this causes a change in the directors who control or manage the corporation.

4.   Preferred stock usually carries a preference for dividends, meaning that preferred shareholders are allocated their dividends before any dividends are allocated to common shareholders.

5.   A premium on stock occurs when a corporation sells its stock for more than par value.

6.   Dividend payment involves three important dates: declaration, record, and payment.

7.   A dividend is a payment made by a corporation to its shareholders, usually as a distribution of profits.

8.   A stock dividend does not reduce assets and equity but instead transfers a portion of equity from retained earnings to contributed capital.

VI. Translate the following sentences into English.

1.   独资企业是个人出资经营、归个人所有和控制、由个人承担经营风险和享有全部经营收益的企业。

2.   合伙企业是由两个或两个以上的自然人通过订立合伙协议，共同出资经营、共负盈亏、共担风险的企业组织形式。

3.   公司是指全部资本由股东出资构成，以盈利为目的而依法设立的一种企业组织形式。

4.   股票发行是指符合条件的发行人按照法定的程序，向投资人出售股份、募集资金的过程。

5.   库存股是指已经认购缴款，由发行公司通过购入、赠予或其他方式重新获得，可供再行出售或注销之用的股票。

6.   法定盈余公积和任意盈余公积的区别就在于其各自计提的依据不同，前者以国家的法律或行政规章为依据提取，后者则由企业自行决定提取。

7.   现金股利，是指用现金支付股利的形式，这是支付股利的最主要形式。

8.   股票股利增加了流通在外的普通股的数量，每股普通股的权益将被稀释，从而可能会影响公司股票的市价。

Reading Material 7

Stock Split

A stock split will usually occur when a stock's price is too high. The company will decide that the stock price is not affordable for the average investor so they will split the stock in order to bring the price down. The price is adjusted such that the before and after market capitalization of the company remains the same and dilution does not occur. Options and warrants are included.

Take, for example, a company with 100 shares of stock priced at $50 per share. The market capitalization is 100 × $50, or $5,000. The company splits its stock 2-for-1. There are now 200 shares of stock and each shareholder holds twice as many shares. The price of each share is adjusted to $25. The market capitalization is 200 × $25 = $5,000, the same as before the split.

Ratios of 2-for-1, 3-for-1, and 3-for-2 splits are the most common, but any ratio is possible. Splits of 4-for-3, 5-for-2, and 5-for-4 are used, though less frequently. Investors will sometimes receive cash payments in lieu of fractional shares.

It is often claimed that stock splits, in and of themselves, lead to higher stock prices; research, however, does not bear this out. What is true is that stock splits are usually initiated after a large run up in share price. Momentum investing would suggest that such a trend would continue regardless of the stock split. In any case, stock splits do increase the liquidity of a stock; there are more buyers and sellers for 10 shares at $10 than 1 share at $100. Some companies have the opposite strategy: by refusing to split the stock and keeping the price high, they reduce trading volume. Berkshire Hathaway is a notable example of this.

Other effects could be psychological. If many investors believe that a stock split will result in an increased share price and purchase the stock the share price will tend to increase. Others contend that the management of a company, by initiating a stock split, is implicitly signaling its confidence in the future prospects of the company.

In a market where there is a high minimum number of shares, or a penalty for trading in so-called odd lots (a non multiple of some arbitrary number of shares), a reduced share price may attract more attention from small investors. Small investors such as these, however, will have negligible impact on the overall price.

When a stock split, many charts show it similarly to a dividend payout and therefore do not show a dramatic dip in price. Taking the same example as above, a company with 100 shares of stock priced at $50 per share. The company splits its stock 2-for-1. There are now 200 shares of stock and each shareholder holds twice as many shares.

Stock split is not unusual in reality. In April 2012, Google proposed a 2-for-1 stock split, a plan that would double the number of outstanding shares in the company and halve its stock price. Google stock was trading at about $650 at the time, just as the company announced a 61% jump in first-quarter profit. Almost two years and with Google stock trading at $1,133 — there is a timeline for when the stock split will take effect. The split will also bring the stock price down from its lofty position north of $1,100, potentially making ownership of Google more accessible to small investors.

Answers:

II.	1	A	2	C	3	B	4	C	5	D	6	B	7	D	8	A
	9	C	10	B	11	D										
III.	1	h	2	f	3	a	4	g	5	i	6	b	7	j	8	c
	9	d	10	e												
IV.	1	F	2	M	3	C	4	O	5	L	6	A	7	J	8	I
	9	D	10	B	11	E	12	G	13	H	14	K	15	P		

知识扩展

1. 直接计入所有者权益的利得或损失

按照国际财务报告准则，利得和损失通常计入当期损益，即当期净利润。但是，有一些特殊利得和损失应当直接计入所有者权益，这些项目主要有以下几个方面。

(1) 资产重估增值。

如 IAS 16 允许一些企业采用重估法或者成本法对固定资产进行计价。如果以重估法计价，资产的增值部分直接计入所有者权益，在处置该资产时将资产重估增值转出，计入当期损益。

(2) 金融资产公允价值变动损益。

IAS 39 要求特定的金融资产以公允价值计价且变动计入其他综合收益，也就是说，将由于公允价值变动产生的利得或损失计入所有者权益，在该金融资产终止确认的时候，将累积的公允价值变动损益计入当期损益。

(3) 外币折算差额。

在编制报表时，企业可能需要对境外经营从一种货币折算为另一种货币，产生的外币折算差额不计入当期损益，直接列示为所有者权益的一个项目。只有当投资者处置其在境外经营的权益时才能计入利润表。

2. 我国股票分割与公积金转增股本的特殊情况

在我国，目前各股份公司的股票面值均为 1 元/股。在新股发行时，发行价均大大高于股票面值，使得资本公积金数倍于股本。比如，公司按 15 元/股的价格发行股票，其股本只有 1 元/股，但资本公积金却高达 14 元/股。在这种情况下，再对 1 元/股的面值进行分割也显得意义不大。因此，我国上市公司对股票分割实际上多是采用资本公积金转增股本的形式来进行。虽然，严格地说，资本公积金转增股本并不属于股票分割，但它的确起到与股票分割同样的作用，即股票数量增加的作用。所不同的是，不是分割股票面值，而是摊薄的每股资本公积。

在我国实务中，上市公司往往把资本公积金转增股本与股利分配混在一起，所谓盈利分配公告中的 10 送 2 转 3 就是如此，它表明，公司盈利分配政策为 10 股送 2 股股票股利，另外再用资本公积金转增 3 股股票。由于我国上市公司发行股票时存在大量的资本公积金，因此，在公司上市初期，不少公司均有能力大比例转增股票，以致让不少股票投资者将它视为了一种盈利分配。因此，在我国，虽然不存在对面值进行分割的股票分割情形，但是资本公积金转增股本普遍存在，二者仅仅是表现形式不同而已。

Chapter 8　Financial Statement Analysis
财务报表分析

Learning Objectives

- Under the outline of financial statement analysis 在财务报表分析大纲下
- Understand the trend analysis of financial statement 了解财务报表的趋势分析
- Understand the preparation of the common-size statement and its analysis 了解一般规模报表的编制和分析
- Understand the different categories of financial ratios and their usefulness 了解不同类别的财务比率及其有用性

 Listening Practice　听力练习

Chapter 8 English Listening.mp3

第 8 章原文翻译和答案的音频见右侧二维码。

Dictation: *Listen and complete the passage with the words or phrases according to what you've heard from the speaker.*

As a place for ___1___ retail shopping, with its 24-hour availability, a global reach, the ability to ___2___ and provide customers information and ordering, and multimedia prospects, the Web is rapidly becoming a multibillion dollar source of revenue for the world's ___3___. A number of businesses already report ___4___ success. As early as the middle of 1997, Dell Computers reported orders of a million dollars a day. By early 1999, the gain from e-commerce was millions of dollars and the stocks of the e-commerce companies were increasing rapidly. Although many so-called dotcom ___5___ disappeared in the economic shakeout of 2000, Web retailing at sites such as *Amazon.com*, *CDNow.com*, and *Compudata Online.com* continues to grow.

 Wisdom　至理名言

Give me a lever, and I will move the world. 给我一根杠杆，我能撬动世界。

Mini Case　微型案例

Before she opened her bar, Scarlett consulted with her financer, a CPA, on the amount of cash, the equipment and inventories needed to start operation. Together they worked out the budget as follows:

(1) $14,000 in cash was needed for the normal operations.

(2) Equipment such as refrigerators, hi-fi systems, coffee machines, tables and chairs, etc. might amount to $9,000.

(3) Glassware, tableware and cooking utensils might cost $2,000.

(4) Daily cost of beverages, coffee , tea, pastry, etc. may come to $1,000.

(5) They were determined to pay off their accounts payable within the credit period agreed.

(6) Monthly administrative expenses might be $2,500.

(7) Wages every month come to $6,000.

(8) They thought it was advisable to borrow from the bank so as to eliminate fund tie-up.

Is such investment budget workable? Let's look into her first month operation.

The process of financial statement analysis consists of the application of analytical techniques to financial statements in order to derive from them measurements and relationships that are significant and useful for decision making. Thus, financial statement analysis, first and foremost, serves the essential function of converting data into useful information.

There are numerous methods for financial analysis, and we will introduce three of them: trend analysis, common-size statement analysis and ratio analysis.

8.1   An Introduction to Financial Statement Analysis
财务报表分析概述

A conversation between A—an accountant and S—a freshman majoring in accounting.

S: What's the major objective of financial analysis?

A: The major objective is to evaluate the past performance, analyze the current financial position, and forecast opportunities and challenges of the future.

S: What are the methods of financial analysis?

A: There are numerous methods for financial analysis, and new methods keep emerging.

S: Then tell me some basic methods.

A: Basic methods may roughly fall into three categories, that is, horizontal analysis, vertical analysis, and ratio analysis. Under horizontal analysis, financial statement amounts are placed together, and percentages between one year and others are computed.

S: What about vertical analysis?

A: Each item is shown as a percentage of a base amount. For instance, on the income statement, the sales revenue is assumed to be 100%, and then a calculation is made of the percentages of the cost of goods sold, net income and other items to the sales revenue.

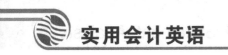

 An Outline of Financial Statement Analysis

Financial statement analysis is the process of understanding the risk and profitability of a firm through analysis of reported financial information, by using different accounting tools and techniques. One purpose of financial statement analysis is to use the past performance of a company to predict its future profitability and cash flows. Another purpose of financial statement analysis is to evaluate the performance of a company with an eye toward identifying problem areas. [1] Financial statement analysis is the foundation for evaluating and pricing credit risk and for doing fundamental company valuation.

Financial statement analysis consists of (1) **reformulating** reported financial statements, (2) analysis and adjustments of measurement errors, and (3) financial analysis on the basis of reformulated and adjusted financial statements. The first two steps are often dropped in practice, meaning that financial analysis is just calculated on the basis of the reported numbers, perhaps with some adjustments.[2]

(1) Financial statement analysis typically starts with reformulating the reported financial information. In relation to the income statement, one common reformulation is to divide reported items into **recurring** or normal items and **non-recurring** or **extraordinary** items. In this way, earnings could be divided into normal or core earnings and **transitory** earnings. The idea is that normal earnings are more permanent and hence more relevant for prediction and valuation. Normal earnings are also divided into net operational profit after taxes and net financial costs. The balance sheet is grouped in net operating assets, net financial debt and equity. [3]

(2) Analysis and adjustment of measurement errors question the quality of the reported accounting numbers.[4] The financial reporting system is not perfect. Economic events and accounting entries do not correspond precisely; they **diverge** across the dimensions of timing, recognition, and measurement. Financial analysis and investment decisions are further complicated by variations in accounting treatment among countries in each of these dimensions. For example, long-lived assets are **written down**, most of the time, in the fiscal period of management's choice. The period of recognition may be neither the period in which the impairment took place nor the period of sale or disposal. Another example is to adjust the reported numbers when the analyst suspects earnings management.

(3) Financial analysis should be based on regrouped and adjusted financial statements. In respect of the quantitative data presented in the financial statements, three techniques used widely to assist decision makers in understanding the external statements are: **trend analysis**, **common-size statement** analysis, and **ratio analysis**. [5] We will briefly introduce the first two method, and the focus of this chapter will be on how ratio analysis help information users interpret and evaluate the data contained in financial statements.

 Trend Analysis

Trend analysis, also known as **horizontal** analysis, is a financial statement analysis technique that shows changes in the amounts of corresponding financial statement items over a period of time. [6] It is a useful tool to evaluate the trend situations. When financial data are available for 3 or more years, trend analysis is a technique commonly used by financial analysts to assess the company's growth prospects. In this analysis, the earliest period is the base period, with all subsequent periods compared with the base.

For example, assume that revenue and cost of goods sold were reported for the 5 years as shown in Table 8-1.

Table 8-1　An Illustration of Trend and Common-size Statement Analysis

	2009	2010	2011	2012	2013
As reported (in $ thousands)					
Revenue	10,021	9,864	10,739	12,677	16,133
Cost of goods sold	2,164	1,695	1,776	2,094	2,528
Gross profit	7,857	8,169	8,963	10,583	13,605
As percentage of 2009 level(trend analysis)					
Revenue	100	99	107	127	161
Cost of goods sold	100	78	82	97	117
Gross profit	100	104	114	135	173
As percentage of revenue(common-size statement analysis)					
Revenue	100	100	100	100	100
Cost of goods sold	22	17	17	17	16
Gross profit	78	83	83	83	84

A base year is selected, 2009 in this case, and the data for all subsequent years are shown as a percentage of base-year data. Relative to 2009, cost of goods sold increased by only 17%, whereas revenue increased by 61% and gross profit increased 73%. It is possible that the company's selling prices are increasing faster than cost of goods sold or the increased gross profit is primarily due to efficiencies in cost of goods sold.

Trend analysis does not fully disclose the weaknesses or strengths of a company. The main purposes of trend analysis are: (1) to see the trend of various income statement and balance sheet figures of a company, (2) to evaluate whether the management is achieving its objectives or not, (3) to investigate unexpected increases or decreases in financial statement items, and (4) to evaluate overall performance of the company.

Common-Size Statement Analysis

Common-size statement analysis, also called **vertical** statement analysis, is one technique that financial managers use to analyze the financial statements. Common-size financial statements usually involve the balance sheet and the income statement. These two financial statements become "common-size" when their amounts are expressed in percentages.

For example, a common-size balance sheet will report all of the balance sheet amounts as a percentage of the total assets amount. If cash was $80,000 and total assets were $1,000,000 then cash will appear as 8% and total assets will appear as 100%.

A common-size income statement will show all of the income statement amounts as a percentage of revenue. In Table 8-1, revenue in 2013 was $16,133,000 and the cost of goods sold was $2,528,000, the common-size income statement would report net sales as 100% and the cost of goods sold as 16%. As a percentage of revenue, cost of goods sold decreased from 22% of revenue in 2009 to 15% of revenue in 2013. This statement confirms our previous findings, and it also indicates that the company might employ a **high-margin** strategy to generate profits.

Common-size statement allows for easy analysis between companies or between time periods of a company. The common size statement can also be a helpful tool in comparing the financial structures and operation strategies of two different companies. <u>The use of percentages in the common-size statements removes the issue of which company generates more revenue, and brings the focus on how the revenue is utilized within each of the two businesses.</u> [7] Often, the use of a common-size statement in this manner can help to identify areas where each company is utilizing resources efficiently, as well as areas where there is room for improvement.

Vocabulary

financial statement analysis	财务报表分析
reformulate	*vt.* 再用形式表示，重新表述，重新制定
recurring	*adj.* 循环的；经常的，复发的
non-recurring	*adj.* 不重现的，非经常性的
extraordinary	*adj.* 非常的；非凡的，特别的；意外的
transitory	*adj.* 不持续的；短暂的，转瞬即逝的
diverge	*vi.* 分开，叉开；分歧；偏离，背离 & *vt.* 使发散
write down	减低账面价值；写下；记下
trend analysis	趋势分析
common-size statement	共同比报表
ratio analysis	比率分析
horizontal	*adj.* 水平的，卧式的 & *n.* 水平线；水平面
vertical	*adj.* 垂直的，竖立的 & *n.* 垂直线，垂直面
high-margin	*n.* 高利润率

Notes

[1] Another purpose of financial statement analysis is to evaluate the performance of a company with an eye toward identifying problem areas. 　财务报表分析的另一个目的是透过问题的表象评价公司的业绩。

[2] The first two steps are often dropped in practice, meaning that financial analysis is just calculated on the basis of the reported numbers, perhaps with some adjustments. 　前两个步骤在

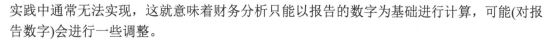

实践中通常无法实现，这就意味着财务分析只能以报告的数字为基础进行计算，可能(对报告数字)会进行一些调整。

[3] Normal earnings are also divided into net operational profit after taxes and net financial costs. The balance sheet is grouped in net operating assets, net financial debt and equity.　正常收益也可划分为税后净经营利润和净财务成本。资产负债表可分组为经营净资产、净财务负债和权益。

[4] Analysis and adjustment of measurement errors question the quality of the reported accounting numbers.　计量错误的分析和调整是指要对会计报告中的数字持怀疑态度。

[5] In respect of the quantitative data presented in the financial statements, three techniques used widely to assist decision makers in understanding the external statements are: trend analysis, common-size statement analysis, and ratio analysis.　就列示在财务报表中的定量性数据而言，广泛地用于帮助决策者理解对外财务报表的三种方法是：趋势分析、共同比报表分析以及比率分析。

[6] Trend analysis, also known as horizontal analysis, is a financial statement analysis technique that shows changes in the amounts of corresponding financial statement items over a period of time.　趋势分析，也称水平分析，是利用一段时期内相应财务报表事项金额的变化对财务报表进行分析的方法。

[7] The use of percentages in the common-size statements removes the issue of which company generates more revenue, and brings the focus on how the revenue is utilized within each of the two businesses.　共同比报表中百分比的使用，使关注点发生转移，从关注哪个公司创造了更多的收入，变为关注两个公司对于收入的使用。

8.2   Financial Ratio
财务比率

A conversation between A—an accountant and S—a freshman majoring in accounting.

S: We often speak of the company's solvency. Could you explain it to me?

A: Solvency refers to the company's ability to pay debts to the creditors. The degree of solvency directly affects the survival and development of the company. Therefore, accountants should pay close attention to relative indicators.

S: Relative indicators are a series of ratios, aren't they?

A: Yes. The major indicators for evaluating the company's short term solvency include current ratio, quick ration and so on. The major indicators for evaluating the company's long-term solvency include debt ratio and times interest earned.

S: Is current ratio relevant to current assets or current liabilities?

A: Yes. The computation of current ratio is to divide current assets by current liabilities. It's the most common ratio used to evaluate a company's liquidity and short-term debt paying ability.

S: The higher the ratio is, the better. Right?

A: Not exactly. This ratio measures the margin of safety provided by the liquid resources relative to obligations rather than expected cash flows. Poor receivables or inventory turnover limit the usefulness of the current ratio.

Financial ratios are used to compare the risk and return of different companies in order to help equity investors and creditors make intelligent investment and credit decisions. They convert huge amount of data into workable form, thus making the information more meaningful. However, we should emphasize that a ratio in **isolation** means very little. Its utility comes from comparing it to some standards. The standards could be the same ratio for prior periods, an industry average, or some other benchmark. [1]

It is important to note that the ratios presented here and their modes of calculation are neither **exhaustive** nor uniquely "correct". The definition of many ratios is not standardized and may vary from analyst to analyst, textbook to textbook, and annual report to annual report. The analyst's primary focus should be the relationships indicated by the ratios, not the details of their calculation.

Generally, there are four broad ratio categories that measure the different aspects of risk and return relationships:

(1) **Activity analysis**: evaluates revenue and output generated by the company's assets.

(2) **Liquidity analysis**: measures the adequacy of a firm's cash resources to meet its near-term cash obligations.

(3) Long-term debt and **solvency analysis**: examines the company's capital structure, including the mix of its financing sources and the ability of the firm to satisfy its longer term debt and investment obligations.

(4) **Profitability analysis**: measures the income of the firm relative to its revenues and invested capital.

Activity Analysis

Activity ratios, also known as **turnover ratios**, can help one evaluate how well a firm is managing and controlling its assets. They can also **aid** one in estimating the amount of capital necessary to generate sales.

(1) **Total Asset Turnover**

The total asset turnover ratio helps the analyst appraise the overall efficiency of asset employment and the level of **capital intensity**. It is computed as follows:

$$\text{Total asset turnover} = \frac{\text{Sales revenue}}{\text{Average total assets}}$$

The higher the ratio, the more efficient in managing and controlling assets.

(2) **Accounts Receivable Turnover**

This turnover ratio helps one judge if a change in receivable turnover is due to a change in sales or to something else such as a lengthening of the time it takes customers to pay. [2] It is computed as follows:

$$\text{Accounts receivable} = \frac{\text{Sales revenue}}{\text{Average accounts receivable}}$$

Analysts can compare this turnover ratio of different periods, decease in this ratio indicates that receivables have increased at a greater rate than sales, implying either that customers are taking longer to pay or a company is granting longer credit terms.

(3) Inventory Turnover

The inventory turnover ratio helps judge how well inventory is controlled and managed. It assists one in evaluating whether a change in inventory is due to a change in sales or to some other factor such as slowdown in the time it takes for the firm to produce and sell its inventory. [3] It is derived as follows:

$$\text{Inventory turnover} = \frac{\text{Costs of goods sold}}{\text{Average inventory}}$$

If there is a decline of inventory turnover ratio, it could be a signal of purchasing problems or even worse, obsolete inventory.

Liquidity Analysis

Ratios in this category are designed to assist one in judging if a firm can pay its current liabilities when due.

(1) Current Ratio

Current ratio is widely used to test a firm's ability to meet its short-term obligation. It is computed as follows:

$$\text{Current ratio} = \frac{\text{Current assets}}{\text{Current liabilities}}$$

Generally speaking, the higher the ratio, the greater ability of a firm pays off its current liabilities. A widely used rule of thumb is that a firm with a current ratio of 2 or more is in good shape in terms of being able to pay maturing current liabilities. [4] Most experienced analysts realize this rule may be misleading.

(2) Quick Ratio

The quick ratio is designed to provide a more **rigorous** test than the current ratio of a firm's ability to pay its current liabilities on time. It does this by excluding relatively illiquid current assets from the **numerator** as shown below:

$$\text{Quick ratio} = \frac{\text{Cash} + \text{marketable securities} + \text{Accounts receivable}}{\text{Current liabilities}}$$

Long-Term Debt and Solvency Analysis

These ratios provide insight into the extent to which a firm is relying on debt financing. They can also aid one in judging a firm's ability to raise additional debt and its capacity to pay its long-term debt on time.

(1) Debt to Assets Ratio

This ratio is derived in the following manner:

$$\text{Debt to assets ratio} = \frac{\text{Total liabilities}}{\text{Total assets}}$$

The higher the ratio, the greater risk will be associated with the firm's operation. In addition, high debt to assets ratio may indicate low borrowing capacity of a firm, which in turn will lower the firm's financial flexibility.

(2) Capitalization Ratio

The capitalization ratio focuses on long-term debt usage. It is calculated as follows:

$$\text{Capitalization ratio} = \frac{\text{Long-term debt}}{\text{Long-term debt} + \text{Owners' equity}}$$

Many analysts calculate both debt to assets ratio and capitalization ratio, because together they can help isolate the source of change in debt usage. [5] For example, if a firm financed the purchase of a building with short-term debt, the debt to assets ratio would be affected but not the capitalization ratio. It is dangerous to finance permanent needs like a building with temporary source of funds like a short-term bank loan.

(3) Debt to Equity Ratio

The debt to equity ratio is derived as follows:

$$\text{Debt to equity ratio} = \frac{\text{Total debt}}{\text{Total equity}}$$

This ratio can be derived from the debt to assets ratio and provides essentially the same information.

(4) Interest Coverage Ratio

The interest coverage ratio also known as **times interest earned** is designed to help one evaluate a firm's capacity to meet interest payments. It is calculated as follows:

$$\text{Interest coverage ratio} = \frac{\text{Earnings before interests and taxes}}{\text{Interest expense}}$$

The higher the ratio is, the greater ability of a firm uses its earnings to pay its interest in a regular manner.

Profitability Analysis

Ratios in this category can assist one in appraising management's ability to control expenses and to earn a return on the resources committed to the business.

(1) Return on Assets

Return on assets is derived as follows:

$$\text{Return on assets} = \frac{\text{Net income}}{\text{Average total assets}}$$

Return on assets reflects the combined effects of cost control and asset utilization. A high

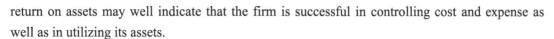
return on assets may well indicate that the firm is successful in controlling cost and expense as well as in utilizing its assets.

(2) **Return on Equity**

This ratio is regarded as a fundamental test of profitability. It relates income to the investment that was committed by the owners to earn the income. It is computed as follows:

$$\text{Return on equity} = \frac{\text{Net income}}{\text{Average owners' equity}}$$

This ratio is particularly useful measure of profitability from the viewpoint of the owners because it relates the two fundamental factors in any investment situation—the amount of the owners' investment and the return earned for the owners on that investment.

(3) **Profit Margin**

This ratio is based on two income statement amounts. It is computed as follows:

$$\text{Profit margin} = \frac{\text{Net income}}{\text{Sales revenue}}$$

This profitability test is simply the percentage of each sales dollar, on average, that represents profit. <u>Care must be exercised in analyzing the profit margin because it does not take into account the amount of resources employed (i.e. total investment) to produce the income.</u>[6]

(4) **Earnings Per Share (EPS)**

EPS are probably the most widely available and commonly used corporate performance statistic for listed companies. This ratio evaluates profitability strictly from the common shareholders' point of view. Rather than based on the dollar amount of the investment, it is based on the number of shares of common stock outstanding. EPS on common shares is computed as follows:

$$\text{Earnings per share} = \frac{\text{Net income}}{\text{Average number of shares of stock outstanding}}$$

 Vocabulary

isolation	*n.* 隔离；隔离状态；孤独；孤立状态
exhaustive	*adj.* 彻底的，透彻的；消耗的，使枯竭的；详尽的
activity analysis	活动分析，活性分析，业务活动分析
liquidity analysis	流动性分析
solvency analysis	偿债能力分析
profitability analysis	盈利能力分析
turnover ratio	周转率
aid	*vt. & vi. & n.* 帮助；资助；救助；促进
total asset turnover	总资产周转率
capital intensity	资本强度，资本集约度，资本应用的密度
accounts receivable turnover	应收账款周转率
inventory turnover	存货周转率

current ratio	流动比率
quick ratio	速动比率
rigorous	*adj.* 严密的；缜密的；严格的
numerator	*n.* (分数的)分子
debt to assets ratio	资产负债率，负债对资产比率
capitalization ratio	长期资本负债率，资本结构比率
debt to equity ratio	产权比率，债务股本比
interest coverage ratio	利息保障比率，利息保障倍数
times interest earned	利息保障倍数
return on assets	资产报酬率
return on equity	股本回报率，产权收益率，产权报酬率，净资产报酬率
profit margin	利润率
earnings per share	每股收益

Notes

[1] The standards could be the same ratio for prior periods, an industry average, or some other benchmark.　这些标准可以是前期相同比率、行业平均水平或是其他基准。

[2] This turnover ratio helps one judge if a change in receivable turnover is due to a change in sales or to something else such as a lengthening of the time it takes customers to pay.　这一周转率有助于判断应收账款周转的变化是源于销货收入的变化还是源于诸如顾客延缓付款等其他原因。

[3] It assists one in evaluating whether a change in inventory is due to a change in sales or to some other factor such as slowdown in the time it takes for the firm to produce and sell its inventory.　它可以帮助人们评价存货的变动是源于销货收入的变化，还是源于诸如企业生产和销售存货的速度放慢等其他原因。

[4] A widely used rule of thumb is that a firm with a current ratio of 2 or more is in good shape in terms of being able to pay maturing current liabilities.　通常采用的经验法则是，流动比率为 2 或更高时，意味着企业在支付到期流动负债方面处于良好状态。

[5] Many analysts calculate both debt to assets ratio and capitalization ratio, because together they can help isolate the source of change in debt usage.　许多分析者既计算资产负债率，也计算长期资本负债率，因为将这两者结合应用有助于识别出举债来源的变化。

[6] Care must be exercised in analyzing the profit margin because it does not take into account the amount of resources employed (i.e. total investment) to produce the income.　分析利润率时必须谨慎，因为这一比率没有考虑创造收益所使用的资源(即投资总额)。

Exercises

I. Discuss the following questions in English.

1. What is the purpose of financial statement analysis?
2. What are various tools used to analyze financial statement?
3. What does trend analysis mean?
4. How are items in common-size statements presented in a financial statement?
5. Why is a common size statement useful tool in financial performance evaluation?
6. How do we calculate the inventory turnover ratio? Why shall we use the average amount of the inventory rather than the end balance?
7. What is the difference between the current ratio and the quick ratio?
8. What does the interest cover ratio mean? And why is it categorized into long-term debt and solvency ratios?
9. What are the main variables that affect the profit margin?
10. What do we mean when we say earning per share valuates profitability strictly from the common shareholders' point of view?

II. Choose the best word or phrase that fits the sentence.

1. One purpose of financial statement analysis is to use the _____ of a company to predict its future profitability and cash flows.
    A. balance sheet   B. income statement
    C. past performance   D. statement of cash flow
2. Earnings could be divided into normal or core earnings and _____ earnings.
    A. terminal   B. temporary
    C. transferred   D. transitory
3. Economic events and accounting entries do not correspond precisely, and they may diverge across the _____ of timing, recognition, and measurement.
    A. definitions   B. dimensions
    C. difference   D. discussions
4. Trend analysis, also known as _____ analysis, is a financial statement analysis technique that shows changes in the amounts of corresponding financial statement items over a period of time.
    A. horizontal   B. vertical
    C. even   D. level
5. A common-size income statement will show all of the income statement amounts as a percentage of _____.
    A. net income   B. operating profit
    C. revenue   D. cost of goods sold

6. The definition of many ratios is not standardized and may _____ from analyst to analyst, textbook to textbook, and annual report to annual report.

    A. vary   B. change

    C. alter   D. shift

7. The total asset turnover ratio helps the analyst appraise the overall efficiency of asset employment and the level of _____.

    A. financial leverage   B. capital intensity

    C. financial flexibility   D. capital structure

8. If there is a decline of inventory turnover ratio, it could be a signal of purchasing problems or even worse, _____ inventory.

    A. stock   B. substantial

    C. obsolete   D. defective

9. The quick ratio is designed to provide a more _____ test than the current ratio of a firm's ability to pay its current liabilities on time.

    A. strict   B. rigorous

    C. rigid   D. hard

10. The interest coverage ratio, also known as _____, is designed to help one evaluate a firm's capacity to meet interest payments.

    A.time interest coverage   B. interest earned ratio

    C. interest earned times   D. times interest earned

11. _____ is probably the most widely available and commonly used corporate performance statistic for listed companies.

    A. Earnings per share   B. Return on equity

    C. Return on assets   D. Profit margin

III. Match each word on the left with its corresponding meaning on the right.

A	B
1. margin	(a) the relative magnitudes of two quantities
2. isolation	(b) the extent to which something is covered
3. exhaustive	(c) parallel to or in the place of the horizon or a base line
4. diverge	(d) very thorough
5. vertical	(e) the net sales minus the cost of goods and services sold
6. turnover	(f) the ability to meet maturing obligations as they come due
7. ratio	(g) be at variance with
8. horizontal	(h) the ratio of the number of workers that had to be replaced in a given time period to the average number of workers
9. coverage	(i) upright in position or posture
10. solvency	(j) a state of separation between persons or groups

IV. Fill in the blanks with words or phrases from the list below.

A.	distort	B.	leverage	C.	dissect	D.	substitute
E.	identity	F.	mitigate	G.	down	H.	generate
I.	unsatisfactory	J.	created	K.	more	L.	course
M.	net	N.	perform	O.	incremental	P.	turnover

DuPont analysis examines the return on equity (ROE) analyzing profit margin, total asset turnover, and financial leverage. It was (1)＿＿ by the DuPont Corporation in the 1920s.

The DuPont analysis is also referred to as the DuPont (2)＿＿.

In a DuPont analysis, the formula for ROE is:

ROE = Profit margin × Total asset turnover × Equity multiplier

The formula breaks (3)＿＿ further to:

$$ROE = \frac{Net\ income}{Revenue} \times \frac{Revenue}{Total\ assets} \times \frac{Total\ assets}{Equity}$$

DuPont model tells that ROE is affected by three things:

- Operating efficiency, which is measured by (4)＿＿ profit margin;
- Asset use efficiency, which is measured by total asset (5)＿＿;
- Financial (6)＿＿, which is measured by the equity multiplier.

If ROE is (7)＿＿, the DuPont analysis helps locate the part of the business that is underperforming.

The method goes beyond profit margin to understand how efficiently a company's assets (8)＿＿ sales or cash and how well a company uses debt to produce (9)＿＿ returns.

Using these three factors, a DuPont analysis allows analysts to (10)＿＿ a company, efficiently determine where the company is weak and strong and quickly know what areas of the business to look at (i.e., inventory management, debt structure, margins) for (11)＿＿ answers. The measure is still broad, however, and is not a (12)＿＿ for detailed analysis.

The DuPont analysis looks uses both the income statement as well as the balance sheet to (13)＿＿ the examination. As a result, major asset purchases, acquisitions, or other significant changes can (14)＿＿ the ROE calculation. Many analysts use average assets and shareholders' equity to (15)＿＿ this distortion, although that approach assumes the balance sheet changes occurred steadily over the (16)＿＿ of the year, which may not be accurate either.

V. Translate the following sentences into Chinese.

1. Financial statement analysis compares ratios and trends calculated from data found on financial statements.

2. The study of percentage changes from year to year is called horizontal analysis.

3. By having all of the balance sheet and income statement amounts as a percentage, we can compare the company's percentage to the industry's, to any other company's, or to different periods of itself.

4.   A primary advantage of ratios is that they can be used to compare the risk and return relationships of companies of different sizes.

5.   Activity ratios describe the relationship between the firms' level of operation and the assets needed to sustain operating activities.

6.   Short-term lenders and creditors must assess the ability of a firm to meet its current obligations.

7.   The analysis of a firm's capital structure is essential to evaluate its long-term risk and return prospects.

8.   Profitability can be measured in several differing but interrelated dimensions.

VI. Translate the following sentences into English.

1.   财务报表分析是以企业基本活动为对象、以财务报表为主要信息来源、以分析和综合为主要方法的系统认识企业的过程，其目的是了解过去、评价现在和预测未来，以帮助报表使用者改善决策。

2.   趋势分析就是分析期与前期或连续数期项目金额的对比，这种对财务报表项目纵向比较分析的方法是一种动态的分析。

3.   财务比率是用倍数或比例表示的分数式，它反映各会计要素的相互关系和内在联系，代表了企业某一方面的特征、属性或能力。

4.   共同比报表是用百分率表示某一报表项目的内部结构，它反映该项目内各组成部分的比例关系，代表了企业某一方面的特征、属性或能力。

5.   一般说来，销售增加会拉动应收账款、存货、应付账款增加，不会引起周转率的明显变化。

6.   由于债务按到期时间分为短期债务和长期债务，所以偿债能力分析分为流动性分析和长期偿债能力分析两部分。

7.   资产负债率反映总资产中有多大比例是通过负债取得的，它可以衡量对企业在清算时保护债权人利益的程度。

8.   资产报酬率是指净利润与总资产的比率，它反映公司从 1 元资产中得到的净利润。

Reading Material 8

Red Flags in Financial Statement Analysis

Red flag is an indicator of potential problems with a security. Most often used to refer to a stock, a red flag can be any undesirable characteristic that stands out to an analyst. There is no universal standard for identifying red flags is the method used will depend on the investment methodology being employed.

A red flag is anything that marks a stock as undesirable. Because there are many different methods used to pick stocks, there are many different types of red flags. What is a red flag for one person might even be considered desirable by another?

The red flags, in no particular order, are:

(1) A several-year trend of declining revenues.

While a company can improve profitability by eliminating wasteful spending, cutting unnecessary headcount, improving inventory management, and so forth, long-term growth is dependent on sales growth. A company with 3 or more consecutive years of declining revenues is a questionable investment—any cost efficiencies can usually be realized over that period of time. More often, declining revenue is an indicative of a declining business—rarely a good investment.

(2) A several-year trend of declining gross, operating, net, and/or free cash flow margins.

Declining margins may indicate that a company is becoming bloated, or that management is chasing growth at the expense of profitability. A declining macro-economic picture or a cyclical company can lower margins without indicating any intrinsic decline in operations. If you can't reasonably attribute margin weakness to outside factors, beware.

(3) Excessively rising outstanding share count.

Watch out for companies whose share count consistently raises more than 2%~3% per year. This indicates that management is giving away the company and diluting your stake through options or secondary stock offerings. The best case here is to see share count declining 1%~2% per year, showing that management is buying back stock and increasing your stake in the enterprise.

(4) Rising debt-to-equity and/or falling interest coverage ratios.

Both of these are an indication that the company is taking on more debt than its operations can handle. Although there are few hard targets in investing, take a closer look if debt-to-equity is over 100% or interest coverage ratio is 5 or less. Take an even closer look if this red flag is accompanied by falling sales and/or falling margins. If so, this stock may not be in very good financial health.

(5) Rising accounts receivable and/or inventories, as a percentage of sales.

The purpose of a business is to generate cash from assets. When accounts receivable are rising faster than sales, it indicates that customers are taking longer to give you cash for products. When inventories rise faster than sales, it indicates that your business is producing products faster than they can be sold. In both cases, cash is tied up in places where it cannot generate a return. This red flag can indicate poor supply chain management, poor demand forecasting, and too loose credit terms for customers. As with most of these red flags, look for this phenomenon over a several year period, as short-term issues are sometimes due to uncontrollable market factors (like today).

(6) Free cash to earnings ratios consistently under 100%.

This is closely related to the above red flag. If free cash flow is consistently coming in under reported earnings, some serious investigation is needed. Usually, rising accounts receivable or inventory is the culprit. However, this red flag can also be indicative of accounting tricks such as capitalizing purchases instead of expensing them, which artificially inflates the income statement net profit number. Remember, only the cash flow statement shows you discrete cash

values—everything else is subject to accounting "assumptions".

(7) Very large "other" line items on the income statement or balance sheet.

These include "other expenses" on the income statement, and "other assets"/"other liabilities" on the balance sheet. Most firms have these, but the value given to them is small enough to not be a concern. However, if these line items are significant as a percentage of total business, dig deep to find out what's included. Are the expenses likely to recur? Is any part of these "other" items shady, such as related party deals or non-business related items? Large "other" items can be a sign of management trying to hide things from investors. We want transparency, not shadiness.

(8) Lots of non-operating or one-time charges on the income statement.

Good companies have very easy to understand financial statements. On the other hand, firms that are trying to play tricks or hide problems often bury charges in the aforementioned "other" categories, or add numerous line items for things like "restructuring", "asset impairment", "goodwill impairment", and so forth. A several year pattern of these "one-time" charges is a concern. Management will tout their improving non-GAAP, results—but in truth there has been little improvement. These charges are a way of confusing investors and trying to make things look better than they are. Watch the cash flow statement instead.

(9) Current ratio under 100%, especially for cyclical companies.

This is another financial health measure, calculated as (current assets/current liabilities). This measures a company's liquidity, or their ability to meet their obligations over the next 12 months. A current ratio under 100% is not a huge concern for firms that have a stable business and generate lots of cash. But for very cyclical companies that could see 25% of their revenues disappear in one year, it's a huge concern. Cyclical + low current ratio = recipe for disaster.

Answers:

II.	1	C	2	D	3	B	4	A	5	C	6	A	7	B	8	C
	9	B	10	D	11	A										
III.	1	e	2	j	3	d	4	g	5	i	6	h	7	a	8	c
	9	b	10	f												
IV.	1	J	2	E	3	G	4	M	5	P	6	B	7	I	8	H
	9	O	10	C	11	K	12	D	13	N	14	A	15	F	16	L

 知识扩展

在财务报表分析中常用的比率

1. 反映偿债能力的财务比率

(1) 短期偿债能力。短期偿债能力是指企业偿还短期债务的能力。一般来说, 企业应该

以流动资产偿还流动负债，所以用流动资产与流动负债的数量关系来衡量短期偿债能力。比率高一般表明企业短期偿债能力较强。常用比率有：

$$流动比率=流动资产/流动负债$$

$$速动比率=(流动资产-存货-待摊费用)/流动负债$$

$$现金比率=(现金+有价证券)/流动负债$$

(2) 长期偿债能力。长期偿债能力是指企业偿还长期利息与本金的能力。通常以负债比率和利息保障倍数两项指标衡量企业的长期偿债能力。负债比率越高，债权人所受的保障就越低。利息保障倍数考察企业的营业利润是否足以支付当年的利息费用，它从企业经营活动的获利能力方面分析其长期偿债能力。

$$负债比率=负债总额/资产总额$$

$$利息保障倍数=经营净利润/利息费用$$

$$=(净利润+所得税+利息费用)/利息费用$$

2. 反映营运效率的财务比率

营运效率是以企业各项资产的周转速度来衡量企业资产利用的效率。周转速度越快，表明企业的各项资产进入生产、销售等经营环节的速度越快，其形成收入和利润的周期就越短，经营效率越高。常用比率有：

$$应收账款周转率=赊销收入净额/应收账款平均余额$$

$$存货周转率=销售成本/存货平均余额$$

$$流动资产周转率=销售收入净额/流动资产平均余额$$

$$固定资产周转率=销售收入净额/固定资产平均净值$$

$$总资产周转率=销售收入净额/总资产平均值$$

3. 反映盈利能力的财务比率

盈利能力是各方面关心的核心，也是企业成败的关键，只有长期盈利，企业才能真正做到持续经营。常用比率有：

$$毛利率=(销售收入-成本)/销售收入$$

$$营业利润率=营业利润/销售收入=(净利润+所得税+利息费用)/销售收入$$

$$净利润率=净利润/销售收入$$

$$总资产报酬率=净利润/总资产平均值$$

$$权益报酬率=净利润/权益平均值$$

$$每股收益=净利润/流通股总股份$$

Chapter 9　Management Accounting
管理会计

Learning Objectives

- Understand the definition of management accounting 理解管理会计的定义
- Compare management accounting with financial accounting and cost accounting 管理会计与财务会计、成本会计的比较
- Understand different types of costs, such as manufacturing costs and non-manufacturing costs, product costs and period costs, direct costs and indirect costs, and varialble costs and fixed costs 了解不同类型的成本，如制造成本和非制造成本，产品成本和期间成本，直接成本和间接成本，可变成本和固定成本
- Understand some cost concepts relating to decision making 理解与决策相关的成本概念
- Understand cost-volume-profit analysis 了解成本－数量－利润分析
- Determine the break-even point 确定收支平衡点
- Understand the margin of safety 了解安全边际
- Understand the definition of budget 理解预算的定义
- Understand master budget and capital budget 了解总预算和资本预算
- Understand fixed and flexible budgets 理解固定预算和灵活预算
- Understand zero-based budget 了解从零开始的预算

 Listening Practice　听力练习

第 9 章听写原文翻译和答案的音频见右侧二维码。

Chapter 9 English Listening.mp3

Dictation: *Listen and complete the passage with the words or phrases according to what you've heard from the speaker.*

We have seen many of the start-ups coming over from the initial states. And actually I think that the market place is going to ____1____ fundamentally towards the more traditional ____2____. They now have the benefit of all of the ____3____ that those have learnt. There have been many articles about it. The ____4____ who once worked for these companies are no longer involved in those organizations. They are working in the ____5____ companies as these companies have made a policy of recruiting these people to assist and advise them in the launch of their own initiatives.

至理名言

> You, academician, worry about making good decisions. In business, we also worry about making decisions good. 你，院士，要考虑做出正确的决定。在商业中，我们也担心如何做出正确的决定。

微型案例

Do you remember the anxiety you felt in school on report card day? You had planned to make straight A's, but your report card contained a B in one subject and a C in another. What happened? You probably evaluated reasons for the difference and made changes so that your grade expectations for the next report card stood a greater chance of being met. Businesses also have report cards in the form of performance reports. Managers prepare budget describing the expected performance for a period. At the end of the period, actual performance is compared against the budgets, and any variance is explained. Then, corrective action is taken. When a company's performance report in a period is disappointing, would you shed some light on what happened and give some suggestions?

Financial accounting and management accounting are both important tools for a business, but serve different purposes. A business uses accounting to determine operational plans in the future, to review past performance and to check current business functions. Financial accounting and management accounting have different audiences, as investors are not usually involved in the day-to-day operations of the business but are concerned about their investment, whereas managers need information quickly to make daily business decisions.

Management accounting is the process of preparing management reports and accounts that provide accurate and timely financial and statistical information required by managers to make day-to-day and short-term decisions.

In this chapter, we will focus on the management accounting and its basic concepts, such as cost behaviour, cost-volume-profit analysis, budgeting and cost concepts related to decision making.

9.1 An Introduction to Management Accounting
管理会计概述

> A conversation between A—an accountant and S—a freshman majoring in accounting.
>
> S: What are the main specialized fields of accounting?

A: They are financial accounting and management accounting.

S: What is the difference between financial accounting and management accounting?

A: Financial accounting focuses on tabulating the numbers and reporting this information. Management accounting focuses on providing information for decision making.

S: Oh, I see. Is there any standard for management accounting?

A: No. Management accounting is an internal business function, so it is not required to follow any accounting standard. Management accounting can employ whatever accounting rules it finds most useful for its own purpose, without worrying about whether these conform to some outside standards.

S: Since the managerial accountant needs not to follow the up-to-date accounting standards, in comparison with financial accounting, managerial accounting is easier, isn't it?

A: Not necessarily. A management accountant need to coordinate with all concerned departments to make an overall analysis of a company's functioning capital and availability of funds, and then he or she has to report all the information to senior management and the board of directors. Is that easier?

S: Of course not.

What is Management Accounting

Management accounting or **managerial accounting** is the process of identification, measurement, accumulation, analysis, preparation and communication of financial information used by management to plan, evaluate, and control within the organization and to assure appropriate use of and accountability for its resources.[1]

Companies need management accountants to know the efficiency of their budget, the cost of their operations and then allocate funds accordingly in production, sales and investment. The role of a management accountant is thus, very crucial for a firm's well being. Their roles and responsibilities are so huge that even a single miscalculation or underestimation of any business plan by a management accountant can put a company's future in danger.

The roles of management accountants include collecting, recording and reporting financial data from several units of an organization, observe and analyze their budget and suggest their funding and allocation. This includes estimation of cost of raw material, labor, manufacturing, sales and advertising, social media networking, **lobbying** and the company's internal operation cost.

Comparison of Financial Accounting and Management Accounting

Accounting information is diversely used by both internal and external parties, and has therefore been classified into two subfields, namely financial accounting and management accounting. Unlike financial accounting, which produces annual reports mainly for external **stakeholders**, management accounting generates monthly or weekly reports for an organization's internal audiences such as department managers and the chief executive officer (CEO). [2]

In contrast to financial accountancy information, management accounting information is: (1) primarily **forward-looking**, instead of historical; (2) model based with a degree of **abstraction** to support decision making **generically**, instead of case based; (3) designed and intended for use by managers within the organization, instead of being intended for use by shareholders, creditors, and public regulators; (4) usually **confidential** and used by management, instead of publicly reported; (5) computed by reference to the needs of managers, often using management information systems, instead of by reference to general financial accounting standards.

 ## Comparison of Cost Accounting and Management Accounting

Cost accounting is an approach for evaluating the overall costs of conducting business. Its goal is to advise the management on the most appropriate course of action based on the cost efficiency and capability. Cost accounting provides the detailed cost information that management needs to control current operations and plan for the future.

Cost accounting and managerial accounting, unlike financial, are more analytical in nature and are internal accounting systems and are not usually disclosed to the public. From the point of view of practical **hierarchy**, cost accounting is considered to be a part of managerial accounting. Cost accounting can be most beneficial as a tool for management in budgeting and in setting up cost control programs, which can improve net margins for the company in the future. [3]

Practically speaking, cost accounting involves computation of cost per unit with different angles. For example, cost accounting in a **steel mill** will principally involve the computation of cost of one ton of steel. For this, a **foreman**'s salary that contributed to the production of that ton of steel is computed. The **coke**, power, workman's salary, premises and factory machinery cost, are some other items that are adding to prime costs (cost of raw material which in this case is iron and other metals). The primary responsibilities of a cost accountant include accumulating the manufacturing costs, reviewing the overhead costs, determining the total product cost for individual products and recommending cost reduction actions the company might take.

Management accounting goes one step forward and makes a further comparative analysis and statements of figures that are derived by financial accounting and costing. Other management accounting functions include the analysis of every possible transaction and projecting the trend of transactions. A management accountant should apply his or her professional knowledge and skill in the preparation and presentation of financial and other decision oriented information, in such a way as to assist management in the formulation of policies and in the planning and control of the operation of the undertaking. [4]

 ## Vocabulary

managerial accounting	管理会计
lobby	*vi.* 为了支持或抵制某项特定目标游说

stakeholder	*n.* 股东；利益相关者
forward-looking	*adj.* 有远见的，向前看的
abstraction	*n.* 抽象；出神；抽象概念；抽象化
generically	*adv.* 一般地
confidential	*adj.* 秘密的；机密的
hierarchy	*n.* 分层，层次；等级制度
steel mill	钢厂
foreman	*n.* 工头，领班，作业组长
coke	*n.* 焦炭，焦煤

Notes

[1] Management accounting or managerial accounting is the process of identification, measurement, accumulation, analysis, preparation and communication of financial information used by management to plan, evaluate, and control within the organization and to assure appropriate use of and accountability for its resources. 管理会计是确认、计量、收集、分析、编制、解释并传递财务信息的过程，用于管理层对企业组织内部的计划、评价和控制，以确保资源合理使用和计量。

[2] Unlike financial accounting, which produces annual reports mainly for external stakeholders, management accounting generates monthly or weekly reports for an organization's internal audiences such as department managers and the chief executive officer (CEO). 与主要为外部利益相关者提供年报的财务会计不同，管理会计面向组织内部使用者，如部门经理和首席执行官，每月或每周向他们提供报告。

[3] Cost accounting can be most beneficial as a tool for management in budgeting and in setting up cost control programs, which can improve net margins for the company in the future. 在管理者进行预算和制定未来可提高公司净利的成本控制计划时，成本会计是最有利的工具。

[4] A management accountant should apply his or her professional knowledge and skill in the preparation and presentation of financial and other decision oriented information, in such a way as to assist management in the formulation of policies and in the planning and control of the operation of the undertaking. 管理会计师应该运用专业知识和技能，编制并列报财务信息以及其他与决策相关信息，来帮助管理者制定政策和计划，控制企业经营。

9.2　The Classification of Costs
成本的分类

A conversation between A—an accountant and S—a freshman majoring in accounting.

S: What are the purposes of cost classification?

A: The purposes of cost classification are to be more useful for the costing of products and services, for cost control, and for a variety of other purposes.

S: Could you give me an example?

A: For budgeting purposes, as well as other forms of cost control, it is further desirable to identify costs by the types of expenses within specific departments or cost centers. Thus, the individuals at these levels of management may have this information for control purposes and be held accountable for cost performance.

S: For the purpose of preparing external financial statements, how should cost be classified?

A: Costs should be classified as period costs or product costs. Period costs are expensed in the time period in which they are incurred. All selling and administrative costs are typically considered to be period costs. Product costs are added to units of product as they are incurred and are not treated as expenses until the units are sold. This can result in a delay of one or more periods between the time in which the cost is incurred and when it appears as an expense on the income statement.

In cost or management accounting, the term cost is used in many different ways. The reason is that there are many different types of costs, and these costs are classified differently according to the immediate needs of management.

Manufacturing Costs and Non-Manufacturing Costs

Costs are associated with all types of organizations-business, non-business, service, retail, and manufacturing. Generally, the kinds of costs that are incurred and the way in which these costs are classified will depend on the types of organization involved.

Traditionally, most of the focus of cost accounting has been on **manufacturing costs** and activities. The reason is probably traceable to the complexity of manufacturing operations and to the need for carefully developed costs for pricing and other decisions.[1] However, costing techniques are now coming into use in many non-manufacturing areas, as firms attempt to get better control over their costs and to provide management with more usable cost data.

The cost of a manufactured product may be subdivided into the followings:

(1) **Direct materials**

Direct materials are the acquisition costs of all materials that are identified as part of the product cost and that may be easily traced to the product in an economically feasible way. The acquisition cost of direct materials includes delivery charges and **custom duties** but excludes minor items such as **solder** and **glue**.

(2) **Direct labor**

Direct labor is the labor cost that can be identified in an **economically feasible** way with a product. Labor of machine operators and assemblers are examples of direct labor cost.

(3) **Manufacturing overhead**

All manufacturing costs that cannot be identified with or traced to the product cost in an economically feasible way. Included within this classification one would expect to find such costs as indirect materials, indirect labor, heat and light, **property taxes**, insurance, depreciation on factory facilities, repairs, maintenance, and all other costs of operating the manufacturing division of a company. Manufacturing overhead is known by various names. Sometimes it is called manufacturing expense, factory expense, overhead, factory overhead, or factory burden. All of these terms are **synonymous** with "manufacturing overhead". [2]

Generally, non-manufacturing costs are sub-classified into two categories: **marketing or selling costs**, and **administrative costs**.

Marketing or selling costs would include all costs necessary to secure customer orders and get the finished product or service into the hands of the customer. Since marketing costs relate to contracting customers and providing for their needs, these costs are often referred to as order-getting and order-filling costs. [3] Examples of marketing costs would include advertising, shipping, sales travel, sales commissions, sales salaries, and costs associated with finished goods warehoused.

Administrative costs would include all executive, organizational, and clerical costs that cannot logically be included under either production or marketing. Examples of such costs would include executive compensation, general accounting, secretarial, public relations, and similar costs having to do with the overall, general administration of the organization as a whole. [4]

Product Costs and Period Costs

A manufacturer's **product costs** are the direct materials, direct labor, and manufacturing overhead used in making its products. The product costs are also "inventoriable" costs, since these are the necessary costs of manufacturing the products. Product costs are costs assigned to the manufacture of products and recognized for financial reporting when sold.

Period costs are not a necessary part of the manufacturing process. As a result, period costs cannot be assigned to the products or to the cost of inventory. The period costs are usually associated with the selling function of the business or its general administration. The period costs are reported as expenses in the accounting period in which they best match with revenues, when they expire, or in the current accounting period. In addition to the selling and general administrative expenses, most interest expense is a period expense.

Direct Costs and Indirect Costs

A major question regarding costs is whether the costs have a direct or an indirect relationship to a specific cost object. **Direct costs** are the costs that can be identified with or traced to a given cost object in a cost effective way. **Indirect costs** are the costs that cannot be identified with or traced to a given cost objective in a cost effective way.

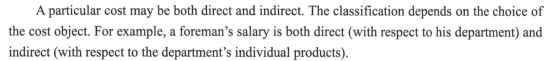

A particular cost may be both direct and indirect. The classification depends on the choice of the cost object. For example, a foreman's salary is both direct (with respect to his department) and indirect (with respect to the department's individual products).

The approach to product costing may be termed as the traditional approach. **Activity-based costing** is an approach to **product costing**—an attempt to reflect more accurately in product costs those activities which influence the level of support overheads, such as **inspection**, planning, delivery. We will discuss the activity-based costing in the reading material of this chapter.

 ## Variable Costs and Fixed Costs

From a planning and control standpoint, perhaps the most useful way to classify costs is by behavior. **Cost behavior** means how a cost will react or respond to changes in the level of business activity. As the activity level rises and falls, a particular cost may rise and fall as well or it may remain constant.

Variable costs are costs that vary, in total, in direct proportion to changes in the level of activities. <u>Although variable costs, in total, rise and fall in proportion to changes in the activity level, they remain constant if expressed on a per unit basis.</u>[5] Examples include direct materials, direct labor, sales commissions and some factory supplies.

Fixed costs are costs that remain constant, in total, regardless of changes in the level of activities. That is, unlike variable costs, fixed costs are not affected by changes in activities from period to period; however, fixed costs do not remain constant if expressed on unit basis. Consequently, as the activity level rises and falls, the fixed costs remain constant in total amount unless influenced by some outside force, such as price changes. Examples of fixed costs included depreciation, insurance, property taxes, rent, supervisory salaries and advertising.

The definition of variable variable costs and fixed costs has important underlying assumptions:

(1) The cost object must be specified (product/department);

(2) The time span must be specified (months/years);

(3) Costs are linear;

(4) All costs are neither variable or fixed;

(5) There is only one cost driver (units produced/units sold);

(6) The relevant range of cost drivers must be specified.

 ## Cost Concepts Relating to Decision Making

Costs are an important feature of many business decisions. There are several other cost concepts with which we should be familiar as we start the study of managerial accounting. These concepts are **relevant costs**, **opportunity costs**, and **sunk costs**.

(1) Relevant costs

A relevant cost (also called **differential cost**) is a cost that differs between alternatives being considered. It is often important for businesses to distinguish between relevant and irrelevant costs when analyzing alternatives, because erroneously considering irrelevant costs can lead to unsound business decisions. Also, ignoring irrelevant data in analysis can save time and effort. Non-cash items, such as depreciation and amortization, are frequently categorized as irrelevant costs, since they do not affect cash flows.

Two common types of irrelevant costs are sunk costs and **future costs** that do not differ between alternatives.

(2) Opportunity costs

In many decision making situation, managers face too many alternatives to analyze thoroughly. Because managers exclude some alternatives from further considerations, the idea of an opportunity cost arises. An opportunity cost can be defined as the potential benefit that is lost or sacrificed when the choice of one course of action requires the giving up of an alternative course of action. [6] Opportunity cost is not usually entered on the books of an organization, but it is a cost that must be considered **explicitly** in every decision that a manager makes.

Although difficult to measure, the concept is of great importance because it emphasizes that decisions are concerned with alternatives, and that the cost of the chosen action plan is the profit **foregone** from the best available alternative.

(3) Sunk costs

A sunk cost is a cost that has already been incurred and that cannot be changed by any decision made now or in the future. Because sunk costs cannot be changed by any decision, they are not relevant costs, and they should not be used in analyzing future course of action.

Vocabulary

manufacturing cost	制造成本，工厂成本，生产成本
direct material	直接材料，直接原料
custom duty	关税
solder	*n.* 焊料，焊锡
glue	*n.* 胶水；胶粘物
direct labor	直接人工
economically feasible	经济可行；经济上合算
manufacturing overhead	制造间接费，制造费用
property tax	财产税，<英>不动产税
synonymous	*adj.* 同义的，类义的；同义词的
marketing (selling) cost	销售成本
administrative cost	管理成本
product cost	产品成本
inventoriable cost	可列入存货的成本；产品成本
period cost	期间成本；当期成本
direct cost	直接成本
indirect cost	间接成本

activity based costing (ABC)	作业成本核算
product costing	产品成本计算
inspection	*n.* 检查；检验；视察；检阅
cost behavior	成本性态，成本特性，成本习性
variable cost	变动成本
fixed cost	固定成本
relevant cost	相关成本
opportunity cost	机会成本
sunk cost	沉没成本，沉淀成本
differential cost	差量成本，差别成本
future cost	未来成本，预测成本
explicitly	*adv.* 明白地，明确地
foregone	*adj.* 先前的，过去的，预知的

Notes

[1] The reason is probably traceable to the complexity of manufacturing operations and to the need for carefully developed costs for pricing and other decisions. 其原因也许可追溯到制造业务的复杂性以及定价和其他决策对精确计算成本的需求。

[2] Sometimes it is called manufacturing expense, factory expense, overhead, factory overhead, or factory burden. All of these terms are synonymous with "manufacturing overhead". 有时被称作制造费用、工厂费用、间接费用、工厂间接费用，或工厂负荷。所有这些术语都与"制造间接费"意思相同。

[3] Since marketing costs relate to contracting customers and providing for their needs, these costs are often referred to as order-getting and order-filling costs. 由于营销成本与同客户签约以及满足其需求有关，这些成本往往也被称作订货取得成本或订货供应成本。

[4] Examples of such costs would include executive compensation, general accounting, secretarial, public relations, and similar costs having to do with the overall, general administration of the organization as a whole. 这类成本的例子包括经理人员酬金，通用会计、秘书、公关以及与整个组织的总体和一般管理有关的类似成本。

[5] Although variable costs, in total, rise and fall in proportion to changes in the activity level, they remain constant if expressed on a per unit basis. 虽然变动成本在总额上与作业量的变化成比例地上升或下降，但若表述为单位成本，它们则保持不变。

[6] An opportunity cost can be defined as the potential benefit that is lost or sacrificed when the choice of one course of action requires the giving up of an alternative course of action. 机会成本可定义为：因选择一个行动方案而放弃另一个行动方案时所丧失或牺牲的潜在利益。

实用会计英语

9.3 Cost-Volume-Profit Analysis
本量利分析

A conversation between A—an accountant and S—a freshman majoring in accounting.

S: Have you heard of CVP analysis? What does it mean?

A: It's the abbreviation for cost-volume-profit analysis. CVP analysis examines the behavior of total revenues, total costs, and profits as changes occur in the output level, selling price, variable costs per unit, and fixed costs of a product. In CVP analysis, we are looking at the effect of three variables on one variable—profit.

S: So the three variables are fixed costs, variable costs and sales volume, right?

A: Right. The profit is equal to the difference between total revenues and total costs. And if the profit is zero, it is said that the break-even point is reached.

S: What is break-even point?

A: The break-even point is a term used in business and accounting. It is the point when a company makes enough profit that they have no losses at all. CVP analysis can be used in many situations in a manager's decision making, and the break-even analysis is the most common one.

S: Does CVP analysis differs from break-even analysis?

A: Their objectives are not the same. The underlying objective of break-even analysis determines the output level that will result in neither profit nor loss. On the other hand, CVP analysis seeks to determine what will be the effect on sales, cost and profit when there is a change in activity level.

What is Cost-Volume-Profit Analysis

Cost-volume-profit (CVP) analysis is a systematic method of examining the relationship between changes in volume and changes in total revenue, total cost and profit. [1] As a model of these relationships CVP analysis simplifies the real-world conditions that a firm will face.

CVP analysis is a key factor in many decisions, including choice of product lines, pricing of products, marketing strategy, and utilization of productive facilities. The concept is so pervasive in managerial accounting that it touches on virtually everything that a manager does.

CVP analysis is sometimes referred to simply as **break-even analysis**. This is unfortunate, because break-even analysis is just one part of the entire CVP concept. However, it is often a key part, and it can give the manager many insights into the data with which he or she is working.

Basic Assumptions

Any CVP analysis or break-even analysis is based on assumptions about the behavior of revenues, cost, and volumes.

The following underlying assumptions will limit the reliability of a given CVP analysis:

(1) The behavior of total revenues and total costs has been reliably determined;

(2) Total revenue and total cost are linear over the relevant range;

(3) Selling prices are constant;

(4) All costs can be subdivided into fixed and variable elements;

(5) Total fixed costs remain unchanged and constant;

(6) Total variable costs are directly proportional to volume over the relevant range;

(7) Productivity is constant;

(8) The analysis either covers a single product or assumes that given product mix will be maintained as total volume changes;

(9) Volume is the only factor affecting costs;

(10) The production volume equals to sales volumes.

CVP analysis is an **oversimplification** and many factors are unjustifiably ignored. Business is ever-changing, so the users of CVP analysis must constantly challenge and re-examine these assumptions **in light of** changes in business conditions.

 CVP Formulas

The basic CVP formula is:

$$\text{Profits} = \text{Sales} - \text{Variable expenses} - \text{Fixed expenses}$$

In order to better our understanding, this basic equation can be expanded as

$$P = px - bx - a$$

Where P, p, x, b and a represent the means of prodits, unit selling price, number of units sold, variable costs and total fixed cots respectively.

In the CVP formula, there are five factors involved, and this formula can help manager to predict future profit at any specified activity level. From the formula we can see that, if we know any four factors among those five factors, then we can derive the left factor by moving the other four factors to the other side of the equation.[2] A change in any one of those components are very important for decision making.

For example, assume that Lee Sing Company is currently selling watches for $100. The variable cost of each unit of the watches is $56. The company has estimated that the fixed cost will be $720,000 for the year. Current sales are 20,000 units each year. Then according to the formula, we can calculate the profit as below:

$$P = px - bx - a = \$100 \times 20,000 - \$56 \times 20,000 - \$720,000 = \$160,000$$

If the target profit is $260,000, and the selling price, fixed cost, and variable cost remain unchanged, then we can calculate the units needed to meet the profit target as below:

$$x = \frac{a + P}{p - b} = \frac{720,000 + 260,000}{100 - 56} \approx 22,273 \text{ (units)}$$

If the target profit is $260,000, and fixed cost, variable cost and the number of units sold

remain unchanged, then we can calculate the selling price needed to meet the profit target as below:

$$p = \frac{a + bx + P}{x} = \frac{\$720{,}000 + \$56 \times 20{,}000 + \$260{,}000}{20{,}000} = \$105$$

If the target profit is \$260,000, and selling price, fixed cost, and the number of units sold remain unchanged, then we can calculate the variable cost needed to meet the profit target as below:

$$b = \frac{px - a - P}{x} = \frac{\$100 \times 20{,}000 - \$720{,}000 - \$260{,}000}{20{,}000} = \$51$$

If the target profit is \$260,000, and the selling price, variable cost and the number of units sold remain unchanged, then we can calculate the fixed cost needed to meet the profit target as below:

$$a = px - bx - P = \$100 \times 20{,}000 - \$56 \times 20{,}000 - \$260{,}000 = \$620{,}000$$

Break-Even Analysis and Margin of Safety

Break-even analysis is an overview of decision models by examining the interrelationships of changes in costs, volume and profits. The **break-even point** is the point when total revenues equal total costs, which is the point of zero profit, it can be expressed in units or dollar sales volume. From this we can derive the break-even point as follows:

$$\text{Break-even point in units} = \frac{a}{p - b}$$

or,

$$\text{Break-even point in sales} = \frac{a}{p - b} \times p$$

Reconsidering the previous example, we can calculate the break-even points respectively, which are shown in Table 9-1.

The break-even point is of great interest to management. [3] Until break-even sales are reached, the product, service, event, or business segment of interest operates at a loss. Beyond this point, increasing levels of profits are achieved.

In the CVP analysis, we often conveniently assume a world of certainty. However, our estimates and projections are subject to different degrees of uncertainty. We may define uncertainty as the possibility that an actual amount will **deviate from** an expected amount.

Sensitivity analysis is a "what-if" technique that basically asks how a result will be changed if the original data are not achieved of if an assumption changes. In CVP analysis, sensitivity analysis answers such questions as "what will the profit be if variable costs per unit increase by 20%". [4] A tool of sensitivity analysis is the **margin of safety**, which is the excess of budgeted sales over the break-even volume.

Every company has a sales target to reach, at which it will make profits. Break-even points are calculated so managers know when the important no-loss stage is achieved. However, it is equally important to know how far above break-even the sales target is. The distance, measured in units, money or ratio, is termed the margin of safety. The following formula is relevant:

Margin of safety revenue (units) = Budgeted revenue (Units) − Breakeven revenue (units)

or

$$\text{Margin of safety ratio} = \frac{\text{Budgeted revenue (Units)} - \text{Breakeven revenue (units)}}{\text{Budgeted revenue (units)}}$$

Table 9-1.　The Schedule of Break-Even Point and Margin of Safety

	Original data	Increase number of units sold to 22,273	Increase selling price to$105	Decrease variable cost to $51	Decrease fixed cost to $620,000
Unit selling price ($)	100	100	105	100	100
Variable cost per unit ($)	56	56	56	51	56
Total fixed cots ($)	720,000	720,000	720,000	720,000	620,000
Number of units sold (units)	20,000	22,273	20,000	20,000	20,000
Profit ($)	160,000	260,000	260,000	260,000	260,000
Break-even point in units (units)	16,364	16,364	14,694	14,694	14,091
Break-even point in sales ($)	1,636,400	1,636,400	1,542,870	1,469,400	1,409,100
Margin of safety units (units)	3,636	5,909	5,306	5,306	5,909
Margin of safety revenue ($)	363,600	590,900	557,130	530,600	590,900
Margin of safety ratio (%)	18.18	26.53	26.53	26.53	29.55

The calculating results of margin of safety are also shown in Table 9-1. It is obviously that margin of safety and cost structure are always linked, and products with lower fixed costs will always enjoy a high margin of safety.

Vocabulary

cost-volume-profit (CVP) analysis	本量利分析
break-even analysis	保本分析，盈亏平衡分析
oversimplification	n. 过度简化，过度单纯化
in light of	adv. 按照，根据
break-even point	保本点，盈亏平衡点
deviate from	不同于……；背离，偏离……
sensitivity analysis	敏感度分析；灵敏度分析；敏感性分析
margin of safety	安全边际

Notes

[1] Cost-volume-profit analysis is a systematic method of examining the relationship between changes in volume and changes in total revenue, total cost and profit.　本量利分析是指

对业务量变动与收入总额、成本总额及利润变动之间内在关系进行系统分析的方法。

[2] From the formula we can see that, if we know any four factors among those five factors, then we can derive the left factor by moving the other four factors to the other side of the equation. 从公式可以看出，如果知道了公式涉及的 5 个因素中的任何 4 个，就可以通过推导得出第五个因素的计算公式。

[3] The break-even point is of great interest to management. 保本点对企业管理层而言非常重要。

[4] In CVP analysis, sensitivity analysis answers such questions as "what will the profit be if variable costs per unit increase by 20%". 在本量利分析中，敏感性分析能回答如"单位变动成本增长 20%对利润的影响"等此类问题。

9.4 Budgeting
预算

A conversation between A—an accountant and S—a freshman majoring in accounting.

S: What is a budget?

A: A budget is a quantitative expression of the money inflows and outflows that reveal whether a financial plan will meet organizational objectives.

S: I develop a spending plan for a school semester. Is this budgeting?

A: Yes. It is a budget to guide you in allocating your money over a specific period.

S: Some people say that budgets are great for planning but not for control. Do you agree with this sentiment?

A: No, I don't. A budget supports the management roles of planning and control by providing a way to express plans and the foundation for controlling activities. Your spending plan also serves as a control on the behavior by setting limits on what can be spent within each budget category.

S: But there are always some differences between actual results and the budget plan.

A: Exactly. The differences are called variances in cost and management accounting. Variances provide a signal that operations did not go as planned and are part of a large control system for monitoring results.

What is budget

A budget is a quantitative expression of a plan of action. It can help management to **coordinate** and implemet business plans. Budgets may be formulated for the whole organization or for any individual unit.

Budgets convert management's plans into monetary terms and provide the means of communicating plans to all areas of responsibility. [1] Budgets play a key role in the entire work of the manager. However, budgets also serve a lot of additional functions, for example, evaluation performance, coordinating activities, communicating and implementing. Although budgeting systems are most common in larger organizations, it is also a useful tool for smaller organizations. In reality, small companies have a relatively high failure rate. More extensive use of budgets would force these business owners to quantify their plans and directly face the uncertainties of their ventures. Budget systems will be helpful in every organization.

 Master Budget

Master budget is a collection of all smaller budgets used within a company. This includes the individual purchase budgets; production budgets for services and company products; fixed-expense budgets for the business operations; and all of the flexible expenses the business spends on travel, business dining and **marketing campaigns**. All of the budgets are added up by creating specific categories under the master budget. For example, if the marketing budget has an events expense category, the master budget will have an event category where the amount for marketing event expenses will be added. Any other department that has an event category in the budget will be added to the event category in the master budget.

Typically, the master budget is for a one-year period corresponding to the fiscal year of the company. Yearly budgets are broken down into quarterly and monthly budgets. The use of smaller periods allows managers to compare actual data with budgeted data more frequently, so problems may be noticed and solved sooner. [2]

A master budget may have specific features, depending on how large the master budget is for the given business. For example, the master budget may include various charts to organize all of the financial amounts and data or graphs to visually display the numeric values of the business. If the master budget is being compared to an older master budget in order to show how the business has grown, it will most likely **encompass** both graphs and charts, along with the written text that discusses the changes that have occurred.

 Capital budget

Capital budget is how an organization determines if a new project is worth the investment. Capital budget is also known as **investment appraisal**.

Capital budget is the process in which a business determines whether projects, such as building a new plant or investing in a long-term venture, are worth pursuing. Oftentimes, a prospective project's lifetime cash inflows and outflows are assessed in order to determine whether the returns generated meet a sufficient target benchmark.

Ideally, businesses should pursue all projects and opportunities that enhance shareholder value. However, because the amount of capital available at any given time for new projects is limited, management needs to use capital budget techniques to determine which projects will yield the most return over an applicable period of time.

Typical capital budget decisions encountered by the business executive are: cost reduction decisions, plant expansion decisions, equipment selection decisions, lease or buy decisions, equipment replacement decisions and so on. [3]

Popular methods of capital budget include **net present value (NPV)**, **internal rate of return (IRR)** and **payback period.**

Under the NPV method, the present value of all cash inflows is compared against the present vlaue of all cash outflows that are associated with an investment project.[4] The difference in the present value of these cash flows, called net present value, determines whether the project is an acceptable investment or not.

The internal rate of return can be defined as the true interest yield promised by an investment project over its useful life. [5] The IRR is that discount rate which will cause the net present value of a project to be equal to zero.

Payback period tells the number of years over which the investment outlay will be recovered or paid back from the cash inflows if the estimates turn out to be correct. [6]

Fixed Budget and Flexible Budget

A **fixed budget**, also known as a **static budget**, projects static levels of known income and expenses over a set period of time. Fixed budgets are much simpler to create and to read than **flexible budgets** and are generally acceptable for situations where the levels of income and expense are not expected to **fluctuate** through the duration of the budgeting period.

When a fixed budget is adjusted to account for variable results, it can be referred to as a flexible budget. When implemented during the budgeting process, a flexible budget helps a business account for future changes in any expense or income account. Multiple flexible budgets drawn up to forecast various levels of economic activities may be complicated, but prepare a business well for any fluctuations in business levels.[7]

Zero-Based Budget

Zero-based budget is an approach to planning and decision-making which reverses the working process of traditional budgeting. In traditional **incremental budget**, departmental managers justify only variances versus past years, based on the assumption that the "baseline" is automatically approved. By contrast, in zero-based budget, every line item of the budget must be approved, rather than only changes. [8] During the review process, no reference is made to the previous level of expenditure. Zero-based budget requires the budget request be re-evaluated thoroughly, starting from the zero-base. This process is independent of whether the total budget or specific line items are increasing or decreasing.

Advantages of zero-based budget are:

(1) Efficient allocation of resources, as it is based on needs and benefits rather than history;

(2) Driving managers to find cost effective ways to improve operations;

(3) Detecting inflated budgets;

(4) Increasing staff motivation by providing greater initiative and responsibility in decision-making;

(5) Increasing communication and coordination within the organization;

(6) Identifying and eliminates wasteful and obsolete operations;

(7) Identifying opportunities for outsourcing;

(8) Forcing **cost centers** to identify their mission and their relationship to overall goals;

(9) Helping in identifying areas of wasteful expenditure, and if desired, can also be used for suggesting alternative courses of action.

Disadvantages of zero-based budget are:

(1) More time-consuming than incremental budget;

(2) Justifying every line item can be problematic for departments with intangible outputs;

(3) Requiring specific training, due to increased complexity VS incremental budget;

(4) In a large organization, the amount of information backing up the budgeting process may be **overwhelming**.

 Vocabulary

coordinate	*vt.* 使协调，使调和；整合
master budget	总预算，全面预算
marketing campaign	市场运动，营销活动
encompass	*vt.* 包含，包括；包围
capital budget	资本预算
investment appraisal	投资估价，投资评估
net present value (NPV)	净现值
internal rate of return (IRR)	内部收益率，内部盈利率
payback period	回收期
fixed budget	固定预算
static budget	静态预算
flexible budget	弹性预算
fluctuate	*vi.* 波动；涨落 & *vt.* 使波动；使动摇
zero-based budget	零基预算
incremental budget	增量预算
cost center	成本中心
overwhelming	*adj.* 势不可当的，压倒一切的，巨大的

✏ Notes

[1] Budgets convert management's plans into monetary terms and provide the means of communicating plans to all areas of responsibility. 预算将管理层的计划转换成货币形式，并

成为将计划传达给所有责任区域的工具。

[2] The use of smaller periods allows managers to compare actual data with budgeted data more frequently, so problems may be noticed and solved sooner. 较短期的预算有助于管理者经常将实际指标与预算指标相比较，以利于更快地发现问题、解决问题。

[3] Typical capital budget decisions encountered by the business executive are: cost reduction decisions, plant expansion decisions, equipment selection decisions, lease or buy decisions, equipment replacement decisions and so on. 企业主管人员遇到的典型资本预算决策是：成本降低决策、厂房扩建决策、设备选择决策、租赁或购置决策、设备更换决策等。

[4] Under the NPV method, the present value of all cash inflows is compared against the present vlaue of all cash outflows that are associated with an investment project. 当使用净现值法时，把某一投资项目有关的所有现金流入量的现值与所有现金流出量的现值进行比较。

[5] The internal rate of return can be defined as the true interest yield promised by an investment project over its useful life. 内部收益率可定义为某一投资项目在其有效年限内可以赚取的真实报酬率。

[6] Payback period tells the number of years over which the investment outlay will be recovered or paid back from the cash inflows if the estimates turn out to be correct. 如果原先对现金流入量的估计准确，回收期将说明投资支出需要几年才能从现金流入量中得到补偿或回收。

[7] Multiple flexible budgets drawn up to forecast various levels of economic activities may be complicated, but prepare a business well for any fluctuations in business levels. 制定多个弹性预算来预测各种各样经济活动水平可能比较复杂，但是可以帮助企业较好地应对任何业务水平的波动。

[8] By contrast, in zero-based budget, every line item of the budget must be approved, rather than only changes. 相比之下，零基预算中每项预算必须核准，而不只是变化。

Exercises

I. Discuss the following questions in English.

1.　What is the main function of management accounting?

2.　What are the differences between financial accouting and management accounting?

3.　What, if any, are differences between the management accounting information needed in manufacturing organizations and that needed in service organizations?

4.　Why do you agree or disagree with the following statement: "an organizaiton should have the most accurate and complete cost system possible"?

5.　What is an opportunity cost? Give an example.

6.　What is cost profit volume analysis?

7.　What does the term break-even point mean?

8.　What are the major objectives in capital budget?

9.　What is the most widely used approach to computing the cost of capital for evaluating new investments?

10.　What are the differences between fixed and flexible budgets?

11.　What are the differences between zero-based budget and incremental budget?

II. Choose the best word or phrase that fits the sentence.

1.　In contrast to financial accountancy information, management accounting information is usually _____ and used by management, instead of publicly.

    A. confident　　　　　　　　　　B. confidential

    C. confidence　　　　　　　　　　D. confidently

2.　Direct materials are the acquisition costs of all materials that are identified as part of the product cost and that may be easily traced to the product in a(n) _____ way.

    A. workable　　　　　　　　　　B. economical

    C. feasible　　　　　　　　　　　D. economically feasible

3.　A manufacturer's product costs are _____ used in making its products.

    A. the direct materials

    B. the direct materials and direct labor

    C. the direct materials, direct labor, and manufacturing overhead

    D. all direct costs

4.　_____ means how a cost will react or respond to changes in the level of business activities.

    A. Cost behavior　　　　　　　　B. Activity-based costing

    C. Variable cost　　　　　　　　　D. Fixed cost

5.　An opportunity cost can be defined as the potential benefit that is lost or sacrificed when the choice of one course of action requires the giving up of a(n) _____ course of action.

    A. unprofitable　　　　　　　　　B. less profitable

    C. alternative　　　　　　　　　　D. feasible

6.　CVP analysis is a systematic method of examining the relationship between changes in volume and changes in total revenue, total cost and _____.

    A. price　　　　　　　　　　　　B. profit

    C. performance　　　　　　　　　D. product

7.　The _____ point is the point when total revenues equal total costs, that is the point of zero profit.

    A. balance　　　　　　　　　　　B. equalized

    C. break-even　　　　　　　　　　D. no-loss

8.　_____ analysis is a "what-if" technique that basically asks how a result will be changed if the original data are not achieved if an assumption changes.

    A. Sensitivity　　　　　　　　　　B. CVP

    C. NPV　　　　　　　　　　　　D. IRR

9. A budget is a _____ expression of a plan of action.

    A. financial   B. formal

    C. quantitative   D. qualified

10. The _____ budget is a collection of all smaller budgets used within a company.

    A. total   B. master

    C. entire   D. whole

11. Under the _____ method, the present value of all cash inflows is compared against the present vlaue of all cash outflows that are associated with an investment project.

    A. NPV   B. IRR

    C. CVP   D. payback period

12. When a fixed budget is adjusted to account for variable results, it can be referred to as a(n) _____.

    A. adjusted budget   B. revised budget

    C. unfixed budget   D. flexible budget

III. Match each word on the left with its corresponding meaning on the right.

A	B
1. hierarchy	(a) (of words) meaning the same or nearly the same
2. inspection	(b) include in scope
3. encompass	(c) move or sway in a rising and falling or wavelike pattern
4. abstraction	(d) the ability to respond to affective changes in your interpersonal environment
5. opportunity	(e) a formal or official examination
6. custom	(f) available only to persons authorized to see documents so classified
7. synonymous	(g) a concept or idea not associated with any specific instance
8. confidential	(h) a series of ordered groupings of people or things within a system
9. sensitivity	(i) a possibility due to a favorable combination of circumstances
10. fluctuate	(j) money collected under a tariff

IV. Fill in the blanks with words or phrases from the list below.

A.	streamline	B.	brought	C.	setting	D.	involves
E.	allocated	F.	passed	G.	attributed	H.	powers
I.	process	J.	receiveded	K.	achieving	L.	accumulating
M.	investment	N.	prepared	O.	defined	P.	collected

Planning and control are essential for (1)____ good results in any business. Firstly, a budget is (2)____ and, secondly, actual results are compared with budgeted ones. Any difference is made responsibility of the key individuals who were involved in (3)____ standards, given necessary resources and (4)____ to use them.

In order to (5)____ the process, the entire organization is broken into various types of centers, mainly cost center, revenue center, profit center and (6)____ center. The organizational budget is divided on these lines and (7)____ on to the concerned managers. Actual results are (8)____ and displayed in the same form for comparison. Difference, if any, are highlighted and (9)____ to the notice of the management. This (10)____ is called responsibility accounting.

Responsibility accounting (11)____ the creation of responsibility centers. A responsibility center may be (12)____ as an organization unit for whose performance a manager is held accountable. Responsibility accounting enables accountability for financial results and outcomes to be (13)____ to individuals throughout the organization. The objective is to measure the result of each responsibility center. It involves (14)____ costs and revenues for each responsibility center, so that deviation from performance target (typically the budget) can be (15)____ to the individual who is accountable for the responsibility center.

V. Translate the following sentences into Chinese.

1.   A management accountant need to be aware of everything, be it political situation that affect market, inflation, other exposures in market, competition, cost of labor, raw material, internal operations, coordination among different departments within a company as well as its interaction with rest of the business world and social media.

2.   To understand how management accounting information helps increase profits, reduce costs, and improve processes, we must focus on the decisions and informational needs of employees and managers, not external constituencies.

3.   Product costs are incurred to produce the volume and mix of products made during the period.

4.   Cost behavior is associated with learning how costs change when there is a change in an organization's level of activities.

5.   Relevant cost helps provide a consistent basis for the comparison of alternative proposal.

6.   CVP analysis relates the firm's cost structure to sales volume and profitability.

7.   A master budget is a budget which summarises a company's plans and helps to set specific targets for sales and financing activities.

8.   A flexible budget can adapt to changing needs throughout the month or from month to month.

VI. Translate the following sentences into English.

1.   管理会计是从传统会计中分离出来与财务会计并列的、着重为企业改善经营管理、提高经济效益服务的一个企业会计分支。

2.   制造成本是指生产活动的成本，即企业为生产产品而发生的成本。

3.   变动成本是指那些成本的总发生额在相关范围内随着业务量的变动而呈线性变动的成本。

4. 机会成本是指在面临多方案择一决策时，被舍弃的选项中的最高价值者是本次决策的机会成本。

5. 沉没成本是决策非相关成本，在项目决策时无须考虑。

6. 本量利分析是成本——产量(或销售量)——利润依存关系分析的简称，也称为 CVP 分析，是指在变动成本计算模式的基础上，以数学化的会计模型与图文来揭示固定成本、变动成本、销售量、单价、销售额、利润等变量之间的内在规律性的联系，为会计预测决策和规划提供必要的财务信息的一种定量分析方法。

7. 全面预算反映的是企业未来某一特定期间(一般不超过一年或一个经营周期)的全部生产、经营活动的财务计划。

8. 零基预算，是指对任何一个预算期，任何一种费用项目的开支，都不是从原有的基础出发，即根本不考虑基期的费用开支水平，而是一切以零为起点，从零开始考虑各费用项目的必要性，确定预算收支，编制预算。

Reading Material 9

Activity-Based Costing

Activity-based costing (ABC) is a system for assigning costs to products based on the activities they require. In this case, activities are those regular actions performed inside a company. "Talking with customer regarding invoice questions" is an example of an activity inside most companies.

Companies may be moved to adopt ABC by a need to improve costing accuracy, that is, understand better the true costs and profitability of individual products, services, or initiatives. ABC gets closer to true costs in these areas by turning many costs that standard cost accounting views as indirect costs essentially into direct costs. By contrast, standard cost accounting typically determines so-called indirect and overhead costs simply as a percentage of certain direct costs, which may or may not reflect actual resource usage for individual items.

Under ABC, accountants assign 100% of each employee's time to the different activities performed inside a company (many will use surveys to have the workers themselves assign their time to the different activities). The accountants then can determine the total cost spent on each activity by summing up the percentage of each worker's salary spent on that activity.

A company can use the resulting activity cost data to determine where to focus their operational improvements. For example, a job-based manufacturer may find that a high percentage of its workers are spending their time trying to figure out a hastily written customer order. Via ABC, the accountants now have a currency amount pegged to the activity of "Researching Customer Work Order Specifications". Senior management can now decide how much focus or money to budget for resolving this process deficiency. Activity-based management includes (but is not restricted to) the use of ABC to manage a business.

ABC systems use a simple two-stage approach that is similar to but more general than the structure of tranditional cost system. Tranditional cost system use actual departments or cost centers for accumulating and redistributing costs. ABC system, instead of using cost centers for accumulating costs, use activities; that is rather than asking how to allocate a service department expense to a production departmant, the ABC system designer asks what activities are being performed by the service department's resources. The resource expenses are assigned to activities based on how much of them are required or used to perform the activities. While ABC may be able to pinpoint the cost of each activity and resources into the ultimate product, the process could be tedious, costly and subject to errors.

As it is a tool for a more accurate way of allocating fixed costs into product, these fixed costs do not vary according to each month's production volume. For example, an elimination of one product would not eliminate the overhead or even direct labor cost assigned to it. ABC better identifies product costing in the long run, but may not be too helpful in day-to-day decision making.

Answers:

II.	1	B	2	D	3	C	4	A	5	C	6	B	7	C	8	A
	9	C	10	B	11	A	12	D								
III.	1	h	2	e	3	b	4	g	5	i	6	j	7	a	8	f
	9	d	10	c												
IV.	1	K	2	N	3	C	4	H	5	A	6	M	7	F	8	P
	9	B	10	I	11	D	12	O	13	E	14	L	15	G		

 知识扩展

1. 标准成本的分类

标准成本是指在正常和高效率的运转情况下制造产品的成本，而不是指实际发生的成本，是有效经营条件下发生的一种目标成本，也叫"应该成本"。标准成本按其制定所依据的生产技术和经营管理水平，分为理想标准成本和正常标准成本；在标准成本系统中广泛使用正常标准成本。

西方企业采用的标准成本有多种，按照制定标准成本所依据的生产技术和经营水平分类，分为理想标准成本，正常标准成本和现实标准成本。

理想标准成本是现有生产条件所能达到的最优水平的成本，这种成本难于实际运用；正常标准成本是根据正常的工作效率，正常的生产能力利用程度和正常价格等条件制定的标准成本，它一般只用来估计未来的成本变动趋势；标准成本按其适用期，分为现行标准成本和基本标准成本。由于基本标准成本不按各期实际修订，不宜用来直接评价工作效率和成本控制的有效性；现实标准成本，是根据适用期合理的耗费量，合理的耗费价格和生产能力可能利用程度等条件制定的切合适用期实际情况的一种标准成本，标准成本法一般采用这种标准成本。

2. 标准成本的用途

(1) 作为成本控制的依据。

成本控制的标准有两类：一类是以历史上曾经达到的水平为依据；另一类是以应该发生的成本为依据，如各种标准成本。

(2) 代替实际成本作为存货计价的依据。

由于标准成本中已去除了各种不合理因素，以它为依据，进行材料在产品和产成品的计价，可使存货计价建立在更加健全的基础上。而以实际成本计价，往往同样实物形态的存货有不同的计价标准，不能反映其真实的价值。

(3) 作为经营决策的成本信息。

由于标准成本代表了成本要素的合理近似值，因而可以作为定价依据，并可作为本量利分析的原始数据资料，以及估算产品未来成本的依据。

(4) 作为登记账簿的计价标准。

使用标准成本来记录材料，在产品和销售账户，可以简化日常的账务处理和报表的编制工作。在标准成本系统中，上述账户按标准成本入账，使账务处理及时简单，减少了许多费用的分配计算。

Chapter 10　Auditing
审计

Learning Objectives

- Understand the nature of auditing 了解审计的本质
- Understand distinction between auditing and accounting 理解审计和会计的区别
- Understand CPAs and the role of CPA firms 了解注册会计师和注册会计师事务所的作用
- Understand different types of audits 了解不同类型的审计
- Understand professional ethics and fundamental principles of auditing 了解审计职业道德和审计基本原则
- Understand the four phrases of audit process 理解审计过程的四个阶段
- Understand different types of audit reports 了解不同类型的审计报告

Listening Practice 听力练习

第 10 章听写原文翻译和答案的音频见右侧二维码。

Chapter 10 English
Listening.mp3

Dictation: *Listen and complete the passage with the words or phrases according to what you've heard from the speaker.*

Make retirement planning corrections when necessary. If you find through the ____1____ that you are not currently saving enough to support your ____2____ goals, then some corrections may be necessary. You can use the Budgeter to help you trim down your ____3____. Or you may want to think about creating multiple streams of ____4____ for yourself through businesses or other means. Or you may choose to move your ____5____ to areas that could provide higher returns.

Come back to the retirement topic yearly. Now that you've done all this work to get your retirement planned out, make sure you revisit this area at least once a year. This gives you the opportunity to hold yourself accountable and stay focused on your goals.

Wisdom 至理名言

If you cannot measure it, you cannot improve it. 如果你不能衡量它，你就不能改进它。

With the growth of the business, Scarlett is thinking of a way to better the management. Is there any way to achieve the objectives of effectiveness and efficiency in operations? How to increase the reliability of financial reporting? How to comply with applicable laws and regulations? She really needs some kinds of policies and procedures or useful tools to solve the possible problems during the management. On the other hand, if she is trying to attract more funds for her business, what kind of qualification will be helpful?

Auditing is a vital part of accounting. Traditionally, audits were mainly associated with gaining information about financial systems and the financial records of a company or a business.

Financial audits are performed to ascertain the validity and reliability of information, as well as to provide an assessment of a system's internal control. The goal of an audit is to express an opinion of the person, organization or system in question, under evaluation based on work done on a test basis.

This chapter will provide background for performing financial audits, including a general overview of auditing, the audit process and audit report.

10.1　An Overview of Auditing
审计学概述

A conversation between A—an accountant and S—a freshman majoring in accounting.

A: "In God we trust, all others we audit." This quote sums up a basic viewpoint of some professionals towards auditing.

S: I know that the financial statements of listed companies must be audited annually. Is there any other organization or individual that should be audited?

A: Yes. The object of an audit can be a person, organization, system, process, enterprise, project or product. For example, a compliance audit (合规性审计) is conducted to determine whether the auditee is following specific procedures, rules, or regulations set by some higher authority.

S: Then what is auditing?

A: Auditing is defined as a systematic and independent examination of data, statements, records, operations and performances of an enterprise for a stated purpose.

S: But the financial statement audit is the most common one, isn't it?

A: Yes. The primary focus of most auditing textbooks is on financial statement audits.

S: What is the objective of financial statement audits?

A: According to International Standards on Auditing (ISA) 200, "the objective of an audit of financial statements is to enable the auditor to express an opinion whether the financial statements are prepared, in all material respects, in accordance with an identified financial reporting framework".

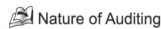Nature of Auditing

Auditing is the accumulation and evaluation of evidence about information to determine and report on the degree of **correspondence** between the information and established criteria.[1] Auditing should be done by a competent, independent person. For ease of understanding, we will discuss the terms in a different order than they occur in the above description.

To do an audit, there must be information in a verifiable form and some criteria by which the auditor can evaluate the information. Information can and does take many forms. Auditors routinely perform audits of quantifiable information, including company's financial statements and individuals' income tax returns. Auditors also audit more subjective information, such as the effectiveness of computer system and the efficiency of manufacturing operations. The criteria for evaluating information vary depending on the information being audited.

Evidence is any information used by the auditor to determine whether the information being audited is stated in accordance with the established criteria. Evidence takes many different forms, including electronic and documentary data about transactions, written and electronic communication with outsiders, observations by the auditor and oral **testimony** of the **auditee**. To satisfy the purpose of the audit, auditors must obtain a sufficient quality and volume of evidence.

The auditor must be qualified to understand the criteria used and must be competent to recognize the types and amount of the accumulated evidence for reaching the proper conclusion after examining the evidence.[2] The auditor must also have an independent mental attitude, even though such auditors are paid fees by the auditees. The competence of those performing the audit is of little value if they are biased in the accumulation and evaluation of evidence.

The final stage in the auditing process is preparing the **audit report**, which communicates the auditor's findings to users. Reports differ in nature, but all must inform readers of the degree of correspondence between the information audited and established criteria.

Distinction between Auditing and Accounting

Many financial statement users and the general public confuse auditing with accounting. The confusion results because most auditing is usually concerned with accounting information, and many auditors have considerable **expertise** in accounting matters. The confusion is increased by giving the title "certified public accountant(CPA)" to many individuals who perform audits.

We have mentioned that "accounting is a system that identifies, measures, records, and communicates relevant, reliable, and comparable information about an organization's business activities". To provide relevant, reliable, and comparable information, accountants must have a thorough understanding of the principles and rules that provide the basis for preparing the accounting information. In addition, accountants must develop a system to make sure that the entity's economic events are properly recorded on a timely basis and a reasonable cost.

When auditing accounting data, auditors focus on determining whether recorded information properly reflects the economic events that occurred during the accounting period. <u>Because Chinese or international accounting standards provide the criteria for evaluating whether the accounting information is properly recorded, auditors must thoroughly understand those accounting standards.</u> [3]

In addition to understand accounting, auditor must possess expertise in the accumulation and interpretation of audit evidence. It is the expertise that distinguishes auditors from accountants. Determining the proper audit procedures, deciding the number and types of items to test, and evaluating the results are unique to the auditor.

Types of Audits

<u>Although the audit process of obtaining and evaluating evidence and communicating the results to interested users applies to all audit applications, the objectives of auditing vary depending on the needs of users of the audit report.</u>[4] **Internal audit**, **governmental audit**, and **external audit** all serve different objectives.

Internal audit is defined as an independent appraisal function established within an organization to examine and evaluate its activities as a service to the organization to examine and evaluate its activities as a service to the organization in the effective discharge of their responsibilities. <u>To this end, the internal audit furnishes them with analysis, appraisals, **recommendations, counsel**, and information concerning the activities reviewed.</u> [5]

Governmental audit covers a wide range of activities on the national, provincial, and local levels and numerous regulatory agencies. Governmental auditors not only examine financial statements but also determine whether government program objectives are met and whether certain government agencies and private enterprises comply with applicable laws and regulations.

External audit involves reporting on financial statements prepared by management for external users or third parties. The third parties include shareholders, creditors, bankers, potential investors, and regulatory agencies. External audits are performed by independent **CPA firms**. Although the audit fee for an external audit is paid by the company being audited, external auditors, unlike internal auditors, are not employees of the company being audited—they must be independent of the company and its management. <u>If external auditors do not maintain personal integrity and objectivity regarding the audit client, the audit report will lack credence from the viewpoint of third party users. Independence is, therefore, the backbone of external auditing.</u> [6]

Certified Public Accountants

Certified Public Accountant (CPA) is the **statutory** title of qualified accountants who have passed the CPA Exam and have met additional education and experience requirements for certification as a CPA. Individuals who have passed the Exam but have not accomplished the required on-the-job experience are permitted the designation "CPA inactive" [7] or an equivalent phrase. In China, only CPAs who are licensed are able to provide to the public **attestation** (including auditing) opinions on financial statements.

CPA firms are formed as general partnerships, limited partnerships and limited liability partnerships. Different levels of professional personnel within a CPA firm may include partners, directors, senior managers, managers, senior accountants, and staff accountants. [8]

CPA firms provide audit services, as well as other attestation and assurance services. Additional services commonly provided by CPA firms include:

(1) Accounting and bookkeeping services

Many small clients with limited accounting staff rely on CPA firms to prepare their financial statements. Thus, CPA firms perform a variety of accounting and bookkeeping services to meet the needs of these clients. In many cases in which the financial statements are to be given to a third party, a review or even an audit is also performed.

(2) Tax service

CPA firms prepare corporate and individual tax returns for both audit and non-audit clients. Almost every CPA firm performs tax services, which may include **estate tax**, **tax planning**, and other aspects of tax services.

(3) Management consulting services

Most CPA firms provide certain services that enable their clients to operate their businesses more effectively. These services are called management consulting or management advisory services. These services give simple suggestions in improving the client's accounting system as well as in the risk management, information technology and e-commerce system design, mergers and acquisitions, and business valuations.[9] Many large CPA firms have departments involved exclusively in management consulting services with little interaction with the audit or tax staff.

The four largest international CPA firms are called the "Big Four", which we will discuss in the reading material of this chapter.

Professional Ethics and Fundamental Principles

Ethics can be defined broadly as a set of moral principles or value. Over the years, the ethical requirements for auditors have increased significantly, as the auditing and reporting requirements for companies have been extended. The Chinese Institute of Certified Public Accountants (CICPA) has its own ethical guide, which establishes ethical requirements for CPA and provide a conceptual framework for all CPA to ensure compliance with the six fundamental principles of professional ethics. These principles are:

(1) **Integrity**

A professional accountant should be straightforward and honest in all professional and business relationships. Integrity also implies fair dealing and truthfulness.

(2) Independence

Independence refers to the independence of the internal auditor or of the external auditor from parties that may have a financial interest in the business being audited. The CICPA requires independence only for attestation engagements. For example, a CPA firm can perform management services for a company in which the partner owns stock. Of course, if the CPA firm also performs an audit, it violates the independence requirements for attestation services.

(3) Objectivity and fairness

A professional accountant should be fair and should not allow bias, conflict of interest or undue influence of others to **override** professional or business judgments.

(4) Professional competence and due care

A professional accountant should perform professional services with due care, competence and **diligence**, and have a continuing duty to maintain professional knowledge and skill at the level required to ensure that a client or employer receives competent professional service. [10]

(5) Confidentiality

A professional accountant should respect the confidentiality of information acquired as a result of professional and business relationships and should not disclose any such information to third parties without proper and specific authority unless there is a legal or professional right or duty to disclose.

(6) Professional behavior

A professional accountant should act in a manner consistent with the good reputation of the profession and refrain from any conduct which might bring discredit to the profession.

Vocabulary

correspondence	*n.* 一致，符合；对应
testimony	*n.* 证词；证明，表明；声明，
auditee	*n.* 被审计单位
audit report	审计报告
expertise	*n.* 专门知识；专门技术；专家的意见
internal audit	内部审计
governmental audit	政府审计
external audit	外部(独立)审计
recommendation	*n.* 推荐；推荐信；建议；可取之处
counsel	*n.* 协商，讨论；建议；策略
CPA firms	会计师事务所
statutory	*adj.* 法定的，法令的；依照法令的
attestation	*n.* 证明；证据
estate tax	房地产遗产税
tax planning	税收筹划，税务规划，纳税计划
ethic	*n.* 伦理；道德规范

integrity	*n.* 诚信；正直；诚实；廉正
independence	*n.* 独立性，独立，自主
override	*vt.* 推翻，无视；践踏；优先于；
professional competence	专业胜任能力
due care	应有的关注；行为准则
diligence	*n.* 勤勉，勤奋
confidentiality	*n.* 机密性
professional behavior	职业行为

Notes

[1] Auditing is the accumulation and evaluation of evidence about information to determine and report on the degree of correspondence between the information and established criteria.   审计是为了确定和报告信息与建立标准之间的符合程度，而对信息证据的收集和评价。

[2] The auditor must be qualified to understand the criteria used and must be competent to recognize the types and amount of the accumulated evidence to for reaching the proper conclusion after examining the evidence.   审计人员必须能够理解所用的标准，在审查证据后必须知道能够得出适当结论所需收集证据的类型和数量。

[3] Because Chinese or international accounting standards provide the criteria for evaluating whether the accounting information is properly recorded, auditors must thoroughly understand those accounting standards.   因为中国或国际会计准则为评价会计信息是否被适当记录提供了标准，所以审计人员必须完全理解那些会计准则。

[4] Although the audit process of obtaining and evaluating evidence and communicating the results to interested users applies to all audit applications, the objectives of auditing vary depending on the needs of users of the audit report.   虽然获取和评价证据并向有利益关系的使用者传送审计结果的审计程序适用于所有的审计应用过程，但审计目标却因审计报告使用者的需求不同而有所差异。

[5] To this end, the internal audit furnishes them with analysis, appraisals, recommendations, counsel, and information concerning the activities reviewed.   为达到这个目的，内部审计向他们提供审查活动的有关的分析、评价、建议、咨询和信息。

[6] If external auditors do not maintain personal integrity and objectivity regarding the audit client, the audit report will lack credence from the viewpoint of third party users. Independence is, therefore, the backbone of external auditing.   如果外部审计师不能与被审计的客户保持公正和客观，那么在第三方使用者看来，审计报告就将缺乏可信性。所以，独立性是外部审计的基础。

[7] CPA inactive   参考翻译"非执业注册会计师"。"inactive"的含义为"不活动的，不活跃的"。

[8] Different levels of professional personnel within a CPA firm may include partners, directors, senior managers, managers, senior accountants, and staff accountants.   在会计师事务所，不同级别的职业人员可能包括合伙人、总监、高级经理、经理、高级会计师(审计员)

和会计师(审计员)。

[9] These services give suggestions in improving the client's accounting system as well as in the risk management, information technology and e-commerce system design, mergers and acquisitions, and business valuations. 这些服务包括建议客户改进会计系统，也包括在风险管理、信息技术、电子商务系统设计、企业并购和企业价值评估方面提出建议。

[10] A professional accountant should perform professional services with due care, competence and diligence, and have a continuing duty to maintain professional knowledge and skill at the level required to ensure that a client or employer receives competent professional service based on current developments in practice, legislation and techniques. 执业会计师应该以应有的关注、专业胜任能力、勤勉尽责的态度提供专业服务，并持续了解和掌握专业知识和技能，以确保客户或雇主能够得到称职的专业服务。

10.2　Audit Process
审计程序

A conversation between A—an accountant and S—a freshman majoring in accounting.

S: When a company desires an audit, it will approach a CPA firm. What will happen next? Do they need to sign an audit contract first?

A: No. First, the CPA firm will examine the company's accounting records, its system of internal control, and the previous year's audit report, if any.

S: Why does the CPA firm examine these things first, instead of obligating the client?

A: Because accountants have legal responsibility for their work, the CPA firm should inquire about the management through various sources to determine the reputation of the company.

S: If the CPA firm decides to accept the client, they will sign the contract. Is that right?

A: Not exactly. Based on its preliminary findings, an estimate is prepared budgeting the total number of hours and the cost range for the audit. Once the client has engaged the CPA firm to perform the audit, the CPA firm will send an engagement letter confirming the arrangement for the audit. The engagement letter signed by the CEO of the client becomes the audit contract that describes the responsibilities of the auditor and the client.

Auditing is essentially a practical task and no audit will be identical to any other. There could be several specific phases in the audit process that should be followed to ensure a successful financial statement audit. The audit process, as described in the text, has four specific phases, as shown in Figure 10-1. A brief introduction to each of the four phases of the audit process will be provided in the following.

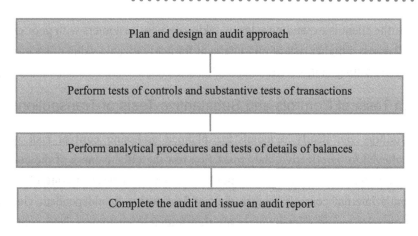

Figure 10-1   Four Phases of a Financial Statement Audit

 Plan and Design an Audit Approach

Concern for sufficient appropriate evidence and cost control necessitates planning the engagement. The plan should result in an effective audit approach at a reasonable cost. Planning and designing an audit approach can be broken down into several parts. Three key aspects are introduced here.

(1) Obtain an understanding of the entity and its environment

To adequately assess the risk of **misstatements** in the financial statements and to interpret information obtained throughout the audit, the auditor must have a thorough understanding of the client's business and related environment, including knowledge of strategies and processes. The auditor should study the client's business model, perform analytical procedures and make comparisons to competitors.[1] The auditor must also understand any unique accounting requirements of the client's industry. For example, when auditing an insurance company, the auditor must understand how **loss reserves** are calculated.

(2) Understand internal control and assess control risk

The risk of misstatement in the financial statements is reduced if the client has effective controls over computer operations and transaction processing. The nature, extent, and timing of the audit work to be performed on a particular engagement depend largely on the effectiveness of the client's system of internal control in preventing material errors in the financial statements. [2] The auditor identifies internal controls and evaluates their effectiveness, a process called assessing control risk. If internal controls are considered effective, planned assessed control risk can be reduced and the amount of audit evidence to be accumulated can be significantly less than when internal controls are not adequate.

(3) Assess risk of material misstatement

The auditor uses the understanding of the client's industry and business strategies, as well as the effectiveness of controls, to assess the risk of misstatements in the financial statements. This assessment will then impact the audit plan and the nature, extent, and timing of audit procedures.

For example, if the client is expanding sales by taking on new customers with poor **credit ratings**, the auditor will assess a higher risk of misstatement for net realizable value of accounts receivable and plan to expand testing in this area.

Perform Tests of Controls and Substantive Tests of Transactions

Before auditors can justify reducing the planned assessing **control risk** when internal controls are believed to be effective, they must first test the effectiveness of the controls. [3] The procedures for this type of testing are commonly referred to as **tests of controls**. For example, assume a client's internal controls require the verification by an independent clerk of all unit selling prices on sales before sales invoices are transmitted to customers. This control is directly related to the accuracy transaction-related **audit objectives** for sales. The auditor might test the effectiveness of this control by examining the sales transaction file for evidence that the unit selling price was verified.

Auditors also evaluate the client's recording of transactions by verifying the monetary amounts of transactions, a process called **substantive tests** of transactions. For example, the auditor might use computer software to compare the unit selling price on **duplicate** sales invoices with an electronic file of approved prices as a test of the accuracy objective for sales transactions. Like the test of control in the preceding paragraph, this test satisfies the accuracy transaction-related audit objective for sales. For the sake of efficiency, auditors often perform tests of controls and substantive tests of transactions at the same time. [4]

Perform Analytical Procedures and Tests of Details of Balances

There are two general categories of phase III procedures. **Analytical procedures** use comparisons and relationships to assess whether account balances or other data appear reasonable. For example, to provide some assurance for the accuracy objective for both sales transactions (transaction-related audit objective) and accounts receivable (balance-related audit objective), the auditor might examine sales transactions in the sales journal for unusually large amounts and also compare total monthly sales with prior years. [5] If a company is consistently using incorrect sales prices or improperly recording sales, significant differences are likely.

Tests of details of balances are specific procedures intended to test for monetary misstatements in the balances in the financial statements. An example related to the accuracy objective for accounts receivable (balance-related audit objective) is direct written communication with the client's customers to identify incorrect amounts. Tests of details of ending balances are essential to the conduct of the audit because most of the evidence is obtained from a source independent of the client and therefore is considered to be of high quality.

Complete the Audit and Issue an Audit Report

After the auditor has completed all procedures for each audit objective and for each financial statement account and related disclosures, it is necessary to combine the information obtained to reach an overall conclusion as to whether the financial statements are fairly presented. Since the audit report represents an acceptance of considerable responsibility by the CPA firm, a partner must first review the **working papers** from the engagement to ascertain that a thorough examination has been completed and to form an opinion on the financial statements. [6] This highly subjective process relies heavily on the auditor's professional judgment. When the audit is completed, the CPA must issue an audit report to accompany the client's published financial statements. These reports will be discussed in the following.

Vocabulary

misstatement	*n.* 错报，误述，虚伪陈述
loss reserve	赔款准备金，损失准备金
credit rating	*n.* 信用评级
control risk	控制风险
test of control	控制测试，符合性测试
audit objective	审计目标
substantive test	实质性测试，大量测试
duplicate	*adj.* 复制的，副本的；(与另一个)完全相同的
analytical procedure	分析性程序
tests of detail	细节测试
working paper	工作底稿

Notes

[1] The auditor should study the client's business model, perform analytical procedures and make comparisons to competitors. 审计员应该研究客户的经营模式，实施分析程序，与其竞争对手进行比较。

[2] The nature, extent, and timing of the audit work to be performed on a particular engagement depend largely on the effectiveness of the client's system of internal control in preventing material errors in the financial statements. 因某项委托而必须开展的审计工作，其性质、范围和时间安排在很大程度上取决于委托人的内部控制系统在防止财务报表出现重大错误方面的有效程度。

[3] Before auditors can justify reducing the planned assessing control risk when internal controls are believed to be effective, they must first test the effectiveness of the controls. 当内部控制被认为有效时，审计员在做出减少原计划评估风险控制的决定之前，必须首先测试控制的有效性。

[4] For the sake of efficiency, auditors often perform tests of controls and substantive tests of transactions at the same time. 基于(内控)有效，审计员通常同时实施控制测试和交易的实质性测试。

[5] For example, to provide some assurance for the accuracy objective for both sales transactions (transaction-related audit objective) and accounts receivable (balance-related audit objective), the auditor might examine sales transactions in the sales journal for unusually large amounts and also compare total monthly sales with prior years. 例如，以确保销售交易(交易相关的审计目标)与应收账款(余额相关的审计目标)的准确性为目标，审计员可以通过在销售日记账中检查超大额的销售交易，也可以把每月总销售与以前年度同期进行比较。

[6] Since the audit report represents an acceptance of considerable responsibility by the CPA firm, a partner must first review the working papers from the engagement to ascertain that a thorough examination has been completed and to form an opinion on the financial statements. 由于审计报告代表着会计师事务所承担的相当大的责任，合伙人必须首先检查该项审计委托的工作底稿，以确保全面审查已完成，并对财务报表提出意见。

10.3 Audit Report
审计报告

> A conversation between A—an accountant and S—a freshman majoring in accounting.
>
> S: How many types of audit reports are there?
>
> A: There are four basic types of audit reports. They are "unqualified opinion", "qualified opinion", "adverse opinion" and "disclaimer of opinion".
>
> S: In what circumstance may an audit issue an unqualified audit report?
>
> A: The large majority of audit reports are unqualified reports. An unqualified opinion should be issued when the auditor concludes that the financial statements are presented fairly, in all material respects, in accordance with the identified financial reporting framework.
>
> S: Oh, I see. Which type is the rarest one?
>
> A: Issuance of an adverse opinion. An adverse opinion states that the financial statements taken overall are not fair presentations. Usually the auditor and the client are able to resolve the accounting problems that might mandate an adverse opinion through arbitration (仲裁). The client cannot afford an adverse opinion if it sells stock to the public, the stock exchanges would suspend trading in the company's stock with resulting serious financial repercussions (后果).

Reports are essential to audit and assurance engagements because they communicate the auditor's findings. Users of financial statements rely on the audit report to provide assurance on the company's financial statements. Such report acts as a bridge taking the large volume of information possessed by the auditor and conveying it to the shareholders in much abbreviated form. There are four basic types of audit reports, under certain specific conditions, may be issued by auditors. They are "**unqualified opinion**", "**qualified opinion**", "**adverse opinion**" and "**disclaimer of opinion**".

Standard Unqualified Audit Report

The **standard unqualified audit report** is issued when the following conditions have been met:

(1) <u>The financial statements presented fairly overall financial position, results of operations and cash flows in conformity with Chinese Accounting Standards or other standards of accounting.</u>[1]

(2) The general standards have been followed in all aspects on the engagement.

(3) Sufficient appropriate evidence has been accumulated, and the auditor has conducted the engagement in a manner that enables him or her to conclude that the standards of **field work** have been met.

(4) The financial statements have adequate information disclosures. This also means that adequate disclosures have been included in the notes and other parts of the financial statements.

(5) There are no circumstances requiring the addition of an explanatory paragraph of the report.

When these conditions are met, the standard unqualified audit report, as shown in Table 10-1, is issued.

Table 10-1　An Illustration of Standard Unqualified Audit Report

AUDITOR'S REPORT (Report title)

To the **addressee** (usually addressed to the shareholders, or the board of directors)

We have audited the accompanying balance sheet of the ABC Company as December 31, 2013, and the related statements of income, changes in owners' equity and cash flows for the year then ended. These financial statements are the responsibility of the Company's management. Our responsibility is to express an opinion on these financial statements based on our audit. **Introductory Paragraph**

We conducted our audit in accordance with Chinese Auditing Standards. Those standards require that we plan and perform the audit to obtain reasonable assurance about whether the financial statements are free of **material misstatement**. An audit includes examining, on a test basis, evidence supporting the amounts and disclosures in the financial statements. An audit also includes assessing the accounting principles used and significant estimates made by management, as well as evaluating the overall financial statement presentation. We believe that our audit provides a reasonable basis for our opinion. **Scope Paragraph**

In our opinion, the financial statements present fairly, in all material respect, the financial position of ABC Company as of December 31, 2013 and the results of its operations and its cash flows for the year then ended. **Opinion Paragraph**

Auditors (the personal names of the auditor and the signatures)

Name of CPA firm

Address (the city where the auditor maintains the office that has responsibility for the audit)

Audit report date (the completion date of the audit)

Unqualified Audit Report with Explanatory Paragraph

In certain situations, an unqualified audit report on the financial statements is issued, but the wording deviated from the standard unqualified report. The unqualified audit report with **explanatory paragraph** meets the criteria of a complete audit with satisfactory results and financial statements that are fairly presented, but the auditor believes it is important or is required to provide additional information. [2] In a qualified, adverse, or disclaimer report, the auditor could not perform a satisfactory audit, because the financial statements have not been fairly presented. The followings are the most important causes of the addition of an explanatory paragraph of the standard unqualified reports:

(1) Emphasis of going-concern problems by drawing attention to the note in the financial statements that discloses the matter.

(2) Situations in which there is significant uncertainty, the resolution of which is dependent on future events that are not under the direct control of the entity.

(3) Other situations such as where the prior financial statements turn out to be materially misstated, and the corresponding figures are properly restated in the current period.

In each case, the three standard report paragraphs are included without modification, and a separate explanatory paragraphs follows the opinion paragraph.

Table 10-2 presents an explanatory paragraph because of changes in accounting principle.

Table 10-2　An Illustration of Explanatory Paragraph

AUDITOR'S REPORT

(Same introductory, scope, and opinion paragraphs as the standard report)

Explanatory Paragraph

As discussed in Note 8 to the financial statements, the Company changed its methods of computing depreciation in 2013.

(Same auditors, name of CPA firm, address, audit report date as the standard report)

Conditions Requiring a Departure from an Unqualified Opinion

It is essential that auditors and readers of audit reports understand the circumstances when an unqualified report is inappropriate and the type of audit report issued in each circumstance. The two conditions requiring a **departure** are briefly summarized in the following:

(1) The scope of the audit has been restricted (**scope limitation**)

When the auditor has not accumulated sufficient appropriate evidence to conclude whether financial statements are stated in accordance with accounting standards, a scope restriction exists. There are two major causes of scope restriction: restrictions imposed by the client and those caused by circumstances beyond either the client's or auditor's control. An example of a client restriction is management's refusal to permit the auditor to confirm material receivables or to physically examine inventory. An example of a restriction caused by circumstances is when the auditor is not appointed until after the client's year end. It may not be possible to physically observe inventories, confirm receivables, or perform other important procedures after the balance sheet date.

(2) The financial statements have not been prepared in accordance with accounting standards

For example, if the client insists on using **replacement costs** for fixed assets or values inventory at selling prices rather than historical costs as required by accounting standards, a departure from the unqualified report is required.

When any of the two conditions requiring a departure from an unqualified report exists and is material, a report other than an unqualified report must be issued.

 Types of Opinion Other than Unqualified

Three main types of audit reports are issued under the above conditions: qualified opinion, adverse opinion, and disclaimer of opinion.

(1) Qualified opinion

A qualified opinion report can result from a limitation on the scope of the audit or failure to follow the accounting standards. A qualified opinion report can be used only when the auditor concludes that the overall financial statements are fairly stated. A disclaimer or an adverse report must be used if the auditor believes that the condition being reported on is highly material. Therefore, the qualified opinion is considered the least severe type of departure from an unqualified report.

A qualified report can take the form of a **qualification** of both the scope and the opinion or of the opinion alone. <u>A scope and opinion qualification can be issued only when the auditor has been unable to accumulate all of the evidence required by accounting standards.</u>[3] Therefore, this type of qualification is used when the auditor's scope has been restricted by the client or when circumstances exist that prevents the auditor from conducting a complete audit. The use of a qualification of the opinion alone is restricted to situations in which the financial statements are not stated in accordance with accounting standards.

When an auditor issues a qualified report, he or she must use the term "except for" in the opinion paragraph. The implication is that the auditor is satisfied that the overall financial statements are correctly stated "except for" a specific aspect of them. It is unacceptable to use the phrase "except for" with any other type of audit opinion.

(2) Adverse opinion

An adverse opinion is used only when the auditor believes that the overall financial statements are so materially misstated or misleading that they do not present fairly the financial position or results of operations and cash flows in conformity with accounting standards. [4] The adverse opinion report can arise only when the auditor has knowledge, after an adequate investigation, of the absence of conformity. This is uncommon and thus the adverse opinion is rarely used.

(3) Disclaimer of opinion

A disclaimer of opinion is issued when the audit has been unable to satisfy himself or herself that the overall financial statements are fairly presented. The necessity for disclaiming an opinion may arise because of a severe limitation on the scope of the audit. The situation prevents the auditor from expressing an opinion on the financial statements as a whole. The auditor also has the opinion to issue a disclaimer of opinion for a going concern problem.

The disclaimer is distinguished from an adverse opinion in that it can arise only from a "lack of knowledge" by the auditor, whereas to express an adverse opinion, the auditor must have knowledge that the financial statements are not fairly stated.[5] Both disclaimers and adverse opinions are used only when the condition is highly material.

Materiality

The common definition of materiality applies to accounting and therefore to audit reporting is: a misstatement in the financial statements can be considered material if knowledge of the misstatement will affect a decision of a reasonable user of the statements [6]. Materiality is an essential consideration in determining the appropriate type of report for a given set of circumstances. For example, if a misstatement is immaterial relative to the financial statements of the entity for the current period, it is appropriate to issue an unqualified report. A common instance is the immediate expensing of office supplies rather than carrying the unused portion in inventory because the amount is insignificant.

The situation is totally different when the amounts are of such significance that the financial statements are materially affected as a whole. In these circumstances, it is necessary to issue a disclaimer of opinion or an adverse opinion, depending on whether a scope limitation or standards departure is involved. In situations of lesser materiality, a qualified opinion is appropriate.

Table 10-3 summarizes the relationship between materiality and the type of opinion to be issued.

Table 10-3　Relationship between Materiality and Type of Opinion

Materiality Level	Significance in Terms of Reasonable Users' Decisions	Type of Opinion
Immaterial	Users' decisions are unlikely to be affected	Unqualified
Material	Users' decisions are likely to be affected only if the information in question is important to the specific decisions being made. The overall financial statements are presented fairly.	Qualified
Highly material	Most or all users' decisions based on the financial statements are likely to be significantly affected.	Disclaimer or Adverse

 Vocabulary

unqualified opinion	无保留意见
qualified opinion	保留意见
adverse opinion	否定意见
disclaimer of opinion	无法表示意见
standard unqualified audit report	标准无保留审计报告，标准审计报告
field work	调查工作，现场工作
addressee	*n.* 受信人，收件人
introductory paragraph	引言段
scope paragraph	范围段，审计范围部分
opinion paragraph	意见段
material misstatement	重大错报
explanatory paragraph	说明段，强调段，审查报告的解释说明部分
departure	*n.* 背离，离开，离去
scope limitation	范围限制
replacement costs	重置成本
qualification	*n.* 限制，保留

Notes

[1] The financial statements presented fairly overall financial position, results of operations and cash flows in conformity with Chinese Accounting Standards or other standards of accounting. 财务报表公允地反映了公司符合中国会计准则或其他会计原则的总体财务状况、经营成果及现金流量的情况。

[2] The unqualified audit report with explanatory paragraph meets the criteria of a complete audit with satisfactory results and financial statements that are fairly presented, but the auditor believes it is important or is required to provide additional information. 具有说明事项段的无保留意见审计报告应符合的标准为：整体审计应具有满意的效果，且公允地列示财务报表。但审计员认为提供附加信息是很重要的，或必须的。

[3]　A scope and opinion qualification can be issued only when the auditor has been unable to accumulate all of the evidence required by accounting standards.　只有当审计人员不能获取所有会计原则所要求的证据时，才可以发表范围和意见受限的保留意见。

[4] An adverse opinion is used only when the auditor believes that the overall financial statements are so materially misstated or misleading that they do not present fairly the financial position or results of operations and cash flows in conformity with accounting standards.　只有当审计人员认为财务报表整体存在重大错报或误导，财务状况或经营成果及现金流量没有依照会计准则公允地列报时，才可以使用否定意见。

[5] The disclaimer is distinguished from an adverse opinion in that it can arise only from a "lack of knowledge" by the auditor, whereas to express an adverse opinion, the auditor must have knowledge that the financial statements are not fairly stated.　无法表示意见与否定意见的区别在于，无法表示意见只能是由"了解不足(未收集到足够审计证据)"造成的，而发表否定意见则是因为审计人员判定财务报表未被公允列报。

[6] a misstatement in the financial statements can be considered material if knowledge of the misstatement will affect a decision of a reasonable user of the statements.　如果错报的知晓将会影响报表使用者的理性决策，那么这一财务报表错报可以认定为是实质性的。

Exercises

I. Discuss the following questions in English.

1.　What is the main function of auditing? Explain the importance of auditing in reducing information risk.

2.　What types of auditing careers are available to those who are competent?

3.　What major characteristics of the organization and conduct of CPA firms permit them to fulfill their social function competently and independently?

4.　Why is there a special need for ethical behavior by CPA professionals?

5.　Identify the four phases of the audit.

6.　What are the functions of planning and designing an audit approach?

7.　What five circumstances are required for a standard unqualified audit report to be issued?

8.　What are the purposes of the opinion paragraph in the audit report? Identify the most important information included in the opinion paragraph.

9.　What type of opinion should an auditor issue when the financial statements are not in accordance with the accounting standards because such adherence would result in misleading statements?

10. How does the auditor's opinion differ between scope limitations caused by client restrictions and limitations resulting from conditions beyond the client's control? Under which of these two will the auditor be most likely to issue a disclaimer of opinion?

11.   How does materiality affect audit reporting decisions?

II. Choose the best word or phrase that fits the sentence.

1.   To do an audit, there must be information in a(n) _____ form and some criteria by which the auditor can evaluate the information.

     A. flexible   B. available

     C. verifiable   D. confident

2.   Many financial statement users and the general public confuse auditing with _____.

     A. accounting   B. audit

     C. account   D. CPA

3.   The highest level of professional personnel within a CPA firm is _____.

     A. manager   B. partner

     C. director   D. CEO

4.   The CICPA requires independence only for _____ engagements.

     A. assurance   B. auditing

     C. attestation   D. formal

5.   The _____ of misstatement in the financial statements is reduced if the client has effective controls over computer operations and transaction processing.

     A. risk   B. probability

     C. possibility   D. danger

6.   Auditors also evaluate the client's recording of transactions by verifying the monetary amounts of transactions, a process called _____ of transactions.

     A. analytical procedure   B. substantive tests

     C. tests of details   D. tests of controls

7.   Since the audit report represents an acceptance of considerable responsibility by the CPA firm, a partner must first review the _____ from the engagement to ascertain that a thorough examination has been completed and to form an opinion on the financial statements.

     A. financial statements   B. financial statements and audit report

     C. working papers   D. audit report and audit contract

8.   The _____ meets the criteria of a complete audit with satisfactory results and financial statements that are fairly presented, but the auditor believes it is important or is required to provide additional information.

     A. standard unqualified   B. unqualified audit report with explanatory paragraph

     C. qualified   D. qualified audit report with explanatory paragraph

9.   When an auditor issues a qualified report, he or she must use the term "_____" in the opinion paragraph.

     A. except for   B. in addition

     C. besides   D. all but

10.   The necessity for disclaiming an opinion may arise because of a _____ limitation on

the scope of the audit.

    A. high   B. total

    C. material   D. severe

11. _____ is an essential consideration in determining the appropriate type of report for a given set of circumstances.

    B. Scope limitation   B. Materiality

    C. Departure   D. Independence

III. Match each word on the left with its corresponding meaning on the right.

A	B
1. counsel	(a) a variation that deviates from the standard or norm
2. client	(b) denial of any connection with or knowledge of
3. testimony	(c) someone who pays for goods or services
4. disclaimer	(d) something that provides direction or advice as to a decision or course of action
5. misstatement	(e) the evidence by which something is attested
6. expertise	(f) something that serves as evidence
7. qualified	(g) a statement that contains a mistake
8. adverse	(h) skillfulness by virtue of possessing special knowledge
9. attestation	(i) in an opposing direction
10. departure	(j) restricted in meaning

IV. Fill in the blanks with words or phrases from the list below.

A.	systematic	B.	code	C.	body	D.	cornerstone
E.	effectiveness	F.	administrative	G.	performing	H.	employed
I.	achieved	J.	industries	K.	consulting	L.	apply
M.	board	N.	similar	O.	mandated	P.	governance

Internal auditors are (1)____ by the organizations they audit. They work for government agencies (federal, state and local); for publicly traded companies; and for non-profit companies across all (2)____.

The internationally recognized standard setting (3)____ for the profession is the Institute of Internal Auditors(IIA). The IIA has defined internal auditing as follows: "Internal auditing is an independent, objective assurance and (4)____ activity designed to add value and improve an organization's operations. It helps an organization accomplish its objectives by bringing a (5)____, disciplined approach to evaluate and improve the (6)____ of risk management, control, and governance processes". Thus professional internal auditors provide independent and objective audit and consulting services focused on evaluating whether the (7)____ of directors, shareholders, stakeholders, and corporate executives have reasonable assurance that the organization's (8)____, risk management, and control processes are designed adequately and function effectively.

Internal audit professionals (Certified Internal Auditors—CIAs) are governed by the international professional standards and (9) _____ of conduct of the Institute of Internal Auditors. While internal auditors are not independent of the companies that employ them, independence and objectivity are a (10) _____ of the IIA professional standards; and are discussed at length in the standards and the supporting practice guides and practice advisories. Professional internal auditors are (11) _____ by the IIA standards to be independent of the business activities they audit. This independence and objectivity are (12) _____ through the organizational placement and reporting lines of the internal audit department.

Internal auditors of publicly traded companies in the United States are required to report functionally to the board of directors directly, or a sub-committee of the board of directors (typically the audit committee), and not to management except for (13) _____ purposes. As described often in the professional literature for the practice of internal auditing (such as Internal Auditor, the journal of the IIA), or other (14) _____ and generally recognized frameworks for management control when evaluating an entity's governance and control practices; and (15) _____ COSO's "Enterprise Risk Management-Integrated Framework" or other similar and generally recognized frameworks for entity-wide risk management when evaluating an organization's entity—wide risk management practices. Professional internal auditors also use control self-assessment as an effective process for (16) _____ their work.

V. Translate the following sentences into Chinese.

1. Auditing is a systematic process of objectively and evaluating evidence reagarding assertions about economic actions and events to ascertain that degree of correspondence between those assertions and established criteria and communicating the results to interested users.

2. Audit can have a preventive effect. If employees or management know they will be audited, this fact may help prevent an detect errors or irregularities.

3. A professional accountant should be straightforward and honest in all professional and business relationships.

4. To external auditors, the principal reason why internal control interests the auditor is that the reliance on internal control will reduce the amount of substantive testing required.

5. Tests of control by the auditor involve auditors ensuring that the procedures above have been applied.

6. To convey information in a sufficient form, the audit report has become an extremely formalized group of phrases, each of which has special significance.

7. In all cases where a qualified opinion is issued, the auditor should give a clear description of all substantive reasons for the qualification and quantify the effect, unless impracticable.

8. The concept of materiality is fundamental to the presentation and classification of data in financial statements.

VI. Translate the following sentences into English.

1. 审计的目的是提高财务报表预期使用者对财务报表的信赖程度。

2. 内部审计是指由部门、单位内部专职审计机构专职审计人员所进行的审计。

3. 会计师事务所是国家批准成立的依法独立承办注册会计师业务的单位，实行自收自支、独立核算、依法纳税，它是注册会计师的工作机构。

4. 专业胜任能力是指注册会计师具有专业知识、技能和经验，能够经济、有效地完成客户委托的业务。

5. 控制测试是指用于评价内部控制在防止或发现并纠正认定层次重大错报方面运行的有效审计程序。

6. 实质性程序是指注册会计师针对评估的重大错报风险实施的直接用以发现认定层次重大错报风险的审计程序，包括对各类交易、账户余额、披露的细节进行测试以及实质性分析程序。

7. 审计报告是指注册会计师根据审计准则的规定，在执行审计工作的基础上，对财务报表发表审计意见的书面文件。

8. 保留意见是审计人员认为被审计单位的经营活动和财务报表在整体上是公允地，但对某些问题还不能做出肯定或否定，个别方面可能存在的重要错误或问题又不足以使财务报表失效而相应做出保留若干意见的评价。

Reading Material 10

The Big Four

The Big Four are the four largest international professional services networks, offering audit, assurance, tax, consulting, advisory, actuarial, corporate finance, and legal services. They handle the vast majority of audits for publicly traded companies as well as many private companies, creating an oligopoly in auditing large companies. It is reported that the Big Four audit 99% of the companies in the FTSE 100, and 96% of the companies in the FTSE 250, an index of the leading mid-cap listing companies.

This group was once known as the "Big Eight", and was reduced to the "Big Six" and then "Big Five" by a series of mergers. The Big Five became the Big Four after the demise of Arthur Andersen in 2002, following its involvement in the Enron scandal. Here are the brief introductions about them.

● Deloitte Touche Tohmatsu

Deloitte Touche Tohmatsu Limited (also branded as "Deloitte") is the largest private professional services organization in the world. Its global headquarters is located in New York City. According to the organization's website as of 2013, Deloitte has the revenues of $32.4 billion and approximately 200,000 staff at work in more than 150 countries, delivering audit tax, consulting, enterprise risk and financial advisory services through its member firms. Deloitte and each member firm is governed by a set of shared values which guide their actions in everything they do. These are four values—integrity, outstanding value, markets and clients. In 2012, it was reported that in the UK, Deloitte had the largest number of clients among FTSE 250 companies.

● Pricewaterhouse Coopers

PWC(officially Pricewaterhouse Coopers) is a global professional services firm headquartered in London, UK. The firm was formed in 1998 by a merger between Coopers & Lybrand and Price Waterhouse. With a combined headcount of more than 184,000 staff in 776 cities across 159 countries, PwC firms rank the world's second-largest professional services firm (after Deloitte) and one of the "Big Four" accountancy firms. Aggregated revenues in fiscal year 2013 were $32.1 billion, including expenses reimbursed by clients. Their clients range from the world's largest and most complex organizations to some of its most innovative entrepreneurs.

● Ernst & Young

Ernst & Young (EY) is the third largest professional service organization in the world with member firms in more than 150 countries, headquartered in London, UK. It employs over 175,000 and had total revenues of $25.8 billion in 2013. The members of the EY global organization help companies in businesses across all industries—from emerging growth companies to global powerhouses—deal with a broad range of business issues. EY provides a range of services, including accounting and auditing, tax reporting and operations, tax advisory.

● KPMG

KPMG is one of the largest professional services firms in the world and one of the Big Four auditors, along with Deloitte, EY and PWC. Its global headquarters is located in Amstelveen, Netherlands. With around 155,000 staff working in member firms in 148 countries, its total revenues reached $23.4 billion in 2013. Its purpose is to turn knowledge into value for the benefit of its clients, their people, and the capital markets. It plays an important role in the capital markets, and is highly active in supporting positive reform within the industry to strengthen credibility and confidence. It also has senior individuals from Japan, USA, UK and Germany who can deal with country specific issues and provide reports under the relevant national form of Generally Accepted Accounting Practice.

Answers:

II.	1	C	2	A	3	B	4	C	5	A	6	B	7	C	8	B
	9	A	10	D	11	B										
III.	1	d	2	c	3	f	4	b	5	g	6	h	7	j	8	i
	9	e	10	a												
IV.	1	H	2	J	3	C	4	K	5	A	6	E	7	M	8	P
	9	B	10	D	11	O	12	I	13	F	14	N	15	L	16	G

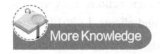

More Knowledge 知识扩展

2016 年我国审计准则修订的主要内容

　　2016 年中国注册会计师协会颁布了 12 项审计准则，此次修订充分体现了准则的国际趋同。其中《中国注册会计师审计准则第 1504 号——在审计报告中沟通关键审计事项》为新制定准则，《中国注册会计师审计准则第 1501 号——对财务报表形成审计意见和出具审计报告》《中国注册会计师审计准则第 1502 号——在审计报告中发表非无保留意见》《中国注册会计师审计准则第 1503 号——在审计报告中增加强调事项段和其他事项段》《中国注册会计师审计准则第 1151 号——与治理层的沟通》《中国注册会计师审计准则第 1324 号——持续经营》和《中国注册会计师审计准则第 1521 号——注册会计师对其他信息的责任》6 项准则做出实质性修改，还有《中国注册会计师审计准则第 1111 号——就审计业务约定条款达成一致意见》《中国注册会计师审计准则第 1131 号——审计工作底稿》《中国注册会计师审计准则第 1301 号——审计证据》《中国注册会计师审计准则第 1332 号——期后事项》《中国注册会计师审计准则第 1341 号——书面声明》5 项是为保持审计准则体系的内在一致性而做出相应文字调整。

　　《中国注册会计师审计准则第 1501 号——对财务报表形成审计意见和出具审计报告》不再以"标准审计报告""非标准审计报告"表述报告类型，并改变了传统审计报告的行文顺序为先表述审计意见、形成审计意见的基础和关键审计事项，之后才是责任段。其次，新颁布的《中国注册会计师审计准则第 1504 号——在审计报告中沟通关键审计事项》要求注册会计师在上市实体审计报告中增加关键审计事项部分，披露审计工作中的重点难点等审计项目的个性化信息，并规范了关键审计事项的恰当表述。而其他实质性修订主要是明确与关键审计事项的关系，以及强化审计人员对持续经营及其他信息等的责任界限。

Chapter 11   International Accounting Harmonization
国际会计协调

Learning Objectives

- Understand the definition of international accounting 了解国际会计的定义
- Understand accounting harmonization and its purpose 了解会计协调及其目的
- Understand international dimension of accounting 了解会计的国际维度
- Know several organizations that have been key players in setting international accounting standards and in promoting international accounting harmonizations, such as IASB, EU, IOSCO, IFAC, ISAR and OECD 了解一些在制定国际会计准则和促进国际会计统一方面发挥关键作用的组织，如国际会计准则理事会、欧盟、国际证监会组织、国际会计咨询委员会、会计标准专家组和经合组织
- Know the web sites addresses of major international organizations and national regulatory and accountancy organizations 了解主要国际组织和国家监管和会计组织的网址
- Understand IFRS Framework 理解国际财务报告准则框架
- Know IASs and IFRSs 了解国际会计准则和国际财务报告准则

 听力练习

Chapter 11 English Listening.mp3

第 11 章听写原文翻译和答案的音频见右侧二维码。

Dictation: *Listen and complete the passage with the words or phrases according to what you've heard from the speaker.*

ACCA offers three qualifications － a professional qualification entitling members to the ____1____ chartered certified accountant; a technician level ____2____; and a diploma for managers who are non-accountants but who need to acquire operational and strategic finance skills. For each of these qualifications, ACCA combines the benefits of traditional ____3____ skills with a wide ranging and forward looking syllabus, which recognizes that finance professionals are increasingly required to demonstrate ____4____ thinking, excellent communication, people skills and fluency with information technology. This was recently confirmed by a poll of ____5____ business leaders commissioned by ACCA from the independent research firm MORI.

Wisdom 至理名言

The globe is not a level playing field. 这个世界不是一个公平的竞争环境。

Mini Case 微型案例

Huawei was founded in 1987. The company's initial development kept in step with the national policies. However, due to the fact that China was basically under a fixed exchange rate system before the exchange rate reform, the operators' awareness of preventing foreign exchange risks is not strong enough. With the implementation of the floating exchange rates since 2005, the foreign exchange risk faced by the company's operations increased, and the exchange rate changes brought certain loss of profit to the company. The company began to take some measures to hedge and avoid foreign exchange risks.

However, from the analysis of the subject of net exchange loss from Huawei's financial statements over the years, it can be seen that the company's foreign exchange risk management capability needs to be improved. In 2014 the company's net exchange loss was 2.135 billion *yuan*. In 2015, the net exchange loss increased by 2.26 billion *yuan* to 4.362 billion *yuan*. In 2016, the company's net exchange loss continued to increase to 5.223 billion *yuan*. The company's net exchange losses continued to rise sharply for three years. Although it has a lot to do with the company's overseas business development, it can be seen that the company has not managed foreign exchange risks effectively.

International accounting is the international aspects of accounting, including such matters as accounting principles and reporting practices in different countries and their classification, patterns of accounting development, international and regional harmonization, foreign currency translation, foreign exchange risk, international comparisons of consolidation accounting and inflation accounting, accounting in developing countries, accounting in communist countries, performance evaluation of foreign subsidiaries and so forth.

11.1　An Overview of International Accounting
国际会计概述

A conversation between A—an accountant and S—a freshman majoring in accounting.

S: I can't see any reason to know anything about the international accounting, since I plan to practice in China with Chinese companies using Chinese Accounting Standards and Regulations.

A: That's doubtful. Which kind of company is your favorite?

S: A large company, like China Petroleum and Chemical Corparation.

A: Do you know this corporation is a publicly listed company at home and also abroad?

S: Is that true?

A: Of course. The corporation issued shares in Hong Kong, New York and London in 2000, and then issued A shares in Shanghai Stock Exchange in 2001.

S: Is there any other company that has issued shares abroad?

A: Yes, there are hundreds of companies that issue shares in Hong Kong, Singapore, New York, London and so on.

S: What accounting principles should be used when preparing financial statements for these companies?

A: Do you think it is enough for them to adopt Chinese Accounting Standards only.

S: Of course not.

What is International Acccounting

International accounting deals with accounting issues that are important to those directly or indirectly involves with accounting and financial control in firms with international operations. [1] International accounting might be distinguished among three approaches: a universal system, a descriptive and informative approach covering all the methods and standards of all countries, and accounting practices of **foreign subsidiaries** and **parent companies**. There are the explanations of all three approaches in the followings.

(1) A universal system

International accounting is considered to be a universal system that could be adopted in all countries. A worldwide set of generally accepted accounting principles would be established. Practices and principles would be developed to be applicable to all countries. This concept would be the ultimate goal of an international accounting system.

(2) A descriptive and informative approach covering all the methods and standards of all countries

Under this concept, international accounting includes all varieties of principles, methods and standards of accounting of all countries. A collection of all principles, methods and standards of all contries would be considered as the international accounting system. These variations result from differing georgraphic, social, economic, political and legal influences.

(3) Accounting practices of foreign subsidiaries and parent companies

A reference to a particular country or **domicile** is needed under the concept for effective international financial reporting. The accountant is concerned mainly with the translation and adjustment of subsidiary's financial statements. Different accounting problems arise and different accounting principles are to be followed depending upon which country is used as a refernce for translation and adjustment purpose. [2]

Accounting Harmonization

With the dramatic growth in global trade and the accelerated internationalization of capital markets, financial statements produced in one country are more frequently used in other countries. This has brought accounting **harmonization** to be the forefront issue of international business.

Accounting is a form of communication. As with all types of communication, though, misunderstanding can arise unless meanings are reasonably clear. Harmonization is a process of increasing the **compatibility** of accounting practices by setting limits on how much they can vary. Accounting harmonization has many dimensions – regional versus global, voluntary versus mandated, piecemeal versus comprehensive, and so on. [3] What will emerge as the most likely development path for the near future? There are three ways. One way is the use of **bilateral agreements**. Under this approach, two or more countries agree to recognize each other's national standards on a **reciprocal** basis. Mutual recognition on a regional level is a second possibility, for instance, among the **European Union**. A third scenario places harmonization at the doorsteps of private, professional groups such as IASB. It appears that the third alternative enjoys a slight edge.

Harmonization is nowadays often considered as an **irreversible** process, even if some authors consider it as an impossible and useless dream. Proponents of international harmonization claim that harmonization has many advantages. It is expected to make financial markets more efficient.

Others have argued that financial statement users have difficulty interpreting information produced under non-domestic accounting system. They claim that harmonization will make it more likely that users will interpret the information correctly, and thus make better decisions based on that information. [4]

Increasing evidence shows that the goal of international harmonization has been so widely accepted that the trend towards international harmonization will continue or accelerate. Harmonization is happening as a natural response to economic forces. Growing numbers of companies are voluntarily adopting International Accounting Standards (IAS). Many countries have adopted IAS in their entirety, base their national standards on IAS, or allow the use of IAS.

In China, on 16 Februry 2006, the Ministry of Finance of the People's Republic of China announced that it has adopted a new basic standard and 38 new Chinse Accounting Standards that are substantially in line with IAS, though a few exceptions are noted. The basic standard is akin to a conceptual framework, and the 38 standards address nearly all over the issues covered in the International Financial Reporting Standards.

International Dimensions of Accounting

Although international accounting might sound **mysterious** and **exotic**, it is a well-established area of specialty within accounting and has two major dimensions: comparative and **pragmatic**.

Comparative: examining how and why accounting principles differ from country to country. It discusses the issues such as financial accounting principles and practices in foreign nations and how thses are established, different accounting systems and their major features.

Pragmatic: examining accounting issues encountered by individuals and firms in international business.

The comparative dimention is oriented toward financial accounting, and the pragmatic one tends to be managerial accounting.

<u>The financial accounting topics covered by international accounting include accounting for foreign currency transactions, translation and consolidation of foreign subsidiary's financial statements, financial disclosure, auditing and taxation.</u> [5]

The managerial accounting topics include foreign exchange risk management, foreign investment analysis, accounting information systems, **transfer pricing**, budgeting, performance evaluation, financial control and operational auditing.

Vocabulary

foreign subsidiary	外国子(附属)公司
parent company	母公司，总公司
domicile	*n.* 住处；永久住处
harmonization	*n.* 和谐，协调，相称
compatibility	*n.* 适合；互换性；通用性
bilateral agreement	双边协定
reciprocal	*adj.* 相互的；互惠的
European Union	欧洲联盟，欧盟
irreversible	*adj.* 不可逆的；不能翻转的
mysterious	*adj.* 神秘的；不可思议的；难解的
exotic	*adj.* 异国的；外来的
pragmatic	*adj.* 实际的；实用主义的
transfer pricing	转让定价，转移定价

Notes

[1] International accounting deals with accounting issues that are important to those directly or indirectly involves with accounting and financial control in firms with international operations. 国际会计探讨的是对于直接或间接地参与国际经营的企业会计与财务控制至关重要的会计问题。

[2] Different accounting problems arise and different accounting principles are to be followed depending upon which country is used as a refernce for translation and adjustment purpose. 哪个国家作为折算和调整的基准，选择不同，出现的会计问题有所不同，遵循的会计原则也不同。

[3] Accounting harmonization has many dimensions — regional versus global, voluntary versus mandated, piecemeal versus comprehensive, and so on. 会计协调有许多维度——区域与全球、主动与被动、部分与综合等等。

[4] They claim that harmonization will make it more likely that users will interpret the information correctly, and thus make better decisions based on that information. 他们声称协调更像是使用者正确地解读信息，从而依据这些信息做出更好的决策。

[5] The financial accounting topics covered by international accounting include accounting for foreign currency transactions, translation and consolidation of foreign subsidiary's financial statements, financial disclosure, auditing and taxation. 国际会计涵盖的财务会计课题包括外币交易会计、外国子公司财务报表的折算与合并、财务披露、审计和税务。

11.2 Major Accounting Harmonization Organizations Among Governments
主要政府间会计协调组织

A conversation between A—an accountant and S—a freshman majoring in accounting.

S: Is there any organization that attempts to harmonize conflicting accounting standards all over the world?

A: Yes. There are many organizations, such as IASB, EU, IOSCO and IFAC.

S: Could you tell me some details about IASB?

A: International Accounting Standards Board, abbreviated as IASB, is an independent regulatory body, headquartered in the United Kingdom, which aims to develop a single set of global accounting standards.

S: What about EU?

A: EU, European Union, which we call "欧盟" in Chinese, is an economic and political union. In contrast to the IASB, which has no authority to require implementation of its accounting standards, the European Commission has full enforcement powers for its accounting directives throughout the member states.

S: Oh. How many countries are there in the EU?

A: 28 countries exactly. Croatia became the 28th EU country on 1 July 2013.

Six organizations have been key players in setting international accounting standards and in promoting international accounting harmonizations:

(1) International Accounting Standards Board (IASB)

(2) **Commission of the European Union (EU)**

(3) **International Organization of Securities Commissions (IOSCO)**

(4) **International Federation of Accountants (IFAC)**

(5) United Nations Intergovernmental Working Group of Experts on International Standards

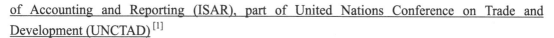

of Accounting and Reporting (ISAR), part of United Nations Conference on Trade and Development (UNCTAD)[1]

(6) Organization for Economic Cooperation and Development Working Group on Accounting Standards (OECD Working Group)[2]

The IASB represents private-sector interests and organizations. The EU Commission, referred to as the European Commission (EC), the OECD Working Group, and the ISAR are political entities that derive their powers from international agreements. IFAC's main activities include issuing technical and professional guidance and promoting the adoption of IFAC and IASB pronouncements. IOSCO promotes high standards of regulation, including harmonized accounting and disclosure standards for cross-border capital raising and trading.

In this part, we will introduce the latter five oranizations, and will explain the first one in detail in the next part.

European Union (EU)

The Treaty of Rome[3] established the EU in 1957, with the goal of harmonizing the legal and economic systems of its member states. As of May 2014, the EU comprises 28 member countries. The European Commission (EC, the governing body of the EU) has full enforcement powers for its accounting **directives** throughout the member states.

One of the EU's goals is to achieve integration of European financial markets. Toward this end, the EC has introduced directives and undertaken major new **initiatives** to achieve a single market for:

(1) raising capital on an EU-wide basis;

(2) establishing a common legal framework for intergrated secutities and derivatives markets;

(3) achieving a single set of accounting standards for listed companies.

The EC **embarked** on a major program of company law harmonization soon after it was formed. EC directives now cover all aspects of company law. Several have a direct bearing on accounting. Of these, many consider the Forth, Seventh, and Eighth Directives to be historically and substantively the most important.

The EU's Fourth Directive, issued in 1978, is the broadest and most comprehensive set of accounting rules within the EU framework. Both public and private companies above certain minimum size criteria must comply. The Fourth Directive requirements apply to individual company accounts and include format rules for financial statements, disclosure requirements, and valuation rules.

The Seventh Directive, issued in 1983, addresses the issue of consolidated financial statements. At the time, consolidated financial statements were the exception rather than the rule. They were the norm in Ireland, the Netherlands, and the United Kingdom, but Germany required consolidation of German subsidiaries (only). However, they were rare elsewhere in Europe.

The Eighth Directive, issued in 1984, addresses various aspects of the qualifications of professionals authorized to carry out legally required (statutory) audits. Essentially, this directive lays down minimum qualifications of auditors.

EC endorsement of IFRS began in 2003 with the adoption of all existing IASB standards and interpretations. The Fourth and Seventh Directives were also amended in 2003 to remove inconsistencies between the old directives and IFRS.

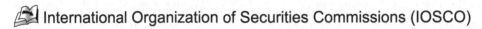 International Organization of Securities Commissions (IOSCO)

IOSCO's membership regulates more than 95% of the world's securities markets. Its members include over 120 securities regulators and 80 other securities markets participants (i.e. stock exchanges, financial regional and international organizations etc.). IOSCO is the only international financial regulatory organization which includes all the major emerging markets **jurisdictions** within its membership.

The member agencies currently assembled together in the International Organization of Securities Commissions have resolved, through its permanent structures:

(1) to cooperate in developing, implementing and promoting adherence to internationally recognised and consistent standards of regulation, oversight and enforcement in order to protect investors, maintain fair, efficient and **transparent** markets, and seek to address systemic risks;

(2) to enhance investor protection and promote investor confidence in the integrity of securities markets, through strengthened information exchange and cooperation in enforcement against misconduct and in supervision of markets and market **intermediaries**;

(3) to exchange information at both global and regional levels on their respective experiences in order to assist the development of markets, strengthen market **infrastructure** and implement appropriate regulation.

IOSCO has worked extensively on international disclosure and accounting standards to facilitate the ability of companies to raise capital efficiently in global securities markets. In 1998 IOSCO published a set of non-financial disclosure standards that may eventually enable companies to use a single **prospectus** to offer or list shares on any of the world's major capital markets. Securities regulators worldwide are increasingly adopting these standards.

An IOSCO technical committee focuses on multinational disclosure and accounting. Its main objective is to facilitate the process whereby world-class issuers can raise capital in the most effective and efficient way on all capital markets where investor demand exists. [4]

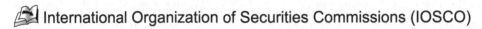 International Federation of Accountants (IFAC)

High-quality auditing standards are necessary to ensure that accounting standards are rigorously interpreted and applied. Auditors **validate** and add **credibility** to external financial reports. Credible financial reporting is at the core of the efficient functioning of capital markets. Thus, the development of international accounting and auditing standards should be aligned for optimal harmonization to occur.

IFAC is the global organization for the accountancy profession dedicated to serving the public interest by strengthening the profession and contributing to the development of strong international economies. [5] IFAC is comprised of 179 members and associates in 130 countries and jurisdictions, representing approximately 2.5 million accountants in public practice, education, government service, industry, and commerce. IFAC members are professional accountancy organizations recognized by law or general **consensus** within their countries as substantial national organizations. National organizations may apply to become an IFAC associate where the organization is working toward membership.

Organized in 1977, IFAC's mission is to serve the public interest by: contributing to the development of high-quality standards and guidance; facilitating the adoption and implementation of high-quality standards and guidance; contributing to the development of strong professional accountancy organizations and accounting firms and to high-quality practices by professional accountants; promoting the value of professional accountants worldwide; and speaking out on public interest issues.

United Nations Intergovernmental Working Group of Experts on International Standards of Accounting and Reporting (ISAR)

The Intergovernmental Working Group of Experts on ISAR was created by the United Nations Economic and Social Council in 1982, and is the only intergovernmental expert body focused on corporate transparency and accounting issues. [6] Hosted by United Nations Conference on Trade and Development, ISAR's work covers a range of financial and non-financial corporate reporting issues. Its mission is to support sustainable economic development and financial stability by contributing to improvements in corporate transparency.

Its specific mandate is to promote the harmonization of national accounting standards for enterprises. ISAR accomplishes its mandate by discussing and **promulgating** best practices, including those recommended by IASB. ISAR was an early proponent of environmental reporting and recent initiatives have focused on corporate governace and accounting by **small and medium-sized enterprises**. It has also conducted technical assistance projects in a number of areas such as accounting reform and retraining in the Russian Federation, Azerbaijan and Uzbekistan, and designing and developing a long-distance learning program in accountancy for French-speaking Africa.

Organization for Economic Cooperation and Development (OECD)

The OECD was officially born on 30 September 1961, when the Convention entered into force. Today, 34 OECD member countries worldwide regularly turn to one another to identify problems, discuss and analyze them, and promote policies to solve them.

OCED is the international organization of the industrialized, market economy countries. It functions through its governing body, the OECD Council, and its network of about 250 committees, working groups and expert groups. [7] Some 40,000 senior officials from national administrations go to OECD committee meetings each year to request, review and contribute to work undertaken by the OECD Secretariat. Once they return home, they have online access to documents and can exchange information through a special network.

OECD uses its wealth of information on a broad range of topics to help governments to foster **prosperity** and fight **poverty** through economic growth and financial stability. We help ensure the environmental implications of economic and social development are taken into account. OECD's work is based on continued monitoring of events in member countries as well as outside OECD area, and includes regular projections of short and medium-term economic development. The OECD Secretariat collects and analyzes data, after which committees discuss policy regarding this information, the Council makes decisions, and then governments implement recommendations.

 Major Websites

There are many other important organizations, which have effect on setting international accounting standards and promoting international accounting harmonizations, such as **International Federation of Stock Exchanges (FIBV), International Monetary Fund (IMF)** and **World Bank**. Refer to Table 11-1 for Websites offering information about major international organizations.

Table 11-1   Websites Offering Information about Major International Organizations

Organization	Website Adress
Bank for International Settlements	www.bis.org
Confederation of Asian and Pacific Accountants (CAPA)	capa.com.my
Deloitte IAS Plus Web site	www.iasplus.com
European Union (EU)	europa.eu/index_en.htm
Fédération des Experts-comptables Européens – Federation of European Accountants (FEE)	www.fee.be
International Accounting Standards Board (IASB)	www.ifrs.org
International Association of Insurance Supervisions (IAIS)	www.iaisweb.org
International Federation of Accountants (IFAC)	www. ifac.org
International Federation of Stock Exchanges (FIBV)	www.fibv.com
International Financial Risk Institute (IFRI)	www.ifri.ch
International Monetary Fund (IMF)	www.imf.org
International Organization of Securities Commissions (IOSCO)	www.iosco.org
Organization for Economic Cooperation and Development (OECD)	www.oecd.org
United Nations Conference on Trade and Development (UNCTAD)	unctad.org
World Bank	www.worldbank.org
World Trade Organization (WTO)	www.wto.org

Note: All websites begin with http://, and this listing was correct when this book went to press. Website addresses often change, and occasionally are discontinued.

Table 11-2 presents the Web site addresses of national regulatory and accountancy organizations, many of which are actively involved in accounting harmonization activities.

Table 11-2　Websites of Selected Regulatory and Accountancy Organizations

Organization	Website adress
Government and Regulatory Organizations	
UK Financial Conduct Authority (FCA)	*fca.org.uk*
UK Prudential Regulation Authority	*bankofengland.co.uk*
US Securities and Exchange Commission (SEC)	*sec.gov*
French Autorité des Marchés Financiers (AMF)	*amf-france.org*
National Professional Accountancy Organizations	
Argentina—Federación Argentina de Consejos Profesionales de Ciencias Económicas	*www.facpce.org.ar*
Barbados—The Institute of Chartered Accountants of Bardados	*icab.bb*
Belgium—Institut des Experts Comptables	*accountancy.be*
Canada—Chartered Professional Accountant of Canada	*cpacanada.ca*
China—Chinese Institute of Certified Public Accountants	*cicpa.org.cn*
Cyprus—The Institute of Certified Public Accountants of Cyprus	*icpac.org.cy*
Czech Republic—Union of Accountants of the Czech Repulic	*svaz-ucetnich.cz*
France—Conseil supérieur de l'ordre des experts-comptables	*experts-comptables.com*
Germany—Institut der Wirtschaftsprufer in Deutschland	*idw.de*
Hong Kong SAR—Hong Kong Institute of Certified Public Accountants	*hkicpa.org.hk*
India—Institute of Chartered Accountants of India	*icai.org*
Ireland—Institute of Chartered Accountants in Ireland	*charteredaccountants.ie*
Japan—Japanese Institute of Certified Public Accountants	*jicpa.or.jp*
Jordan—Arab Society of Certified Public Accountants	*ascasociety.org*
Kenya—Institute of Certified Public Accountants of Kenya	*icpak.com*
Korea—Korean Institute of Certified Public Accountants	*kicpa.or.kr*
Malaysia—Malaysian Institute of Accountants	*mia.org.my*
Malta—Malta Institute of Accountants	*miamalta.org*
Mexico—Instituto Mexicano de Contadores Públicos	*imcp.org.mx*
Nepal—Institute of Chartered Accountants of Nepal	*ican.org.np*
New Zealand—Institute of Chartered Accountants of New Zealand	*icanz.co.nz*
Nigeria—Institute of Chartered Accountants of Nigeria	*icanig.org*
Norway—Den norske Revisorforening	*revisornett.no*
Pakistan—Institute of Cost and Management Accountants of Pakistan	*icmap.com.pk*
Pakistan—Institute of Chartered Accountants of Pakistan	*icap.org.pk*
Philippines—Philippine Institute of Certified Public Accountants	*picpa.com.ph*

Table 11-2(Continued)

Organization	Website adress
Romania—Corpul Expertilor Contabili si Contabililor Autorizatidin Romania	*ceccar.ro*
Singapore—Institute of Singapore Chartered Accountants	*accountants.org.sg*
South Africa—South African Institute of Chartered Accountants	*saica.co.za*
Sweden—Föreningen Auktoriserade Revisorer	*far.se*
Turkey—Union of Chambers of Certified Public Accountants of Turkey	*turmob.org.tr*
UK—Institute of Chartered Accountants in England & Wales	*icaew.com*
US—American Institute of CPAS	*aicpa.org*
Zimbabwe	*icaz.org.zw*
Accounting Standards-Setting Bodies	*icaew.co.uk*
Australia—Accounting Standards Board (AASB)	*aasb.com.au*
France—Conseil National de la Comptabilité (CNC)	*finances.gouv.fr*
Germany—German Accounting Standards Committee	*drsc.de*
Japan—Accounting Standards Board (ASBJ)	*asb.org.jp*
New Zealand—Accounting Standards Board	*icanz.co.nz*
UK—Accounting Standards Board (ASB)	*asb.org.uk*
US—Financial Accounting Standards Board (FASB)	*fasb.org*

Note: All websites begin with http://www, and this listing was correct when this book went to press. Websites often change, and occasionally are discontinued.

 Vocabulary

Commission of the European Union (EU)	欧盟委员会(欧盟)
International Organization of Securities Commissions (IOSCO)	国际证券事务监察委员会组织
International Federation of Accountants (IFAC)	国际会计师联合会
directive	*n.* 指令 & *adj.* 指示性的，指导性的
initiative	*n.* 倡议 & *adj.* 自发的；创始的
embark	*vt.* 使从事，使着手
jurisdiction	*n.* 司法权；管辖权
transparent	*adj.* 透明的；含义清楚的，显而易见的
intermediary	*n.* 中间人；媒介；调解人
infrastructure	*n.* 基础设施；基础建设
prospectus	*n.* 内容说明书；内容介绍，简介
validate	*vt.* 使合法化，使有法律效力；使生效；批准，确认
credibility	*n.* 可靠性，可信性；确实性

consensus	*n.* 一致；舆论；一致同意，合意
promulgate	*vt.* 宣扬(某事物)；传播；公布；颁布
small and medium-sized enterprises	中小企业
prosperity	*n.* 繁荣；兴旺，昌盛；成功
poverty	*n.* 贫穷；缺乏，不足；贫瘠，不毛；低劣
International Federation of Stock Exchanges (FIBV)	国际证券交易所联会
International Monetary Fund (IMF)	国际货币基金组织
World Bank	世界银行

✎ Notes

[1] United Nations Intergovernmental Working Group of Experts on International Standards of Accounting and Reporting (ISAR), part of United Nations Conference on Trade and Development (UNCTAD)   联合国会计与报告国际准则政府间专家工作组，联合国贸易和发展会议的一部分

[2] Organization for Economic Cooperation and Development Working Group on Accounting Standards (OECD Working Group)   经济合作与发展组织会计准则工作组

[3] Treaty of Rome   罗马条约：1957 年 3 月 25 日，在欧洲煤钢共同体的基础上，法国、联邦德国、意大利、荷兰、比利时和卢森堡 6 国政府首脑和外长在罗马签署《欧洲经济合作条约》和《欧洲原子能共同体条约》，后来人们称这两条约为《罗马条约》。

[4] Its main objective is to facilitate the process whereby world-class issuers can raise capital in the most effective and efficient way on all capital markets where investor demand exists.   它的主要目标是加快进程，借以使世界级的发行者可以在所有的投资需求存在的资本市场以最有效和高效的途径来筹集资本。

[5] IFAC is the global organization for the accountancy profession dedicated to serving the public interest by strengthening the profession and contributing to the development of strong international economies.   国际会计师联合会(IFAC)是一个全球化的会计专业组织，通过加强职业建设和促进强大的国际经济发展，致力于为公共利益服务。

[6] The Intergovernmental Working Group of Experts on International Standards of Accounting and Reporting (ISAR) was created by the United Nations Economic and Social Council in 1982, and is the only intergovernmental expert body focused on corporate transparency and accounting issues.   会计与报告国际标准政府间专家工作组(ISAR)是在 1982 年由联合国经济社会理事会所建立的，它是唯一一个关注于公司透明度与会计问题的政府间专家机构。

[7] It functions through its governing body, the OECD Council, and its network of about 250 committees, working groups and expert groups.   它通过它的管理团队——经济合作与发展组织会计准则工作组理事会，以及约 250 个委员会、工作组和专家小组的联网——来履行职责。

11.3 International Accounting Standards Board
国际会计准则委员会

A conversation between A—an accountant and S—a freshman majoring in accounting.

S: Have Chinese Accounting Standards (CAS) and IFRS completely converged in the rules of financial statement presentation?

A: Not yet. The good news is that they are the same or similar in most rules. For beginners their differences are negligible.

S: What are their similarities?

A: Quite a lot. For example, the components of a complete set of statements include: the balance sheet, the income statement, the statement of cash flow, the statement of changes in owners' equity and accompanying notes.

S: What are the differences?

A: First, under CAS, elements of financial statements are six. Under IFRS, elements are five, and they are assets, liabilities, equity, income and expenses. Second, unlike CAS, IFRS does not prescribe a standard layout of financial statements, but a list of minimum items.

S: Can I have a look at some samples of IFRS financial statements?

A: If you log onto *www.iasb.org*, the website of International Accounting Standards Board, you can find some samples.

Organization of International Accounting Standards Board

In 1973, the International Accounting Standards Committee (IASC) was formed by professional accounting organizations in nine countries to develop worldwide accounting standards. The early standards of the IASC were primarily catalogs of the diverse accounting practices then used worldwide. The IASC was often blamed in that its standards included too many alternative accounting treatments and were not rigorous enough.

In 1999, IASC approved a report, Recommendations on Shaping IASC for the Future, which recommended that a new structure for the IASC was required to reflect the IASC's increased importance. On April 1st, 2001, the IASC was restructured into the International Accounting Standards Board (IASB) based on recommendations from the report.

The IASB used to consist of 14 members, appointed by the IASC Foundation. In January 2009, the **Trustees** voted to expand the IASB to 16 members by July 2012. At present, IASB is an independent group of 16 experts with an appropriate mix of recent practical experience in setting accounting standards, in preparing, auditing, or using financial reports, and in accounting education. Broad geographical diversity is also required. Members are appointed by the Trustees through an open and rigorous process that includes advertising vacancies and consulting relevant organizations. Doctor Zhang, who previously worked as Chief Accountant and Director

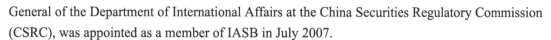

General of the Department of International Affairs at the China Securities Regulatory Commission (CSRC), was appointed as a member of IASB in July 2007.

The IASB has announced that its new standards will be called International Financial Reporting Standards (IFRSs), but the existing standards will continue to be called International Accounting Standards (IASs). [1] In general, the term "IFRSs" refers both to the existing IASs issued by the former IASC and to the IFRSs from the IASB.

Framework for the Preparation and Presentation of Financial Statements

As well as developing its accounting standards, the IASB has adopted an important document setting out the concepts underlying the preparation and presentation of financial statements for external users – The Framework for the Preparation and Presentation of Financial Statements. [2] The Framework was originally developed by the IASC in July 1989, and the history of the Framework is shown in Table 11-3.

Table 11-3   History of Framework for the Preparation and Presentation of Financial Statements

April 1989	Framework for the Preparation and Presentation of Financial Statements (the Framework) was approved by the IASC Board
July 1989	Framework was published
April 2001	Framework adopted by the IASB
September 2010	Conceptual Framework for Financial Reporting 2010 (the IFRS Framework) approved by the IASB

The IFRS Framework also describes the basic concepts that underlie the preparation and presentation of financial statements for external users. The IFRS Framework serves as a guide to the Board in developing future IFRSs and as a guide to resolving accounting issues that are not addressed directly in an International Accounting Standard or International Financial Reporting Standard or Interpretation.

In the absence of a Standard or an Interpretation that specifically applies to a transaction, management must use its judgement in developing and applying an accounting policy that results in information that is relevant and reliable.[3] In making that judgement, IAS 8.11 requires management to consider the definitions, recognition criteria, and measurement concepts for assets, liabilities, income, and expenses in the IFRS Framework. This elevation of the importance of the Framework was added in the 2003 **revisions** to IAS 8.

The following topics are covered in the Framework:

(1) the objective of financial reporting;

(2) the qualitative characteristics of useful financial information;

(3) the reporting entity;

(4) the definition, recognition and measurement of the elements from which financial statements ae constructed;

(5) concepts of capital and **capital maintenance**.

Since the first four topics are introduced in the reading material of this chapter and are similar to the content in Chapter 1, we are only concerned with last issue.

Capital maintenance is an accounting concept based on the principle that income is only recognized after capital has been maintained or there has been a full recovery of costs. Capital maintenance has been reached if the amount of a company's capital at the end of a period is unchanged from that at the beginning of the period, with any excess amount treated as profit.[4] The two basic definitions of capital maintenance are **financial capital maintenance** and **physical capital maintenance**.

According to IFRS, under the definition of financial capital maintenance, a profit is earned only if the amount of net assets at the end of a period exceeds the amount at the beginning of the period, excluding any inflows from or outflows to owners, such as contributions and distributions. It can be measured either in nominal monetary units or constant purchasing power units.

The definition of physical capital maintenance, according to the IFRS, implies that a profit is earned only if the enterprise's productive or operating capacity at the end of a period exceeds the capacity at the beginning of the period, excluding any owners' contributions or distributions.

IASs and IFRSs

There is no substantial difference between IASs and IFRSs. One of the major differences is that the series of standards in the IAS were published by the IASC between International Accounting Standards Board 1973 and 2001, whereas, the standards for the IFRS were published by the IASB, starting from 2001. When the IASB was established in 2001, it was agreed to adopt all IASs, and name future standards as IFRS. One major implication worth noting is that any principles within IFRS that may be contradictory will definitely **supersede** those of the IAS. Basically, when contradictory standards are issued, older ones are usually disregarded.

We may be curious about how we develop IFRSs and how we maintain them.

IFRSs are developed through an international consultation process, the "**due process**", which involves interested individuals and organizations from around the world. The due process comprises six stages, with the Trustees having the opportunity to ensure **compliance** at various points throughout:

(1) setting the **agenda**;

(2) planning the project;

(3) developing and publishing the discussion paper;

(4) developing and publishing the **exposure draft**;

(5) developing and publishing the standard;

(6) after the standard is issued.

Then, the **Interpretations Committee** is responsible for the maintenance of IFRS. The types of issue that the Interpretations Committee is called on to deal with include the identification of divergent practices that have emerged for accounting for particular transactions, cases of doubt about the appropriate accounting treatment for a particular circumstance or concerns expressed by investors about poorly specified disclosure requirements. [5] The objectives of the Interpretations Committee are to interpret the application of IFRS, provide timely guidance on financial reporting issues that are not specifically addressed in IFRS and undertake other tasks at the request of the IASB.

Table 11-4 and Table 11-5 show the list of standards issued by both IASB and IASC.

Table 11-4　The List of International Accounting Standards

#	Name	参考翻译	Issued
IAS 1	Presentation of Financial Statements	财务报表列报	2007*
IAS 2	Inventories	存货	2005*
IAS 3	Consolidated Financial Statements Superseded in 1989 by IAS 27 and IAS 28	合并财务报表 已被于 1989 年生效的 IAS 27 和 IAS 28 取代	1976
IAS 4	Depreciation Accounting Withdrawn in 1999	折旧会计 于 1999 年被撤销	
IAS 5	Information to Be Disclosed in Financial Statements Superseded by IAS 1 effective on 1 July 1998	财务报表应披露的信息 已被于 1998 年 7 月 1 日生效的 IAS 1 取代	
IAS 6	Accounting Responses to Changing Prices Superseded by IAS 15, which was withdrawn in December 2003	针对物价变动的会计应对 被 IAS 15 取代，而 IAS 15 于 2003 年 12 月被撤销	
IAS 7	Statement of Cash Flows	现金流量表	1992
IAS 8	Accounting Policies, Changes in Accounting Estimates and Errors	会计政策、会计估计变更和差错	2003
IAS 9	Accounting for Research and Development Activities Superseded by IAS 38 effective on 1 July 1999	研发活动的会计处理 已被于 1999 年 7 月 1 日生效的 IAS 38 取代	
IAS 10	Events After the Reporting Period	报告期后事项	2003
IAS 11	Construction Contracts	建造合同	1993
IAS 12	Income Taxes	所得税	1996*
IAS 13	Presentation of Current Assets and Current Liabilities Superseded by IAS 1	流动资产和流动负债的列报 已被 IAS 1 取代	
IAS 14	Segment Reporting Superseded by IFRS 8 effective on 1 January 2009	分部报告 已被于 2009 年 1 月 1 日生效的 IFRS 8 取代	1997

Table 11-4(Continued)

#	Name	参考翻译	Issued
IAS 15	Information Reflecting the Effects of Changing Prices Withdrawn in December 2003	反映物价变动影响的信息 于 2003 年 12 月被撤销	
IAS 16	Property, Plant and Equipment	不动产、厂场和设备	2003*
IAS 17	Leases	租赁	2003*
IAS 18	Revenue	收入	1993*
IAS 19	Employee Benefits	雇员福利	2011*
IAS 20	Accounting for Government Grants and Disclosure of Government Assistance	政府补助的会计和政府援助的披露	1983
IAS 21	The Effects of Changes in Foreign Exchange Rates	汇率变动的影响	2003*
IAS 22	Business Combinations Superseded by IFRS 3 effective on 31 March 2004	企业合并 已被于 2004 年 3 月 31 日生效的 IFRS 3 取代	1998*
IAS 23	Borrowing Costs	借款费用	2007*
IAS 24	Related Party Disclosures	关联方披露	2009*
IAS 25	Accounting for Investments Superseded by IAS 39 and IAS 40 effective in 2001	投资会计 已被于 2001 年生效的 IAS 39 和 IAS40 取代	
IAS 26	Accounting and Reporting by Retirement Benefit Plans	退休福利计划的会计和报告	1987
IAS 27	Separate Financial Statements (2011)	单独财务报表(2011)	2011
IAS 27	Consolidated and Separate Financial Statements Superseded by IFRS 10, IFRS 12 and IAS 27 (2011) effective on 1 January 2013	合并和单独财务报表 已被于 2013 年 1 月 1 日生效的 IFRS 10 和 IFRS 12，以及修改后的 IAS(2011)取代	2003
IAS 28	Investments in Associates and Joint Ventures (2011)	对联营和合资经营的投资(2011)	2011
IAS 28	Investments in Associates Superseded by IAS 28 (2011) and IFRS 12 effective in 2013	联营中的投资 已被于修改过后的 IAS 28(2011)和 2013 年生效的 IFRS 12 取代	2003
IAS 29	Financial Reporting in Hyperinflationary Economies	在恶性通货膨胀经济中的财务报告	1989

Table 11-4(Continued)

#	Name	参考翻译	Issued
IAS 30	Disclosures in the Financial Statements of Banks and Similar Financial Institutions Superseded by IFRS 7 effective on 1 January 2007	银行和类似金融机构财务报表中的披露 已被于 2007 年生效的 IFRS 7 取代	1990
IAS 31	Interests In Joint Ventures Superseded by IFRS 11 and IFRS 12 effective in 2013	合营中的权益 已被于 2013 年生效的 IFRS 11 和 IFRS 12 取代	2003*
IAS 32	Financial Instruments: Presentation	金融工具：列报	2003*
IAS 33	Earnings Per Share	每股收益	2003*
IAS 34	Interim Financial Reporting	中期财务报告	1998
IAS 35	Discontinuing Operations Superseded by IFRS 5 effective in 2005	中止经营 已被于 2005 年生效的 IFRS 5 取代	1998
IAS 36	Impairment of Assets	资产减值	2004*
IAS 37	Provisions, Contingent Liabilities and Contingent Assets	准备、或有负债和或有资产	1998
IAS 38	Intangible Assets	无形资产	2004*
IAS 39	Financial Instruments: Recognition and Measurement Superseded by IFRS 9 where IFRS 9 is applied	金融工具：确认与计量 当 IFRS 9 生效后，该准则失效	2003*
IAS 40	Investment Property	投资性房地产	2003*
IAS 41	Agriculture	农业	2001

Table 11-5　The List of International Financial Reporting Standards

#	Name	参考翻译	Issued
IFRS 1	First-time Adoption of International Financial Reporting Standards	首次采用国际财务报告准则	2008*
IFRS 2	Share-based Payment	以股份为基础的支付	2004
IFRS 3	Business Combinations	企业合并	2008*
IFRS 4	Insurance Contracts	保险合同	2004
IFRS 5	Non-current Assets Held for Sale and Discontinued Operations	持有待售的非流动资产和终止经营	2004
IFRS 6	Exploration for and Evaluation of Mineral Assets	矿产资源的勘探和评价	2004
IFRS 7	Financial Instruments: Disclosures	金融工具：披露	2005

Table 11-5(Continued)

#	Name	参考翻译	Issued
IFRS 8	Operating Segments	经营分部	2006
IFRS 9	Financial Instruments	金融工具	2013*
IFRS 10	Consolidated Financial Statements	合并财务报表	2011
IFRS 11	Joint Arrangements	合营安排	2011
IFRS 12	Disclosure of Interests in Other Entities	对其他主体中权益的披露	2011
IFRS 13	Fair Value Measurement	公允价值计量	2011

The above tables list the most recent version (or versions if a pronouncement has not yet been superseded) of each pronouncement and the date that revisions was originally issued. Where a pronouncement has been reissued with the same or a different name, the date indicated in the above tables is the date the revised pronouncement was reissued (these are indicated with an asterisk "" in the tables). The majority of the pronouncements have also been amended through IASB or IFRS Interpretations Committee projects, for consequential amendments arising on the issue of other pronouncements, the annual improvements process, and other factors.

 Vocabulary

Trustees	*n.* 管理委员会
revision	*n.* 修订，修改；修订本
capital maintenance	资本保值，资本保全
financial capital maintenance	财务资本保全
physical capital maintenance	实物资本保全
supersede	*vt.* 取代，代替
due process	法定诉讼程序
compliance	*n.* 顺从，服从承诺
agenda	*n.* 议事日程；待议诸事项一览表
exposure draft	征求意见草案，讨论稿
Interpretations Committee	(国际财务报告准则)解释委员会

Notes

[1] The IASB has announced that its new standards will be called International Financial Reporting Standards (IFRSs), but the existing standards will continue to be called International Accounting Standards (IASs). 国际会计准则委员会宣告，新准则将被称为国际财务报告准则(IFRSs)，但已存在的准则将仍被称为国际会计准则(IASs)。

[2] As well as developing its accounting standards, the IASB has adopted an important document setting out the concepts underlying the preparation and presentation of financial statements for external users — The Framework for the Presparation and Presentation of Financial Statements. 除发布会计准则外，国际会计准则委员会还采纳了一个重要文件，即

提出针对外部使用者的基于财务报表编制和列报的概念——财务报表编制和列报框架。

[3] In the absence of a Standard or an Interpretation that specifically applies to a transaction, management must use its judgement in developing and applying an accounting policy that results in information that is relevant and reliable.　如某项交易缺少可明确应用的准则或解释(应用说明)，管理部门必须自行判断来制定和采用一种具有相关和可靠信息的会计政策。

[4] Capital maintenance has been reached if the amount of a company's capital at the end of a period is unchanged from that at the beginning of the period, with any excess amount treated as profit.　如果公司期末资本与期初相比金额没有变化，资本保全就实现了，超出金额可作为利润。

[5] The types of issue that the Interpretations Committee is called on to deal with include the identification of divergent practices that have emerged for accounting for particular transactions, cases of doubt about the appropriate accounting treatment for a particular circumstance or concerns expressed by investors about poorly specified disclosure requirements.　解释委员会需处理问题的种类包括，特定交易会计处理不同方法的识别，在特定环境或投资者表示没有明确的披露要求的情况下关于适当会计处理的怀疑。

Exercises

I. Discuss the following questions in English.

1.　Why have international accounting issues grown in importance and complexity in recent years?

2.　Some have advocated that a single, widely spoken language be designated as the formal international accounting language. Write a two-paragraph statement in favor of choosing English as the designated language.

3.　Discuss at least three trends that clearly indicate the growing internationalization of financial markets.

4.　In most countries, published financial accounting standards differ from those actually used in practice. What causes such differences and who should be conserned about them?

5.　What is the purpose of accounting harmonization in the European Union (EU)?

6.　Why is the concept of auditing harmonization important? Will international harmonization of auditing standards be more or less difficult to achieve than international harmonization of accounting principles?

7.　Describe IOSCO's work on harmonizing disclosure standards for cross-border offerings and initial listings by foreign issuers. Why is this work important to securities regulators around the world?

8.　What role do the United Nations and the Organization for Eonomic Cooperation and Development play in harmonizing accounting and auditing standards?

9.　What evidence is there that IFRS are becoming widely accepted around the world?

10. What are at least three similarities and at least three differences between IASB standards and Chinese Accounting Standards?

II. Choose the best word or phrase that fits the sentence.

1. A _____ of all principles, methods and standards of all countries would be considered as the international accounting system.

    A. combination   B. collection

    C. consolidation   D. consideration

2. Harmonization is a process of increasing the _____ of accounting practices by setting limits on how much they can vary.

    A. comparability   B. communication

    C. compatibility   D. understandability

3. Although international accounting might sound mysterious and exotic, it is a well-established area of specialty within accounting and has two major dimensions: comparative and _____.

    A. useful   B. valuable

    C. theoretical   D. pragmatic

4. The _____ established the EU in 1957, with the goal of harmonizing the legal and economic systems of its member states.

    A. Treaty of Rome   B. Maastricht Treaty

    C. Treaty of Nice   D. Treaty of Lisbon

5. IOSCO is the only international financial regulatory organization which includes all the major emerging markets _____ within its membership.

    A. fairness   B. government

    C. jurisdictions   D. regulation

6. IFAC members are _____ accountancy organizations recognized by law or general consensus within their countries as substantial national organizations.

    A. public   B. professional

    C. certified   D. charted

7. ISAR accomplishes its mandate by discussing and _____ best practices, including those recommended by IASB.

    A. promoting   B. providing

    C. pronouncing   D. promulgating

8. OECD uses its wealth of information on a broad range of topics to help governments to _____ prosperity and _____ poverty through economic growth and financial stability.

    A. foster; fight   B. foster; resist

    C. enhance; fight   D. enhance; resist

9. On April 1st, 2001, the IASC was _____ into the IASB based on the report Recommendations on Shaping IASC for the Future.

A. reformed

B. restructured

C. recombined

D. reformed

10.　The definition of _____ capital maintenance, according to the IFRS, implies that a profit is earned only if the enterprise's productive or operating capacity at the end of a period exceeds the capacity at the beginning of the period, excluding any owners' contributions or distributions.

A. physical

B. financial

C. material

D. tangible

11.　One major implication worth noting is that any principles within IFRS that may be contradictory will definitely _____ those of the IAS.

A. eliminate

B. cancel

C. remove

D. supersede

III. Match each word on the left with its corresponding meaning on the right.

A	**B**
1. pragmatic	(a) members of a governing board
2. transparent	(b) a negotiator who acts as a link between parties
3. domicile	(c) set out on (an enterprise, subject of study, etc.)
4. intermediary	(d) the residence where you have your permanent home
5. consensus	(e) concerned with practical matters
6. bilateral	(f) easily understood or seen through
7. trustee	(g) concerning each of two or more persons or things; especially given or done in return
8. directive	(h) agreement in the judgment or opinion reached by a group as a whole
9. reciprocal	(i) affecting or undertaken by two parties
10. embark	(j) a pronouncement encouraging or banning some activities

IV. Fill in the blanks with words or phrases from the list below.

A.	current	B.	exchange	C.	owe	D.	result in
E.	adjust	F.	original	G.	owed	H.	sale
I.	currency	J.	debit	K.	gain	L.	loss
M.	receive	N.	credit	O.	translate	P.	purchase

Accounting for foreign (1)___ transactions has two sections. The first section is recording the (2)___ transactions. The second section is recording when the company pays or receives the money in a foreign currency. The foreign currency exchange rate will allow the accountant to (3)___ the foreign currency to his own currency. Any changes in the foreign currency exchange rate will (4)___ a gain or loss on the foreign currency.

Purchases

- Debit "purchases" and credit "accounts payable" by the amount of money owed using the current exchange rate. For example, if the (5)____ exchange rate is 1 euro for $1.50, and a company purchases a product for 400 euros, then the company would debit and (6)____ $600.

- Debit "accounts payable" and credit "foreign currency gain" or debit "foreign currency loss" and credit "accounts payable" at the end of the accounting period to (7)____ the transaction to the current exchange rate. In the example, if the exchange rate changed to 1 euro for $1.25, then the company would (8)____ only $500. Debit and credit $100 to adjust the $600.

- Debit "accounts payable" and credit "cash" and "foreign currency gain" or debit "accounts payable" and "foreign currency loss" and credit "cash" when paying for the purchase. Use the exchange rate on the day you (9)____ the currency.

Sales

- Debit "accounts receivable" and credit "sales" by the amount of money (10)____ using the current exchange rate. For example, if the current exchange rate is 1 euro for $1.50, and a company sells a product for 400 euros, then the company would (11)____ and credit $600.

- Debit "accounts receivable" and credit "foreign currency (12)____" or debit "foreign currency (13)____" and credit "accounts receivable" at the end of the accounting period to adjust the transaction to the current exchange rate. In the example, if the exchange rate changed to 1 euro for $1.25, then the company would (14)____ only $500. Debit and credit $100 to adjust the $600.

- Debit "cash" and credit "accounts receivable" and "foreign currency gain" or debit "cash" and "foreign currency loss" and credit "accounts receivable" when receiving money for the (15)____. Use the exchange rate on the day you received the cash.

V. Translate the following sentences into Chinese.

1. While the effort to reduce international accounting diversity is important in its own right, there are today a number of additional factors that are contributing to the growing importance of studying international accounting.

2. A major accounting issue associated with export and import activities relates to accounting for foreign currency transactions.

3. The factor that has perhaps contributed most to the growing interest in international accounting among corporate executives, investors, market regulators, accounting standard setters and business educations alike is the internationalization of the world's capital markets.

4. The IOSCO Objectives and Principles of Securities Regulation sets out 38 principles of securities regulation, which are based upon three objectives of securities regulation.

5. IFAC's Strategic Plan identifies the organization's strategic direction during the period

of 2013—2016 within the context of the current and anticipated environment.

6.　IASB, formerly the IASC, is an independent private-sector standards-setting body founded in 1973 by professional accounting organizations in nine countries and restructured in 2001.

7.　IAS 1 Presentation of Financial Statements sets out the overall requirements for financial statements, including how they should be structured, the minimum requirements for their content and overriding concepts such as going concern, the accrual basis of accounting and the current/non-current distinction.

8.　The IASB met at its offices in London on 22~25 April 2014. Part of the meeting was held jointly with the Financial Accounting Standards Board (FASB) to discuss the leases project.

VI. Translate the following sentences into English.

1.　全球资本市场和跨境投资活动的迅速增长，意味着对于必须以这样或那样的方式从事这些领域工作的专业人士而言，会计的国际视角更加重要了。

2.　国际会计是指以各国不同的经济组织进行超越国界的经济贸易活动、理财活动和在会计处理和财务报告方面引起的特殊问题为研究对象，谋求各国不同的会计准则、报告准则和会计、审计制度在经济交往中相互协调的会计学科。

3.　国际会计协调是指在一个各国比较能接受的国际会计准则的指导下，推行能使各国理解的较为统一的会计实务，尤其是有关会计揭示、计量方法及单位等方面的实务。

4.　国际会计先后成立了一些组织：国际会计师联合会、国际会计准则委员会、国际会计合作委员会等。

5.　国际会计师联合会于 1977 年 10 月 14 日在德国慕尼黑成立，其前身是于 1972 年在澳大利亚的悉尼召开的第 10 届国际会计师大会上成立的国际会计职业协调委员会。

6.　国际证券事务监察委员会组织是国际间各证券期管理机构所组成的国际合作组织，总部设在加拿大的蒙特利尔市。

7.　国际会计准则委员会旨在制定高质量、易于理解和可行性的国际会计准则，准则要求向公众披露的财务报告应具明晰性和可比性。

8.　通常所说的国际会计准则是一个比较笼统的概念，其含义是指在主要发达国家采用的、对其他国家影响较大的会计概念、方法、程序、做法等，其中美国财务会计准则理事会(FASB)发布的会计准则(FAS)和国际会计准则理事会(IASB)发布的会计准则(IAS)最具影响力。

Reading Material 11

Conceptual Framework for Financial Reporting 2010*

The IFRS Framework addresses:

- the objective of financial reporting

---

* 资料来源于 *http://www.iasplus.com*

- the qualitative characteristics of useful financial information
- the reporting entity
- the definition, recognition and measurement of the elements from which financial statements are constructed
- concepts of capital and capital maintenance

Chapter 1: The Objective of General Purpose Financial Reporting

The primary users of general purpose financial reporting are present and potential investors, lenders and other creditors, who use that information to make decisions about buying, selling or holding equity or debt instruments and providing or settling loans or other forms of credit.

The primary users need information about the resources of the entity not only to assess an entity's prospects for future net cash inflows but also how effectively and efficiently management has discharged their responsibilities to use the entity's existing resources (i.e., stewardship).

The IFRS Framework notes that general purpose financial reports cannot provide all the information that users may need to make economic decisions. They will need to consider pertinent information from other sources as well.

The IFRS Framework notes that other parties, including prudential and market regulators, may find general purpose financial reports useful. However, the Board considered that the objectives of general purpose financial reporting and the objectives of financial regulation may not be consistent. Hence, regulators are not considered a primary user and general purpose financial reports are not primarily directed to regulators or other parties.

Information about a reporting entity's economic resources, claims, and changes in resources and claims

Economic resources and claims

Information about the nature and amounts of a reporting entity's economic resources and claims assists users to assess that entity's financial strengths and weaknesses; to assess liquidity and solvency, and its need and ability to obtain financing. Information about the claims and payment requirements assists users to predict how future cash flows will be distributed among those with a claim on the reporting entity.

A reporting entity's economic resources and claims are reported in the statement of financial position.

Changes in economic resources and claims

Changes in a reporting entity's economic resources and claims result from that entity's performance and from other events or transactions such as issuing debt or equity instruments. Users need to be able to distinguish between both of these changes.

Financial performance reflected by accrual accounting

Information about a reporting entity's financial performance during a period, representing changes in economic resources and claims other than those obtained directly from investors and creditors, is useful in assessing the entity's past and future ability to generate net cash inflows. Such information may also indicate the extent to which general economic events have changed the entity's ability to generate future cash inflows.

The changes in an entity's economic resources and claims are presented in the statement of comprehensive income.

Financial performance reflected by past cash flows

Information about a reporting entity's cash flows during the reporting period also assists users to assess the entity's ability to generate future net cash inflows. This information indicates how the entity obtains and spends cash, including information about its borrowing and repayment of debt, cash dividends to shareholders, etc.

The changes in the entity's cash flows are presented in the statement of cash flows.

Changes in economic resources and claims not resulting from financial performance

Information about changes in an entity's economic resources and claims resulting from events and transactions other than financial performance, such as the issue of equity instruments or distributions of cash or other assets to shareholders is necessary to complete the picture of the total change in the entity's economic resources and claims.

The changes in an entity's economic resources and claims not resulting from financial performance is presented in the statement of changes in equity.

Chapter 2: The Reporting Entity

The chapter on the reporting entity will be inserted once the IASB has completed its re-deliberations following the Exposure Draft ED/2010/2 issued in March 2010.

Chapter 3: Qualitative Characteristics of Useful Financial Information

The qualitative characteristics of useful financial reporting identify the types of information are likely to be most useful to users in making decisions about the reporting entity on the basis of information in its financial report. The qualitative characteristics apply equally to financial information in general purpose financial reports as well as to financial information provided in other ways.

Financial information is useful when it is relevant and represents faithfully what it purports to represent. The usefulness of financial information is enhanced if it is comparable, verifiable, timely and understandable.

Fundamental qualitative characteristics

Relevance and faithful representation are the fundamental qualitative characteristics of useful financial information.

Relevance

Relevant financial information is capable of making a difference in the decisions made by users. Financial information is capable of making a difference in decisions if it has predictive value, confirmatory value, or both. The predictive value and confirmatory value of financial information are interrelated.

Materiality is an entity-specific aspect of relevance based on the nature or magnitude (or both) of the items to which the information relates in the context of an individual entity's financial report.

Faithful representation

General purpose financial reports represent economic phenomena in words and numbers. To be useful, financial information must not only be relevant, it must also represent faithfully the phenomena it purports to represent. This fundamental characteristic seeks to maximize the underlying characteristics of completeness, neutrality and freedom from error.

Information must be both relevant and faithfully represented if it is to be useful.

Enhancing qualitative characteristics

Comparability, verifiability, timeliness and understandability are qualitative characteristics that enhance the usefulness of information that is relevant and faithfully represented.

Comparability

Information about a reporting entity is more useful if it can be compared with a similar information about other entities and with similar information about the same entity for another period or another date. Comparability enables users to identify and understand similarities in, and differences among, items.

Verifiability

Verifiability helps to assure users that information represents faithfully the economic phenomena it purports to represent. Verifiability means that different knowledgeable and independent observers could reach consensus, although not necessarily complete agreement, that a particular depiction is a faithful representation.

Timeliness

Timeliness means that information is available to decision-makers in time to be capable of influencing their decisions.

Understandability

Classifying, characterizing and presenting information clearly and concisely makes it understandable. While some phenomena are inherently complex and cannot be made easy to understand, to exclude such information would make financial reports incomplete and potentially misleading. Financial reports are prepared for users who have a reasonable knowledge of business and economic activities and who review and analyze the information with diligence.

Applying the enhancing qualitative characteristics

Enhancing qualitative characteristics should be maximized to the extent necessary. However, enhancing qualitative characteristics (either individually or collectively) render information useful if that information is irrelevant or not represented faithfully.

The cost constraint on useful financial reporting

Cost is a pervasive constraint on the information that can be provided by general purpose financial reporting. Reporting such information imposes costs and those costs should be justified by the benefits of reporting that information. The IASB assesses costs and benefits in relation to financial reporting generally, and not solely in relation to individual reporting entities. The IASB will consider whether different sizes of entities and other factors justify different reporting requirements in certain situations.

Chapter 4: The Framework: the Remaining Text

Chapter 4 contains the remaining text of the Framework approved in 1989. As the project to revise the Framework progresses, relevant paragraphs in Chapter 4 will be deleted and replaced by new chapters in the IFRS Framework. Until it is replaced, a paragraph in Chapter 4 has the same level of authority within IFRSs as those in Chapters 1~3.

Underlying assumption

The IFRS Framework states that the going concern assumption is an underlying assumption. Thus, the financial statements presume that an entity will continue in operation indefinitely or, if that presumption is not valid, disclosure and a different basis of reporting are required.

The elements of financial statements

Financial statements portray the financial effects of transactions and other events by grouping them into broad classes according to their economic characteristics. These broad classes are termed as the elements of financial statements.

The elements directly related to financial position (balance sheet) are:

- Assets
- Liabilities
- Equity

The elements directly related to performance (income statement) are:

- Income
- Expenses

The cash flow statement reflects both income statement elements and some changes in balance sheet elements.

Definitions of the elements relating to financial position

- **Asset.** An asset is a resource controlled by the entity as a result of past events and from which future economic benefits are expected to flow to the entity.
- **Liability.** A liability is a present obligation of the entity arising from past events, the settlement of which is expected to result in an outflow from the entity of resources embodying economic benefits.
- **Equity.** Equity is the residual interest in the assets of the entity after deducting all its liabilities.

Definitions of the elements relating to performance

- **Income.** Income is the increases in economic benefits during the accounting period in the form of inflows or enhancements of assets or decreases of liabilities that result in increases in equity, other than those relating to contributions from equity participants.
- **Expense.** Expenses are the decreases in economic benefits during the accounting period in the form of outflows or depletions of assets or incurrences of liabilities that result in decreases in equity, other than those relating to distributions to equity participants.

The definition of income encompasses both revenues and gains. Revenue arises in the course of the ordinary activities of an entity and is referred to by a variety of different names including sales, fees, interests, dividends, royalties and rents. Gains represent other items that meet the definition of income and may, or may not, arise in the course of the ordinary activities of an entity. Gains represent the increases in economic benefits and as such are not different in nature from revenue. Hence, they are not regarded as constituting a separate element in the IFRS Framework.

The definition of expenses encompasses losses as well as those expenses that arise in the course of the ordinary activities of the entity. Expenses that arise in the course of the ordinary activities of the entity include, for example, cost of sales, wages and depreciation. They usually take the form of an outflow or depletion of assets such as cash and cash equivalents, inventory, property, plant and equipment. Losses represent other items that meet the definition of expenses and may, or may not, arise in the course of the ordinary activities of the entity. Losses represent the decreases in economic benefits and as such they are not different in nature from other expenses. Hence, they are not regarded as a separate element in this Framework.

Recognition of the elements of financial statements

Recognition is the process of incorporating in the balance sheet or income statement an item that meets the definition of an element and satisfies the following criteria for recognition:

● It is probable that any future economic benefit associated with the item will flow to or from the entity; and

● The item's cost or value can be measured with reliability.

Based on these general criteria:

● **An asset** is recognized in the balance sheet when it is probable that the future economic benefits will flow to the entity and the asset has a cost or value that can be measured reliably.

● **A liability** is recognized in the balance sheet when it is probable that an outflow of resources embodying economic benefits will result from the settlement of a present obligation and the amount at which the settlement will take place can be measured reliably.

● **Income** is recognized in the income statement when an increase in future economic benefits related to an increase in an asset or a decrease in a liability has arisen that can be measured reliably. This means, in effect, that recognition in income occurs simultaneously with the recognition of increases in assets or decreases in liabilities (for example, the net increase in assets arising on a sale of goods or services or the decrease in liabilities arising from the waiver of a debt payable).

● **Expenses** are recognized when a decrease in future economic benefits related to a decrease in an asset or an increase in a liability has arisen that can be measured reliably. This means, in effect, that recognition of expenses occurs simultaneously with the recognition of an increase in liabilities or a decrease in assets (for example, the accrual of employee entitlements or the depreciation of equipment).

Measurement of the elements of financial statements

Measurement involves assigning monetary amounts at which the elements of the financial statements are to be recognized and reported.

The IFRS Framework acknowledges that a variety of measurement bases are used today to different degrees and in varying combinations in financial statements, including:

- Historical cost
- Current cost
- Net realisable (settlement) value
- Present value (discounted)

Answers:

II.	1	B	2	C	3	D	4	A	5	C	6	B	7	D	8	A
	9	B	10	A	11	D										

III.	1	e	2	f	3	d	4	b	5	h	6	i	7	a	8	j
	9	g	10	c												

IV.	1	I	2	F	3	O	4	D	5	A	6	N	7	E	8	C
	9	B	10	G	11	J	12	K	13	L	14	M	15	P

More Knowledge 知识扩展

1. 关贸总协定

20 世纪 30~40 年代，世界贸易保护主义盛行。国际贸易的相互限制是造成世界经济萧条的一个重要原因。第二次世界大战结束后，解决复杂的国际经济问题，特别是制定国际贸易政策，成为战后各国所面临的重要任务。

1946 年 2 月，联合国经社理事会举行第一次会议，会议呼吁召开联合国贸易与就业问题会议，起草国际贸易组织宪章，进行世界性削减关税的谈判。随后，经社理事会设立了一个筹备委员会。

1946 年 10 月，筹备委员会召开第一次会议，审查美国提交的国际贸易组织宪章草案。参加筹备委员会的与会各国同意在"国际贸易组织"成立之前，先就削减关税和其他贸易限制等问题进行谈判，并起草"国际贸易组织宪章"。

1947 年 4~7 月，筹备委员会在日内瓦召开第二次全体大会，就关税问题进行谈判，讨论并修改"国际贸易组织宪章"草案。经过多次谈判，美国等 23 个国家于 1947 年 10 月 30 日在日内瓦签订了"关税及贸易总协定"。

按照原来的计划，关贸总协定只是在国际贸易组织成立前的一个过渡性步骤，它的大部分条款将在"国际贸易组织宪章"被各国通过后纳入其中。但是，鉴于各国对外经济政策方面的分歧以及多数国家政府在批准"国际贸易组织宪章"这样范围广泛、具有严密组织性和国际条约所遇到的法律困难，该宪章在短期内难以被通过。

因此，关贸总协定的 23 个发起国于 1947 年年底签订了《临时议定书》，承诺在今后的国际贸易中遵循关贸总协定的规定。该议定书于 1948 年 1 月 1 日生效。

此后，关贸总协定的有效期一再延长，并为适应情况的不断变化，多次加以修订。于是，"关税及贸易总协定"便成为各国共同遵守的贸易准则，协调国际贸易与各国经济政策的唯一的多边国际协定。

关贸总协定的序言明确规定其宗旨是：缔约各国政府认为，在处理它们的贸易和经济事务的关系方面，应以提高生活水平、保证充分就业、保证实际收入和有效需求的巨大持续增长、扩大世界资源的充分利用以及发展商品生产与交换为目的。通过达成互惠互利协议，大幅度地削减关税和其他贸易障碍，取消国际贸易中的歧视待遇等措施，以对上述目的做出贡献。

2. 世界贸易组织

1994 年 4 月 15 日，在摩洛哥的马拉喀什市举行的关贸总协定乌拉圭回合部长会议决定，成立更具全球性的世界贸易组织，简称"世贸组织"(World Trade Organization，WTO)，以取代成立于 1947 年的关贸总协定 (GATT)。

世贸组织是一个独立于联合国的永久性国际组织，1995 年 1 月 1 日正式开始运作，负责管理世界经济和贸易秩序，总部设在瑞士日内瓦莱蒙湖畔。1996 年 1 月 1 日正式取代关贸总协定临时机构。世贸组织是具有法人地位的国际组织，在调解成员争端方面具有更高的权威性。它的前身是 1947 年订立的关贸总协定。与关贸总协定相比，世贸组织涵盖货物贸易、服务贸易以及知识产权贸易，而关贸总协定只适用于商品货物贸易。目前，世贸组织的贸易量已占世界贸易的 95%以上。

1995 年 7 月 11 日，世贸组织总理事会会议决定接纳中国为该组织的观察员，中国于 2001 年 11 月加入该组织。

世贸组织成员分为四类：发达成员、发展中成员、转轨经济体成员和最不发达成员。2006 年 11 月 7 日世界贸易组织关于接纳越南加入该组织的工作全部完成，11 月 28 日，越南国会批准关于越南加入世界贸易组织的议定书。在这项议定书获得批准 30 天后，越南正式成为世贸组织第 150 个成员。

3. 国际货币基金组织

国际货币基金组织是政府间国际金融组织，1945 年 12 月 27 日正式成立，1947 年 3 月 1 日开始工作，1947 年 11 月 15 日成为联合国的专门机构，在经营上有其独立性，其总部设在华盛顿。该组织的宗旨是通过一个常设机构来促进国际货币合作，为国际货币问题的磋商和协作提供方法；通过国际贸易的扩大和平衡发展，把促进和保持成员方的就业、生产资源的发展、实际收入的高水平作为经济政策的首要目标；稳定国际汇率，在成员方之间保持有秩序的汇价安排，避免竞争性的汇价贬值；协助成员方建立经常性交易的多边支付制度，消除妨碍世界贸易的外汇管制；在有适当保证的条件下，基金组织向成员方临时提供普通资金，使其有信心利用此机会纠正国际收支的失调，而不采取危害本国或国际繁荣的措施；按照以上目的，缩短成员方国际收支不平衡的时间，减轻不平衡的程度等。

该组织临时委员会是世界两大金融机构之一国际货币基金组织的决策和指导机构。该委员会将在政策合作与协调，特别是在制定中期战略方面充分发挥作用。委员由 24 名执行董事组成。国际货币基金组织每年与世界银行共同举行年会。

中国是该组织创始国之一。1980 年 4 月 17 日，该组织正式恢复中国的代表权。中国在该组织中的份额为 33.852 亿特别提款权，占总份额的 2.34%。中国共拥有 34 102 张选票，占总投票权的 2.28%。中国自 1980 年恢复在货币基金组织的席位后单独组成一个选区并派一名执行董事。1991 年，该组织在北京设立常驻代表处。

4. 世界银行

世界银行是国际复兴开发银行 (International Bank for Reconstruction and Development，IBRD) 的简称，它是一个国际组织，其一开始的使命是帮助在"二战"中被破坏的国家重建。今天它的任务是资助国家克服穷困，其资金来自成员方缴纳的基金和世界银行债券。在 1944 年 7 月 1 日到 7 月 22 日的布雷顿森林会议上参加国决定建立世界银行，1945 年 12 月 27 日，在参加国签署其条约后世界银行正式成立。

世界银行的使命是战胜贫困和提高发展中国家人民的生活水平。它是个向低收入和中等收入国家提供贷款、政策建议、技术援助和知识分享服务以减轻贫困的开发银行。世界银行的主要帮助对象是发展中国家，帮助它们建设教育、农业和工业设施。它向成员方提供优惠贷款，同时世界银行向受贷国提出一定的要求，比如减少贪污或建立民主等。

世界银行的工作经常受到非政府组织和学者的严厉批评，有时世界银行内部的审查也对其某些决定提出质疑。往往世界银行被指责为美国或西方国家施行有利于它们自己的经济政策的执行者，此外，往往过快、不正确的、按错误的顺序引入的或在不适合的环境下进行的市场经济改革对发展中国家的经济反而造成破坏。

References

1. Johm J. Wild, Ken W. Shaw, Bathan Chiupeta, Principles of Accounting. 19th ed. 北京：中国人民大学出版社，2009

2. Walter T. Harison Jr., Charles T.Hongren, C. Wiliam Thomas, etc. Financial Acounting, 8th ed. 上海：上海人民出版社，2013

3. 叶建芳，孙红星. 会计英语. 第4版. 上海：上海财经大学出版社，2011

4. ACCA. Financial Accounting (Study Text). Bpp Learning Media, 2012

5. Peter J. Eisen. Accounting, Barron's Educational Series Inc., U.S., 2013

6. Bary Elliolt, Jamie Eliott. Financial Accounting and Reporting, 16th ed. Pearson, 2013

7. 郝绍伦. 会计英语. 第2版. 合肥：中国科学技术大学出版社，2006

8. 孟焰，白蔚秋. 会计英语. 北京：经济科学出版社，2010

9. 黄世忠，陈箭深，葛方雯. 会计英语教程. 厦门：厦门大学出版社，2004

10. 罗殿英，温倩，贺欣. 会计审计专业英语. 北京：机械工业出版社，2008

11. 何丽梅，李宜. 会计英语教程. 北京：电子工业出版社，2010

12. 注册会计师考试研究中心. 英语(2013年度注册会计师全国统一考试辅导教材). 北京：北京人民出版社，2013

13. 侯立新，黄捷，邓雪. 会计英语. 北京：机械工业出版社，2007

14. 孙耀远，祁渊. 会计原理(英文版). 北京：外语教学与研究出版社，2009

15. 葛军. 会计英语. 第2版. 北京：科学出版社，2011

16. Leslie K. Breitner, Robert N. Anthony. Essentials of Accounting. 10th ed. 北京：清华大学出版社，2010

17. Gerald I. White, Ashwinpaul C. Sondhi, Dov Fried. The Analysis and Use of Financial Statements. 3rd ed. 北京：中国人民大学出版社，2007

18. Anthony A. Atkinson, Rajiv D. Banker, Robert S. Kaplan, etc. Management Accounting. 6th ed. 北京：清华大学出版社，2013

19. Alvin A. Arens, Randal J. Elder, Mark S. Beasley. Auditing and Assurance Services: An Integrated Approach.14th ed. 北京：中国人民大学出版社，2013

20. Frederick D.S. Choi, Gary K. Meek. International Accounting. 19th ed. 大连：东北财经大学出版社，2005.

21. 老青，刘五宁，张红琴. 会计英语听力速记实训教程. 北京：世界知识出版社，2011